**"Get your money out of the country,
before your country gets the money out of you!"**
Last Words of W. G. Hill

THE
INVISIBLE
INVESTOR

By:

Peter T. Trevellian

PT Publishing, Inc.
Panama City, Panama

D1600467

The Invisible Investor by **Peter Trevellian**
© International Copyright 1997, PT Publishing, Inc.

Editor & Publisher:
PT Publishing, Inc.
PO Box 6-1097, El Dorado
Panama City, Panama

ISBN 9962-5505-5-6

1st Edition 1997
By: Peter T. Trevellian, Esq. and Dr. W.G. Hill

For questions or further information, contact the publishers.

A Brand New Special Report for people too busy to read books

The
Invisible Investor

"Get your money out of the country before your
country gets the money out of you."
Peter Trevellian's Latest Bombshell

Courts and juries have gone mad — **with million dollar plus verdicts for mildly miffed but otherwise undamaged plaintiffs;**
Government agencies can confiscate and destroy **everything you own, without due process,**
Property rights have been eroded **beyond all recognition . . .**
Selective Prosecution **means that successful people with visible assets run a** high risk of criminal indictment.

Do you need new defenses, new asset protection options? **The INVISIBLE INVESTOR a brilliant, fast moving, easy reading report by the legendary W.G. Hill, (author of 2nd Passport Report and The Perpetual Tourist) and Dr. Peter Trevellian, the world's foremost expert on expatriation of assets will give you** amazing insights into a secret world **you never knew existed, a way of handling your savings and assets so that:**

⟨ **You will never spend another day or a single dime on lawyers, tax preparers, or accountants.** Lawyers, accountants, and bureaucrats will be banished from your life — forever.

⟨ **You, the invisible or anonymous investor can be** insulated and buffered **to the point where** you will never be sued **or waste a moment of your life defending yourself in court. You make yourself** judgment proof **at a stroke and at no cost. [Yes, you read that correctly.] The INVISIBLE INVESTOR SHOWS YOU HOW**

TO MOVE YOUR ASSETS TO ABSOLUTE SAFETY AND (best of all) IT DOES NOT COST ANYTHING. More important, you will make new contacts and much more money on your investments than you ever dreamed possible. You will learn what it means to be a "P.T." or sovereign individual.

- Your private papers and personal records will be invisible and undiscoverable.

- Your assets are likewise invisible and undiscoverable in the custody of big safe banks that do not even know your name.

- Yet, you can cash out any time. Have all your money in your hand instantly, anywhere in the world, without any paper trail or electronic record link. [This information not available in any other publication!]

Estate Planning? Forget it! Billions of dollars find their way into the pockets of lawyers, and state and federal tax collectors. The Invisible Investor shows you how (without any lawyer) to avoid probate costs. At a stroke and at no cost, you will eliminate family squabbles over your money after you have gone. You'll find out how wealthy people preserve and pass on 100% of their hard earned money to the loved ones and good causes they really want to have it — not the State. Taxes? The INVISIBLE INVESTOR'S estate pays no taxes. The heirs pay no inheritance taxes!

Capital Gains Taxes? They are completely eliminated, at a stroke.

Your Personal Income Taxes? They too can be *legally* eliminated, completely if you are willing to move abroad (to a tropical paradise?) part of the year and if you run your existing businesses through an offshore corporation. If you have a net worth of over $250,000 to invest, you can live comfortably on your capital's earnings — without working. We show you how and where.

Risk of Criminal Prosecution? With one in every seven Americans now destined to serve jail time for newly defined victimless crimes, you need to plan your personal escape before becoming enmeshed in the legal process. All criminal (and civil) liability is absolutely eliminated because in the case of trouble, not only your assets are out of the jurisdiction, but your personal paperwork and second passport is arranged so you can follow your assets to highly enjoyable get-away places from where you can't be extradited or even *served* with legal papers. You can be safe and your money can be safe. Read this Special Report, the Invisible Investor! If it is not all we say it is (and more) you get your money back; in addition, you keep the $125 worth of free newsletters as a gift.·

THE INVISIBLE INVESTOR

By: Peter Trevellian, Inspired by W.G. Hill

TABLE OF CONTENTS

Get your money out of the country before your country gets the money out of you

*I*T is legal. It is easy. It's Invisible. It is Offshore. Many years ago, I was in a minor dispute with a government agency. They were wrong. I was right. No question about it. They thought I owed them a few thousand dollars in taxes. I knew they owed me considerably more in rebates and refunds. We figured the case might be heard some years down the line. Maybe in some administrative supervisor's office. Maybe in court. However, the odds were, my high priced Certified Public Accountants would settle the claim. Probably in my favor. That is what I paid them for. It was no worry for me at the start. If the accountants could not work out something, it would go to the lawyers. "My team" would insulate me. I was well insured, and well protected against every contingency. So I thought!

Negotiation and compromise had resolved similar differences of opinion a hundred times before. In those days, I had a sizable business to run: hoards of employees, rents to pay, and a big payroll to meet. There were projects to complete. I was busy! Couldn't be bothered with giving a lot of personal attention to a piddling small tax claim amounting to less than a day's rent for my firm. So maybe I refused to take a call and had staff refer some squeaky voiced government guy to my accountants. I did not even remember the incident. The disputed matter seemed a little thing, like a baby leech on your rear when you are up to your eyeballs in alligators.

The Whole Shebang Hits The Fan

While at my desk, 9:00 a.m. one foggy Monday morning, a good, reliable supplier, "Mrs. Zanadu," burst into my inner office unexpectedly: "How could you do this to me?" She was waiving my bounced check for $75,000. Her people had done a good job and I had authorized full payment for her on the prior Friday. I told her, "Calm down — let's have a look?" I knew our check was written against a good account. We had more than enough on deposit to cover this check several times over. There was a credit line too.

"There's been a mistake," I exclaimed. "You take this downstairs to our good friend, the Bank Manager, Mr. Moneypenny. He'll set things right!" I was writing a memo to Moneypenny, my bank manager about cashing the attached $75,000 check immediately for Mrs. Zanadu, when my ex-wife Lady Morgana De La Fey Trevellian burst in screaming:

Morgana [Fire-Breathing Lady-Dragon] Enters Hissing

"You dirty, low down %$#@#$*. It's enough that you $#@$ me in our divorce, but how could you do this to your own kid?" Her scenes were nothing new. I sent Mrs. Zanadu on her way, and gently but firmly told Morgana the Terrible, "Calm down darling sweetness, have a seat. Have this cup of soothing Tizana Tea I made for myself. Tell me what's on your mind. Please dear. Do not be upset. "$$#@# you + your ^#@$#@!!% your tea" She blurted, angrily, as my peace offering hit the wall breaking the cup into an irretrievable archeological artifact. "The G-men just seized your daughter's Christmas and birthday money: Two-thousand six hundred and thirty six dollars. And if you, you %$$$#@#$, don't hand it over in cash in the next thirty seconds, my lawyers will make you wish you were never born." I knew better than to argue with Morgana, so I went into my petty cash drawer and pulled out $3,000 cash. "No need to threaten me. I do not know how this happened; nevertheless I will take your word for it. Here, these three grand is for our little Snookums. You keep the change and get your pretty hair done up in a Beehive or whatever you like. You always look so beautiful when you're mad."

I said it (about her looking beautiful when she was mad) although it was not true. It was a good line from an old Clark Gable movie. It usually worked to keep the women in my life from sinking into a self-induced hysteria or throwing things. "You're so cute when you're angry." One of my favorite lines. It often brought a smile to their face, tears to their eyes, and after a few minutes of tender embracing, they were firmly in my control — where all beautiful women belong. However, Morgana (still with a magnificent figure) would have none of it. That was how my day started on *disaster Monday.*

She grabbed the money, pushed me away, and said rather calmly, " The smartest thing I ever did was to get a quick divorce from you. So long." She moved towards the door like an angry tornado. Then, she paused. What next? She pouted and cooed: "You'll get your comeuppance some day!" She turned her back to me again and headed slowly towards the door. At the door, she paused again. Aha, she is coming 'round, I hoped. She turned, just her head this time, and gave me the same fleeting smile that once warmed my heart. Then she blew me a kiss. "Bye," she murmured sweetly.

"We sure had some good loving together" I mused. She was wife number three for me (and almost the most expensive of the lot) but I still loved her. Sort of. The next time I was to see her it was in court — again. Ah, well, I digress. Back to the main tale.

The Longest Day

To put that very long and disastrous day in a nutshell, at least fifty people complained of bad checks that Monday. My business went into a dead faint and never woke up again. We had no money, and were locked out! No access to any of our projects. The finished properties and construction projects were all sealed. My workers were greeted with bits of tape and official warnings taped on all entrances:

"Warning do not break this official seal! These properties have been seized, by order of the United States of America, etc., etc."

Every single one of my personal and company bank accounts were empty. Every stock brokerage account was "frozen." I had only the money in my wallet. What the heck had happened? Some pimple faced little twerp in the bowels of some government office building basement, had decided to screw me over real well. He might be a nobody, he might be on a small salary, but he could show some son-of-a-gun rich tycoon like me *who really held the power in our society.* To show whose boss in connection with the disputed claim of a few thousand dollars, he gave an order to place liens on all my properties. All my bank accounts (immediately isolated by computer search) were closed — turned over to his agency for further disposition. Newspapers were notified by official government press releases that this action had been taken because of my uncooperative attitude. [I dared to question the claim!] My special treatment was to serve as a warning to all business and professional people that they must drop everything to kiss the fanny of any junior bureaucrat who wanted to waste their time and make up claims out of thin air. My ex-wife's fury had been provoked because my daughter, then six, had a few thousand dollars in a savings account. Morgana the witch, I mean wife, umm, ex-wife was (at that time) the sole signer on the kid's account. However, my name and identity number was associated with this account. When the kid was only a few days old, I had opened it. Now, six years later, it had been confiscated, along with every other bank account, stock brokerage account, and property I owned or had any interest in.

I had used my security number to open the account six years earlier because the baby didn't have her own I.D. number yet. Now it belonged to the government. Was this a bad dream? The long and short of it was that from that day on, all my employees were out of a job. Mrs. Zanadu and all my creditors (innocent of any wrongdoing — as I was) were to remain forever unpaid. Most of my old contacts would never do business with me again. They blamed me for defaulting on deals that were no longer in my control. I was soon to be held in criminal contempt and sent to jail for being unable to meet my alimony and child support obligations. The government agency, which had tied up hundreds of times more in assets than their claims were worth, insisted I, owed them still more. Other state and local agencies piggybacked onto these claims. I soon had so many civil cases, trumped up fraud charges, and other troubles that there did not seem to be any light at the end of the tunnel.

To PT Or Not To PT

Some would have defenistrated (jumped out of a window). This was the euphemism employed during that period in government "resolution reports" i.e., the conclusion in similar cases. Really — No joke! No defenestration for me! Though not prepared for a totally unexpected battle with the government, I (fortunately) had some experience in operating offshore. I had moved myself and my assets abroad for a short period when I learned Morgana was going to sue me for divorce. After settling with her, my guard was down. Big mistake! It cost me most of my assets.

The Body Is Gone

Six months later, I packed up everything I had left in one small rucksack. I borrowed money from the few friends I still had left, and boarded the first flight to anywhere. What flight? I had no plan, just wanted to get out of the country and have space to think. Fortunately, once I was alone — without the pressures of daily depositions and court appearances, I remembered that I still had one bank account abroad. A long deceased foreign aunt and uncle had established it for me as a child. Their small estate had gone into this account before the Morgana divorce, and it stayed there on the very good advice of a lawyer who told me to leave the funds abroad, "just in case." There was enough money there, safe from government attack, to support me for a few years while I decided what to do next. What had been irrelevant small change in my financial heyday became my survival stash! Not enough to support me for life, but sufficient to allow me to relax, smell the flowers, get out from under, and breathe freely.

Do We Fight Or Do We Let It Go?

It's another story, the litigation's end, but I learned that when your property is seized in litigation (especially when the government is the plaintiff), even if you win — it can be years and years till you get back any part of it. Even if you are judged to be completely in the right, when the smoke clears, any real estate that was mort- gaged has long ago been foreclosed and lost. Maybe it is sold for back (local) taxes. Your business or profession? Forget it. Client's stay away from any lawyer whose client trust accounts are seized and who cannot keep himself out of trouble. Even the big star, F. Lee Bailey hasn't made much of a comeback since 1996 when he served 45 days in jail for contempt until he coughed up $16 million to pay a government claim.

How about your cash and securities? What a joke! Any recovery — when you don't have money to pay lawyers hourly rates — is subject to their fifty per cent contingent attorney fees (if you win), plus costs. You might get 25% net, if you are very lucky. The best case scenario is hardly worth seven or eight years of court appearances, depositions, document searches and long waits in lawyers offices and rat hole hearing rooms. Your business goes to pot. Worst of all, when you have been grievously wronged, there is no one to sue. "The govern- ment acted in good faith," says the judge. Not sometimes. Every time! Besides, says the judge: "As a sovereign, your government officials are immune to any action for damages." Your lawyer? He has got his half. "Maybe you can get a congressman or senator to pass a private bill to have the US Treasury make you whole again." Sure, if you believe in Santa Claus or Easter Bunnies. Had I to do it over again, it would have been better to walk away. Devote all that time and energy spent in courts and in rat-hole depo- sition rooms instead towards new projects and a new life abroad. The past is dead. Let it go.

A Different World, A Different Life

Once upon a time, some fifteen years after Bloody Monday, I met another exile in Europe who had owed me $12,000 for a car I'd sold him just before leaving. He had been a good friend. Later, he had troubles of his own, and like I did, he made a new life for himself abroad. I reminded him of the money he owed me. "Come on my friend," he said, "That was a different world — a different life. For- get it." He was right. I never brought it up again.

It Is Just A Game For The Bureau-Rats, But It Is Your Life They Disrupt

For the little twerp bureau-rat that set up the chain of events that disrupted my universe and ruined me financially, it was all a paper game. I was just one of hundreds of similar lives ruined by him in his brief government career. Such twerps grow up to become politicians or more often amoral private lawyers. They inevitably change sides. Graduating with credentials in advanced harassment, they move on to represent victims instead of setting them up. However, government always holds the winning hand. Their bureaucrats have endless resources, nothing else to do, immunity from counter-suits, friendly judges (who work for the same employer) and special rules of discovery and collection — just for them. They win 98% of all their cases. Even State prosecutors win over 95% of the criminal cases they bring to court. The "O.J. Simpson" acquittal in his first case was a one in ten million event.

Movies and books usually see the innocent person acquitted. In real life, a criminal defendant always loses. Even if he is not convicted, the stress, loss of face, and finally the hemorrhaging attorney fees do irrevocable damage. To me, being caught in the wringer caused my then current marriage to fall apart long before the trial was over. Post-conviction, becoming an exile, a fugitive and being impoverished put me in a position where for many years it was impossible to see my own kids. There was a lot of other damage, but I will not bore you with a six hundred page partial summary.

"Well," says you, dear reader, "You were well educated, healthy, relatively young, had money and friends abroad. What are you complaining about? Other people start far worse off than you were when you left the country.

"Wake Up Call Hey! Wake Up!"

This is not a plea for sympathy. I am not somebody on a crusade — a guy who wants the Justice System to be more just. This is a wake up call FOR YOU. To warn you that there is An Unseen Danger out there. I want to prevent you from ever being caught in a situation

— worse than mine — from where there may be no exit. My story had a happy conclusion. But I was for months in a mental state where it would have been quite easy to blow my brains out or to turn to booze or dope for comfort. Stories like mine do not usually have a happy conclusion. As for me, sure, things worked out. I got a chance to live in Monaco and watch the pretty, topless French girls for a while. Then I found lasting romance, a new family, and a new career in Europe. Sure, I lost many of my possessions. It was down the toilet with everything I had built up over twenty years. I was forced to sever ties with all my old friends. Whatever social position and status I had was gone with the wind. Nevertheless, I was able to make a comeback of sorts — to survive and prosper. "Living well is the best revenge." Part of my success and survival was because I was young and part because I had some mad money abroad. To be quite honest, I think another essential factor was my attitude. I was not going to be beaten. But as with Scarlet O'Hara, a whole good life was taken away from me. It was "Gone With the Wind." I was, in effect, a refugee. For you, if you are mentally financially and paperwork prepared, you probably will never have to leave and to suffer nearly as much as I did. Why? Because you will not be fatally injured when the enemy fires their first volley. This process of learning how to protect yourself takes a bit of understanding. You have only 240 pages to go! But let me give you a hint. Being PT or Prepared Thoroughly involves hiding a large portion of your assets and getting your paperwork in order so that you can disappear (out of the country) and stay out of every computer in the world until things cool off. When the money is gone and the body is invisible, there is nobody to sue, arrest, or harass. You are as free as a ghost, or a soaring soul.

You Become A PT: The Perpetual Traveler

Years later, after a career in quite unrelated matters, I met Dr. W.G. Hill at a seminar in Monte Carlo. We became closely associated (when I volunteered to be his proofreader and editor). He became a legendary guy who earlier on had very similar problems to mine. He too was a tax exile or Perpetual Traveler (PT). By then, he was a successful consultant on "offshore matters." Through him I learned of many other people who did not come out so well — and a few who did much better (financially) than I did. But once you lose a great fortune, the value of money falls more into perspective. You need enough dough to cover the basics, but beyond that, relationships, health, and creative work become much more important than collecting more chips or markers. Much of this book will contain the wisdom of my former mentor who has since gone to the land of five flags where all good PT's go. How about the Five Flags? It goes something like this: Every PT should realize that "his" government exists to exploit him, not to serve him. Accordingly, five (probably new) flags should be chosen. They are:

1. A country that will give you citizenship and a good passport — and not control and tax you when you are gone.

2. A country where you can work or make serious money.

3. A country where you can play or indulge yourself in what gives you pleasure — even though such activities may be considered illegal, immoral, or fattening at the place where you formerly lived.

4. A country where you can have a "legal residence" and where there are no onerous regulations, property taxes nor income taxes. Of course, the country should not require that you actually spend any time there.

5. A country from where your investments and financial dealings can be run by trustworthy employees, institutions or banks. This place must have genuine independence, good secrecy laws, a laissez-faire attitude, and a long tradition of the inviolability of private property.

Each of the above five flags should be different from each other, and certainly different from the country you were born in or are presently a citizen of. What does all this mean to you? Probably nothing, but that is because you have a lot to learn and there is a whole "offshore" world out there that you do not understand at all.

What Is The Purpose Of Learning About This Other World?

What is this new way of thinking? Simply put, the average professional or businessperson doesn't realize that the only thing between him and sudden disaster (like mine) is a thing called "judicial and prosecutorial discretion." Or to say it another way, if anyone gets in a lawsuit or comes to the attention of certain bureaucrats who for any reason doesn't like them, that bureaucrat can pull the plug. Like cancer or an AIDS infection, your life then changes radically. Most people will not believe it can happen to them — until it happens! What to do? Like the Boy Scout Motto says: "Be Prepared!"

Government Isn't The Only Enemy

When you are hit with a lawsuit — maybe just for failure to file an environmental impact report — your whole world can collapse overnight. What about sexual harassment? Today, a suggestive glance (and nothing else) can cost you a million dollars, plus attorney's fees of an equal amount. The plaintiff's award in a sexual harassment case can be more than that if you happen to have any visible serious money. In most communities, hungry lawyers roam the streets like scavengers, trying to stir up "class actions" and other lawsuits that will transfer wealth from the deep pockets of productive people into their own ravenous maws. There is one guy around who has never made any legitimate money from his patents, but he acquired thousands of dormant patents just for their lawsuit potential, he has become a near billionaire by filing many patent infringement suits. Another chap in California gets copyrights on short (sometimes rather prosaic) sayings. Then he sues authors and publishers who use them.

"Beware the slivey toves," Alice in Wonderland was told. "They gire and gimbel in the borogroves." Life and love can be surrealistic these days. Another strong possibility is mistaken identity. You are a saint, but computer error or misidentification targets you as some kind of tax evader, money launderer or criminal. The laws are such that crimes can be tailored to fit any individual who falls into the net. By the time things are resolved, maybe you have spent years in litigation, or at worst, jail. My own personal observation (from having been there) is that at least one third of the people in jail or convicted of felonies do not deserve the abuse they get. Your chance? Fully one in five that you will be accused of a crime during your lifetime. About one in seven that you will be convicted!

For wealthy people who used to be virtually immune from criminal charges, the odds are changing — not in our favor. We are now prime targets. The "undeserving rich" like Mike Milken and Leona Helmsley are the means, the stepping stones by which ambitious bureaucrats become successful politicians. Bureaucrats and politicians produce nothing of value, but they love to destroy those who achieve prominence in productive enterprises. At some time in your life, if you are an entrepreneur or innovative professional, it is extremely likely that you will lose your assets and very possibly serve some hard time. Business risks? We have not even mentioned good old fashioned business risks and economic cycles that have destroyed (or will sooner or later bring down) every economic enterprise that ever existed on Earth.

Assets on deposit abroad, the same "insurance" that will keep you afloat when you are sued, will help you survive and rise again when and if circumstances cause insolvency.

Civil Contempt

Did you know there is a very good chance of your doing time in a non-criminal matter? Several examples will be cited later in this report. Many people, particularly professional people and wealthy people go to jail for "civil contempt." Once, when (after the divorce) I was having a dispute with good old Morgana over visitation and child custody, the judge got disgusted (mainly with her) and said: "I don't think either of you are fit parents. I am taking your "Snookums" into State custody, and putting her into foster care. Now, both of you get out of my courtroom!" he snarled. "Come back in sixty days after you have settled this between yourselves!" The reason we were in court was that we could not settle it between ourselves. We wanted a decision, but not that decision. All I asked was that Morgana should let me have Snookums on alternate weekends — as the court order had provided. Morgana said no. "You'll see the kid only when I say so." Now the judge was going to institutionalize the four-year-old? What kind of thing was this? Of course, I was furious! My baby was only four! I was so shocked by this order; I blurted out, "Your honor, that is the dumbest thing I ever heard. I withdraw my objections. Give Snookums to my wife. Don't send her to an orphanage!" What did that get me? Guess? "That outburst will cost you five days in the county jail and a $500 fine. I am the only one who makes the decisions in this court-room, and don't you forget it!"

Moral Of The Story

The point is that your personal freedom and your control over your own money and your destiny hang by a thread. Any number of jerks like the judge above can cut that thread. These people are often ignorant, uncaring, jealous people with their own agenda. In my opinion, (hereafter IMO) neither state social workers, judges, nor private litigants who come into your life by random chance, should be allowed to have such control. Nobody but you should have power over your kids, your person, and your assets.

In coming pages, I will take you through the hidden trails that lead many of my clients and I, to take complete control over their own destinies. You should have the **right to earn money honestly and to save or dispose of it as you please.** We do not need to be part of an unfair system. We can be individual sovereigns, writing our own rules.

Can you afford to ignore the rest of this story? I do not think so. Do not wait until some capricious event deprives you of your money, your business, your family or your precious personal freedom. My foreign bank account, the one that saved my life, was provided for me in a way that amounted to a lucky — a very lucky, accident. If you don't have a rich uncle abroad who has set you up with survival money, then do it yourself. Opening your own bank or stock broker-age account offshore costs nothing. It is legal, and it might save your life. It is a first step toward becoming an Invisible Investor.

Get your money out of the country before your country gets the money out of you!

Offshore Finance" for Dummies

*W*HAT do people mean when they say "Offshore?"

An "offshore bank" for instance, is nothing more or less than *any bank outside the country or "jurisdiction" where you, the customer lives.* An "offshore" corporation, trust, foundation or any legal entity formed outside the country where YOU live is "Offshore" for you.

You do not have to really know anything else to bluff your way through a cocktail party. But if you stop here, you won't know the real reason why "Offshore" financial planning is a necessity for nearly everyone of substance in most of the world.

"Offshore" For A German Citizen May Be "Domestic" For An American

If "Hans Makler" lives in Germany, he may have his offshore bank account in New York City. There, under the US "Edge Act" his account has bank secrecy! Why? Simply because he is a foreigner. Americans do not get the same protection. If you live in New Orleans or Dallas, an account in New York would not be "offshore" for you, but an account in Frankfurt, Germany would be. Moreover, under German law, you would have greater bank secrecy there, and thus, more protection against the claims of stateside creditors and tax collectors than you would get with a domestic account. Get it? Again, *an offshore account is any account owned by you at a loca-*

tion outside of your present place of residence or citizenship. A foreigner may have his offshore account in your hometown, but you can never have an offshore account in your own hometown.

Offshore Vs Domestic

An account in a foreign bank is called an "offshore account" and an account in your home country is called a "domestic account." If you live in the USA, any account abroad — in Albania, Estonia, Hong Kong Sweden or Zimbabwe is "offshore." An account in Boston, Miami, Honolulu or the Canal Zone is "domestic."

What is the difference between a domestic deposit and an offshore deposit in terms of practical effect?

Advantages Of A Domestic Account

The advantage of a domestic account used to be convenience. You walked over to your corner bank and could make unlimited cash deposits or withdrawals over the counter. You could not do that very easily if your bank was in Hong Kong. Today, with an ATM (Automatic Teller Machine) card, you can make cash withdrawals at any hour of the day or night from any offshore account. You can walk up to the wall at any bank or for that matter, any grocery store or shopping center where they have an ATM machine. You can pull out the cash you need. You cannot move cash abroad very easily, but if you deposit "unusual amounts" of cash (read over $100) domestically, you may ring all sorts of bells. You can make instant transfers to and from offshore accounts by telephone, email, or fax. Same at home. So domestic or offshore, convenience and ease of use is about the same these days.

The only remaining advantage of your domestic banking relationship is that if you want to get an unsecured loan, you probably think your local high street (main street) bank is more likely to give it to you. An offshore bank would want collateral for any loan. Or would they? The usual perceptions are wrong, as usual. Your offshore bank will issue you a credit card. Depending upon the credit card, you may be able to get unsecured cash advances for up to several hundred thousand dollars, unsecured. Then too, certain banks in Europe, especially in the United Kingdom, expect you to run your account with a debit balance (that is, always in the red). Thus, the reality is you can borrow more unsecured, at lower rates "offshore" than at home. Is the offshore bank likely to give you a bigger secured loan on better terms than your home bank, or a bigger home loan? Probably yes. In addition, for anything complicated, like a letter of credit, your offshore bank is probably better equipped to service you than your local, hometown bank. Bottom line? Anything your hometown bank can do, an offshore bank can do better.

Disadvantages Of A Domestic Account

One of the main reasons that offshore banking has become popular is that a domestic account in many jurisdictions, particularly in the USA or Canada is about as private as your most guarded secrets. Your account balance may not be featured in Newsweek's front cover, but it is just as easy to have a look at. Everybody can see into it — your American bank account that is.

Once an attorney representing a potential adversary knows your bank balance, he makes his decision whether to sue or not to sue. Even with a very weak case, he will sue Mr. Deep Pockets. Even with a very strong case, he will not sue Mr. No Account. Accordingly, the main disadvantage of a domestic account is that anyone can find out what's in it, and a government agent can freeze and seize it — often without giving you any notice at all.

Private Civil Cases

In a civil case, if a person suing you for damages, divorce (or whatever), makes a statement that you are a sneaky son-of-a-gun who will hide your money as soon as you get sued, he will normally get a court order *ex parte*, (no notice to you) freezing your account. A *civil plaintiff needs a court order to grab your money.* To get a court order, he must make up a convincing story for the judge. Collection lawyers are experts at that. If you really are perceived as a defendant who is smart enough to move assets out of harm's way, any judge will grant an order tying up your accounts till the lawsuit is over.

You will probably get a notice your money is tied up — after it happens. [Special Note: Keep books such as this one well hidden from potential adversaries. It could be used as evidence of your intention to move money abroad to evade your creditors.]

Government Civil Cases

The government has an easier time grabbing your dough. They do not need a court order to freeze your account. Many government agency junior employees (DEA or Treasury to name just two of dozens) are issued with little pads of forms. They just fill in your account number. The bank or stockbroker holding your money is obliged not only to freeze the account, but also to *transfer it to them without further formality.* The government employee may have created a claim out of thin air because he does not like you, or he made a mistake and confused you with someone of a similar name. Your assets may be your life savings, or loan proceeds committed to an important business deal. It does not matter. They are gone and you won't get them back without a fight that will cost you (in many cases) more than the assets are worth. If it was a government seizure, even if you recover, you get nothing for your legal costs or the years of aggravation you spent in court. Moreover, the latest wrinkle is that your funds may be blocked or seized electronically. Yes, from the bowels of the nearest Federal Building, an eruption of electrons can give the order to separate you from your assets. However, this trick will only work on domestic accounts.

Due Process

Years ago, there was a (long dead) legal concept called "due process." To take your money or property, the government had to notify you in advance. To confiscate your assets they had to have trial. Some years ago, that due process requirement was reduced to "an administrative hearing" in front of a Kangaroo Court of government officials. They always sided with the government. The bureaucrats always felt that even such a stacked hearing was an unnecessary delay of the inevitable. Now to save time, they do not even need to go through the motions of a "fair hearing." These days, the government *simply* takes your money, your safe deposit box contents, or your securities. You will not find out about it until you try to access the money. Even then, your bankers or brokers may have been "gag-ordered" to not say a word about it. So sometimes you cannot even find out who took your money or why, without hiring a lawyer and going to court a long and expensive process. I do not want to be told this does not happen. It has happened to me! It has happened to my clients. Neither my clients nor I had any connection with drugs, money laundering, nor organized crime. The new easy-seizure laws were passed by Congress — justified in order to carry on the "Drug War," but usable against you.

My guess is that 99 out of every hundred asset seizures these days involve people who have absolutely no connection to illicit drugs. Anyone in banking, finance, legal, or accounting services knows what the score is. The government just helps itself to the money of "bad people." *Bad people according to Bureaucrat Rule Number One, is anyone who is not a bureaucrat, politician, or welfare recipient.* Actually, there is no such rule. I just made that up. However, the truth is that the small minority of people reading this book is the productive people of this world.

Anyone not riding the government gravy train really is the target. If you employ people who produce anything besides red tape, you and your assets are not safe. And that's why people like us have gone "offshore."

Another Small Point:

Withholdings (for taxes or otherwise) of part of your "unearned" interest and dividend income can not be taken out of your off-shore account. There is *no reporting* of any interest or dividends to any tax authorities. These things happen with domestic accounts at banks and brokers, but not with offshore accounts. An offshore account is like buried treasure. No one can steal it from you because no one knows about it — unless you tell them!

The Popularity Of Offshore Accounts Is A
Response To The Vulnerability Of Domestic Accounts

How does it work? Why are foreign or offshore accounts safer? If you have a bank or brokerage account with a firm outside your own country, it is not so easy for an adversary either civil or governmental, to find out about it. It is even harder for them to grab it. How safe your offshore account is depends on many factors:

Is your account at a firm owned or controlled by a parent company in your home country? Why is this important? Simple! Say an American has a Panamanian or Swiss bank account at Citibank (an American owned bank). Or a brokerage account at Merrill Lynch (also an American Firm). Obviously, the United States Government can search the company records in the States (accessible to the parent company), and find the owner's name and balance. Seizure of the assets is just as easy because all dollar accounts wherever opened, are always kept in the United States.

Because of treaties and deals with Canada, the USA and Canada are the same. Thus, we come to our first exceptions:

To gain the most important benefits of an offshore account, namely privacy and asset protection, the accounts should be in a country not overly friendly with your own country. They should have no "exchange of information" treaties and they should have a tradition of bank secrecy.

Advantages Of Offshore Accounts

The main advantages of offshore accounts as we have seen, *are privacy and greater security against seizure.* Other advantages are:

Higher Interest Rates

With the whole world to look at, you may well find banks that offer *higher interest rates* and greater security (insofar as the banks are less risky).

Ability To Invest In Foreign Currency Or "Forbidden" Offshore Funds

If a conservative investor in the USA put $100,000 in 8% treasury bonds or a savings account yielding 8%, at the end of a year, inflation robbed him of 6%, State and Federal taxes took half of the interest income. At the end of the year after taxes, he had a nominal $104,000, but the value in purchasing power was under $98,000 in terms of the money he started with. Tax-free bonds were a break-even proposition, with more risk of loss (due to the possibility of a municipality defaulting). With your money in an offshore roll-up fund (in a currency that has less inflation), it is easy to realize a true growth in capital. We do not like bonds or savings accounts very much, because the returns on stock or equity funds are historically two to three times as high as on interest bearing investments. Either way, no one can deny that far more options are open to the investor whose capital is invested from a base or headquarters outside of his home country. For those who are too timid to invest through an alternate identity, the other possibilities are to use a trust, charitable foundation, non-profit corporation, corporation, or other legal form like the Liechtenstein Anstalt or "Institute." This Liechtenstein type legal entity has its own separate identity but takes what ever form the person who sets it up chooses to give it. Most offshore centers now have laws to allow the formation of these Liechtenstein type trusts or foundations. To keep things simple, all you have to understand is that there is more than one way to skin a cat. It is possible to have a nest egg or pension plan abroad that earns more money, pays less taxes, and is not subject to any authority other than your own.

Easier Succession (Inheritance)

A domestic account at a bank or broker (or any domestic asset) may be subject to probate when you die. This involves large administration costs and charges. The judge in charge of your estate may appoint his cronies to "appraise" it at a cost of 3% of total value. An "inventory" may cost another 3%. You get nickeled and dimed for so many 2% and 3% charges for nothing that half your estate just fades away into the pockets of lawyers and bureaucrats. Then there is required publication and notices to all relatives, ex-spouses, and creditors — in other words, the whole world gets an open invitation. "Trouble makers, file your claims." All these requirements have been carefully designed to transfer your wealth to lawyers and bureaucrats. If your legal heirs have the slightest dispute between them, lawyers for the estate will delay things and file so many charges for their mediation services and protection of the estate that these alone could eat up half your estate. Then there is the federal estate and state inheritance taxes. Before they are finished, a multi-million dollar estate could be diminished (I should say "demolished") to shoeshine money.

Even if all you have is one joint domestic savings account that is supposed to pass to a successor, if one joint owner dies, and the other survives, an inheritance tax clearance is needed before the surviving owner can get at the money. In plain English, when you die, it will be necessary for your widow (or kid) to employ an attorney, to argue over how much tax is due. In some cases, your loved ones will pay out over ninety percent of the value of the account to clear probate and settle the tax questions.

What Happens To Your *Offshore* Assets When You Die?

In most of the tax haven foreign jurisdictions, the owner of the account and the person(s) he designates are the only people involved. If one of the signatories on an account dies, there is no question of probate, succession, or taxation. The owner can have a document on file, the equivalent of a will that designates his successor(s). The successor (wife or kid) then has sole signing power over the funds and no courts or government agents are involved in any way. There are NO fees, NO charges, NO taxes, and NO administration. If a relative or other claimant thinks, they are entitled to part of your estate, tough luck. They will not even know that there were any offshore assets.

Escaping Exchange Controls

Every government threatened by its citizens' desire to escape burdensome taxes continually tightens the screws by new impositions on its residents and citizens that would not be tolerated elsewhere. What for instance? A nation often imposes EXIT TAXES on those citizens who simply wish to pick up their chips and depart. The USA has done this.

Beating Travel Restrictions

In most democratic countries, a citizen can go anywhere he wants with his national passport. In the USA, there is always a list of countries to which travel is forbidden. Cashing checks or charging lunches in "forbidden Cuba" for instance would be evidence of your trip and result in felony charges against you. Better to have an offshore account (and a second passport) if you are an American and you want to have freedom to travel.

There May Be Currency Restrictions

How much money can be imported, exported, or spent abroad? There is talk of restrictions being imposed by the USA. Obviously, these are circumvented if you have substantial assets abroad. Nelson Mandela went to jail and stayed in the poky for thirty years because he left South Africa without permission and took a few bucks (Rand) with him. If he had an offshore account, the course of African history would have been different.

Restrictions On Ownership Of Foreign Bank Accounts

Restrictions On Investments Abroad

Registration requirements

Reporting requirements

Penalty Taxes on Accounts held abroad

These can all be avoided if funds are placed abroad in a low profile, correct way.

More Services Are Available From Offshore Banks

In virtually every offshore fiscal center, every financial institution or stockbroker offers a much better package of services than any domestic bank/stockbroker in the United States. Local banks talk about being a "full service bank" but they do not do even a tiny portion of what an offshore bank or financial service organization might be willing to do for you. Let us talk about one of my banks. This bank is not even a proper bank. They call themselves a Financial Services Organization. They give me a credit card, just likes yours does. They pay all my credit card charges automatically for me and check them for accuracy. In the old days when I was into conspicuous consumption, they paid all the bills and hired staff for my racing stables, my yacht, and my personal domestic staff. They still chose what stocks, bonds, and commodities I buy and sell. They would even do the detail and grunt work on real estate deals in odd places like Cuba — if I asked them too.

The Discretionary Account

I let my offshore money managers pick and choose my investments on a discretionary basis. Unlike USA stockbrokers who churned and burned me until my money was gone, I have found excellent money managers offshore. They make me a lot more money trading stocks and bonds than I could make with my own selections. For the last twenty-five years I have averaged about 25% a year net annual income in USA dollars. After inflation, that is a real return of around 15% compounded. They collect rents and manage my property — domestic or abroad. They arrange mortgages and loans when needed. They would prepare my income tax forms if I needed the service (I don't!). They prepared and hold my will, and have arranged for all insurance needs at a discount. They will (if I needed them to — which I don't) set up trusts to protect my spendthrift children and my "special someone" from their own foolishness. They will buy my travel tickets, make hotel reservations, get me theater and concert tickets, find me a maid, and even fix me up with a date if I am lonely. They charge for all this service, but (in the old days) it was nice to have "one stop shopping." These days, I have cut back and have a more uncomplicated, possession-free life. My staff of one is an un-paid love-slave. But the money manager is Panama still runs my finances.

When I visit my "bankers" I am given a special welcome at the airport by an uniformed flunky and whisked through customs (with whatever I am carrying subject to the equivalent of diplomatic immunity). I am driven to my destination in a shiny prestige car. They give me a swell annual simulated leather appointment book and a new computer every year. Plus, computer software to keep track of all my investments. Best of all they try harder. If there is any service I suggest or want they try to please.

I am told that soon, instead of paper statements, I will be able to view my entire investment portfolio with an instant daily update over the Internet by punching in a very secret code. I can also trade from my computer. And what does this all cost me? Nix. Nil. Nada. Nunca. Nichts. Zero. Well, sort of!

There is no free lunch of course. My money manager gets commissions on the trades, and I might pay an overall management fee of ° of one percent per year. On some special deals, they get a percentage of profits, based upon performance. For special services, I also have my account charged. But this is a cost, and I said there was no cost. Was I fibbing? No. Look at it this way: Compared to what I used to earn when I watched the market, traded and didn't know a thing about effective tax planning, I am now netting three times as much. How much? I don't want to tell the world exactly what my net worth is, but lets just say if I was netting for instance $100,000 per year on my investments before going offshore, I am netting $300,000 now. Three times as much! Part of it is better investment performance and lower commissions. Part is less taxes. So why should I worry about the fact that the people who made it happen are getting a chunk of my increased profits. If I could double my income again safely; they could have whatever they felt was fair. My rule is to look at what you get and not worry too much about what the other guy is making. Needless to say, I expect my capital to be preserved even if the market goes to blazes! In the 1987 stock market crash, I was only down (at worst) 10% from the all time highs, and at the bottom I was still slightly ahead of what I had started the year at. Am I happy? I used to say all I need is more money, a younger woman and better luck at the racetrack. Once I became a PT, I got everything I wished for except at the track. So, I changed games. No more racetrack.

It's A Joke

Reminds me of the last time I was in Bangkok. I was walking on the beach and came upon an old oil lamp. I rubbed it and out comes a genie. Said he would grant my every wish. So I made a wish. That night I went into one of the bars and showed the girls what I had received from the genie, a little tiny piano and a tiny guy just over a foot high who sat down and played the piano for everybody. Cute? One of the girls said, "Could I make a wish too?" So I rubbed the lamp, the genie came out, and the bargirl said, "I wish for a million bucks!" A few seconds later lots of little ducks flew in the windows and waddled through the doors until the bar was so full of quacking ducks you could barely move. The girl who made the wish yelled at me in the din: "I asked for a million bucks, not a million ducks!" That is when I told her, my genie has a hearing problem — do you think I wished for a fourteen inch "pianist?" [Joke]

Less Risk Of Bank Failure

It is a myth that a FDIC insured USA bank is safer. Years and years ago I had an account in an USA insured bank. When it failed, it turned out that the mere fact that it was insured meant the bank invested in many risky, even crazy deals because the directors knew the Federal Government would bail them out. But did they? Yes and no. From my point of view, I had invested (back in those high interest days) for a 10% return. I could have gotten the same return in safe but uninsured corporate bonds. But I went for the bank (actually a Savings & Loan) because of the FDIC insurance and a free toaster. When the S&L folded, I did not have full access to my money for four years. I got no interest. On $100,000, I figure I lost $40,000 on my insured account. I got the face value of my money back, but considering inflation; I was down another 50% in purchasing power.

Today, I'd rather keep my money in a strong foreign bank where I get high interest at any strong currency that I want, and were banks in general are far more solid than any other in the USA.

Why Are We Talking So Much About The USA?

We do not want to pick on the USA. The legal systems in some other countries are just as bad — in different ways. In addition, the tax systems in places like Spain or Germany may be even more onerous, ruthless, and more unfair — in different ways. But there are two reasons we single out the USA in this Special Report. The first reason is that this is our English Language Edition and most (70%) of our readers are either Americans, or American Expats. The rest are British. Are you British? We expect to have a British oriented edition out some day. In that book, you will find a lot about John Bull, and very little about Uncle Sam. Because you own this book, we will give you a 50% discount on the British Edition. Remind me of this promise when the new book is announced. Get on our mailing list by simply sending your name and address to the publisher. Say: "Someday I want the British Edition at a 50% discount; Or else!"

The second reason is that I, and so many of my friends have been taken to the cleaners by those Gringo Bureau-rats and judges that I needed to warn the world about Outlaw America. Now that I have done it, and have in this book warned you about Swiss banks, I feel a lot better. Many consulting clients of mine have had similar experiences, and the only answer seems to be to:

"Get your money out of the country, before your country gets the money out of you."

Moreover, while you are at it, think about getting your ducks in a row so that you could leave and live "offshore" with your money — if it ever seems like the right thing to do.

Keep on reading for details on how to do it. Do not peek at the "Resource Section" at the back of this book until you have finished the text.

Chapter 3

The Myth: "No Major Trading Country Can Restrict The Movement Of Money And Remain A Major Force In International Commerce"

*T*HIS (above) quote comes from a smart lawyer's best selling book on Offshore Banking.

The author obviously does not know his history. *Every major trading power has at one time absolutely prohibited the private ownership of foreign currency and the import or export of its own currency.* The United States with its current lack of currency controls (aside from reporting requirements) is the **exception** rather than the rule. The greatest trading nation of all (on a per capita basis), Taiwan, did not allow its own citizens to take vacation trips or invest outside of their own country until recently. China, Korea and Japan currently restrict the movement of money. They all depend upon foreign commerce far more than does the USA and is certainly "a major force in international commerce."

Due to currency restrictions, Great Britain's wealthiest citizens for many years after World War II had to make do on vacation trips with only enough money to pay for accommodations in fleabag hotels. Italians until very recently were forbidden to have any foreign currencies or own any property outside of their own country. Italy is the world's leader in foreign trade on a per capita basis — if their underground economy is included in the statistics.

I predict that within twenty years American citizens will be ordered to repatriate all assets held abroad. There will be jail sentences (no parole) for any persons who do not comply. And I further predict that like in Italy, where there are roughly three forbidden foreign accounts for every Italian man, woman, and child, the attempt at government control will be a flop. Laws destine to be ignored are the ones without popular support.

Of course there will be "good government reasons" given: Foreign holdings will be forbidden to further the battle against drugs, crime, inflation, or bad weather. Mexico did in fact pass such a law about a decade ago. As most rich Mexicans did not comply, this law made virtually every upper class Mexican a criminal — under the laws of his home country. Politicians love to criminalize what was once considered ordinary behavior. It gives the government the right to use prosecutorial discretion and go after anyone they please. What is that? Governments always want the "legal right" to put you and anyone else they choose, behind bars. It comes in handy for controlling dissent. However, do not worry about being a criminal in twenty years. There are so many laws now on the books that those persons reading this book could be jailed or have their assets confiscated TODAY. If a prosecutor wants to get you, he can fit your facts to some legally defined crime and send you away.

Moral: If you want to control your assets and protect a nest egg that cannot be stolen from you by the government, you should, nay you *must* have secret assets abroad.

"Get your money out of the country before your country gets the money out of you!"

Chapter 4

PT - What is it all about?

By W.G. Hill, Harry Schultz & Peter Trevellian
(Excerpt From The *Original*, Manuscript *PT*.
A Few Copies Available from Us. See Back Pages)

Do you want to escape the control over your life and property now held by modern Big Brother government? Our PT concept could have been called Individual Sovereignty, because PT's look after themselves. We do not want or need authorities to dominate every aspect of our existence from cradle to grave. We do not need to be protected. We will not be smothered.

The PT concept is one way to break free. It is a coherent philosophy, a plan for a stress free, healthy, prosperous life — not limited by government interference, the threat of nuclear war, the reality of food and water contamination, litigation, domestic conflicts, taxation, persecution or harassment. Whether your problem is an unacceptable child-custody decree or an unwarranted accusation by some Gestapo-style government agency, PT offers escape. It is a way out of any negative situation created and imposed upon you by any government. Many individuals choose to vent their frustrations with acts of violence. The PT merely avoids conflict by refusing to play in any forum where the rules are unfair.

What Does "PT" Stand For?

PT stands for many things, Perpetual Traveler, or Permanent Tourist, for instance. However, a PT **need not travel** all of the time, or **any** of the time for that matter. A PT merely arranges his or her paperwork in such a way that all governments consider him a tourist, a person who is just **Passing Through.** In the eyes of government officials, a PT is merely on a temporary sojourn or vacation. The advantage is that by being seen as a person who is only Parked Temporarily, the PT is not subject to taxes, military service, lawsuits nor persecution for partaking in innocent, but forbidden pleasures. Unlike most citizens or subjects, the PT will not be persecuted for his beliefs or lack of them.

PT is a concept, a way of life, a way of perceiving the universe, and your place in it. One can be a full-time dedicated PT, a part-time PT, or a mental PT ready to make the right moves when the time comes. PT is elegant, simple **and requires no accountants, attorneys, offshore corporations, nor other complex arrangements.** Preparing for this does not cost money it makes money. It is the Perfect Thing.

The Threat Of Big Brother Government

Governments, under the guise of protecting us, have intruded into every area of life, taking the largest part of our earnings in taxes and then rewarding us with little aside from restrictions and harassment. All modern governments these days have virtually eliminated individual privacy and continue to increase limitations on freedom of choice in many areas of human activity. Each country has its own unique restrictions. Even western democracies are growing increasingly fond of keeping their citizenry on very short leashes, if not completely shackled.

The constitutions of most nations give lip service to the absolute freedom to travel, but in practice, every government severely limits travel with passport, visa and other requirements. By imposing restrictions on foreigners, most nations invite tit-for-tat measures. Personal finances, currency controls, domestic situations, and job requirements make the freedom to go anywhere at anytime just a dream for most people. The properly equipped PT operates outside the usual rules, gaining perfect mobility, and a full slate of human rights. PT is the logical and natural path to freedom from dictators, ambitious politicians, emperors, occupying armies, ruling classes, and in a "democracy," the **tyranny of the majority.** Indeed, freedom from the arbitrary whims of senile judges, deranged politicians and the destructive powers of rampant bureaucracy is the essence of PT.

PT's, People of Talent, can, at a few strokes of the pen, be truly free of Big Brother. Since oppressors and exploiters in the modern world exercise control with paperwork and computers, one of your first and prime objectives is to get off all computer lists and registers of any kind. This is easy to accomplish. PT's disappear from the voter lists, then vanish from the roster of property owners or taxpayers. Your present government will no longer be interested in you if they think you have left the jurisdiction and have ceased to be a citizen. It is the goal of the PT to achieve this invisibility by taking on at least one new nationality and acquiring an offshore address.

This worldview opens up all sorts of previously unknown possibilities for the PT. For instance, US banks are not permitted to encourage US customers to keep accounts in foreign currencies. Foreign banks are not permitted to advertise such accounts in the US. Regulated financial institutions are forbidden to advertise the fact that when the dollar is devalued, all American bank accounts, stocks and real property decline in relative value. A dollar decline of 50 per cent against most other currencies occurred between 1985 and 1987. The vast numbers of US citizens were kept in the dark about the simple procedure for avoiding this predictable loss. They could have made a sure 100 per cent on their money in one year by switching into yen, Swiss francs, or German marks.

Furthermore, PT freedom extends much further than monetary concerns. Government-instigated wars or military service that they would rather avoid need inconvenience neither the PT nor his family. The flexibility and mobility inherent in being a PT means that one will never be an unwilling draftee, victim, jailbird, concentration camp inmate, casualty, refugee or displaced person. PT's choose their own fights and surroundings. They are not swept along in torrents caused by forces beyond their control.

You can rest assured that with the PT theory, you will be able to remain comfortably beyond the reach of Big Brother's ever-extending grasp. It is impossible for any government to attack or wipe out PT's because we are an amorphous group without consistent behavior patterns. From the point of view of any government official, we appear to be the most desirable kind of tourist, respectful of local laws and authority, low profile and prosperous. PT's cannot be identified, classified, or isolated from the general run of tourists. Thus, unlike some publicity seeking individualists or tax rebels, a PT courts no danger and invites no confrontations.

Avoid Taxes Legally

A Canadian investor with a large income from his stocks and bonds would normally be obligated to sacrifice almost half of his earnings to the Canadian government. He could choose to reduce his tax burden in the most common, but ill-advised way, the fiddle. He would then become a criminal, at least in Canada. Many countries have only civil penalties for tax violations, but Canada, the UK and the United States have made tax evasion into a criminal offense, resulting in what are in effect debtors prisons for those who refuse to pay taxes. It would be far more sensible for this Canadian investor to break free and become a PT.

By merely moving abroad and establishing a legally recognized residence and domicile in a tax haven, this Canadian investor would be able to legally avoid handing over half of his income to the bureaucrats. He would then also be free to roam the world as desired, provided he did not remain anywhere outside of his new tax haven home long enough to be considered resident for tax purposes. Thus, the PT avoids all income taxes without resorting to fraud, because it is not necessary. A theoretically perfect PT need never file tax returns, government required disclosure forms or any other paperwork.

The major exception to this scenario is if you are a US passport holder, in whom case you will also have to divest yourself of what is commonly, known as the most expensive passport in the world. I will discuss the particular problems faced by Americans in greater detail later in this report.

If you do not enjoy forcible extraction from your bank account or restrictions on your basic human rights, then **you can easily move and declare yourself a legal resident of anywhere you please.** If you do not like paying taxes, they can legally be avoided. There is no government that has the legal right or the practical ability to tax a PT who neither lives within its borders permanently nor has any assets there.

The PT is free to enrich the world with his talent, skills, invention, industry, or artistry and then enjoy 100 per cent of the fruits of his work or enterprise. Unlimited, untaxed wealth and the power to dispose of it as you please are one of the major benefits of becoming a PT. PT's can produce good things, be paid in full without withholdings or deductions, and then spend their earnings on what gives them pleasure.

PT Possibilities

As PT's, only those restrictions imposed by ourselves can keep us from experiencing the wonders of the world. The PT can and will drive, fly or sail across international frontiers when and where he wants, alone or with anyone he chooses. PT's move freely without exit permits or visas. As PT's we should be mentally, financially and physically prepared to leave anywhere we happen to be and go to the other end of the earth at the first whiff of danger or just in search of greener pastures. The PT is able to move fast and decisively, to disappear, and resurface anywhere, anytime.

As PT's we can **read what we want to read, eat what we want to eat, see what we wish to see, imbibe or ingest as desired and invest anywhere in anything. We are completely free from restrictions placed upon us by governments.** We can buy or sell what we please. We can associate with employ or live with people whom we find agreeable and pleasing. If we want to change friends, employment or climate for any reason, we can do so almost instantaneously without the need to get any sort of permission from the state. Until you become a PT, the range of opportunities denied to you is inconceivable. People don't miss the things of which they are unaware. This report will raise your consciousness as to the nature of freedom. It is one way to rid yourself of limitations.

Upon becoming a PT, I discovered that I could drive at top speed on a public highway without ever getting a ticket. The secret was merely the German autobahn where there are no speed limits. Fast motoring may not be your cup of tea, but the point is whatever your particular pleasure or peculiarity may be, there are always going to be several places in the world where it is legal and available. In Germany, the land of BMW and Porsche, the vast majority of the locals feel that it is their inalienable human right to zip along as fast as their cars can go. A PT need never be tempted to break any laws. If he feels like doing something **illegal,** like playing a hand of high-stakes poker in a town where gambling is not permitted, he simply goes away and does it where it's legal. A PT seeks out places where he can do as he pleases, legally and openly.

Many men and women in Ireland were forced to become PT's because divorce is not allowed. The thought of being forced to stay married for life to a much-disliked spouse was enough to send them across the seas. The Irish still consider many types of physical contact between two consenting adults to be a crime. This list includes adultery (even if his or her spouse deserted one party thirty years ago), fornication (sex before marriage) and even oral sex between married couples. All of these activities are punishable by long jail terms in Ireland and many other Christian countries.

With PT, gone is all the fear of fines, censure or jail for victimless crimes. Gone is the fear of eating turtle soup or roast pork or drinking wine, activities that are illegal in almost half the world. Gone is the fear of violating such laws as prohibition against peeing in a toilet reserved for members of a certain race. I say goodbye to all such laws. Goodbye also, to all censorship and managed news. Goodbye to government forms in quintuplets. Our personal finances, the medical treatment we need, our personal domestic life and relationships are strictly our private affair, not objects to be manipulated by government against our personal interests.

PT Means Real Freedom

As PT's we can study any philosophy, raise, and educate our children in our beliefs and opinions without contradiction from our government-controlled school curriculum. We can pass on our knowledge and point of view according to our inner lights. We need not follow the dictates of an obtuse school commissar who bans our favorite books and forbids mention of those truths we find most self-evident.

As PT's we finally become able to invent, improvise, abandon, reject, or follow any religion, personal morality or way of life we choose. We can shop, have a drink, or eat when we want, not just when the local laws allow restaurants and stores to be open. For those with unconventional thoughts, habits, or beliefs, PT is the answer. Life can be lived spontaneously, free, without state imposed restrictions. Becoming a PT means never again having to ask permission or submit to any higher authority. Life is free of permits, licenses, exit permits, visas, currency restrictions, taxes, record keeping, bureaucrats, social workers, litigation, filing, and reports.

PT's need not put up with rules, regulations or laws they find personally offensive, inconvenient or immoral. Thus if it suits him or her, without any government or church dispensation, the PT may have as many spouse-equivalents as can be managed. The range of possibilities for greater freedom is expanded to whatever can be conceived. A PT may be celibate and need not own a car or acquire any other status symbol unless so desired.

On the other hand, the PT can live in a highly controlled society if he so chooses, if for some reason this sort of community gives him a sense of security or perhaps even superiority. PT is all about options. The more options you have, the more free you are. A PT can live under whichever system suits him best.

This freedom, however, does not mean that a PT should be or can be irresponsible by causing problems, injury, or pain to others. The message of PT is not to encourage greed, lust, irresponsibility, immorality, or any of the other seven deadly sins. On the contrary! To avoid government's heavy hand is to avoid violating local laws and morality. We must go physically to those places where doing what we want to do is accepted as ordinary behavior. No point in spending time where our lifestyle, appearance or conduct will cause moral offense or get us into difficulties with local authorities. Thus, a PT who likes to drive fast can push his Ferrari along at 175 mph on the German autobahn where it is legal but not in California, where more reasonable speeds are called for. The PT concept involves discovering those places where your particular pleasures are legal and accepted. Fortunately, there are few possibilities in human behavior, no matter how bizarre, that are not considered "normal" somewhere on planet earth.

You need not worry any longer about what the neighbors might think because you can move to where your neighbors will think you are just terrific, or where they ignore you. You need not worry if your local laws or politics seem to be irrational. Is the mainstream morality incompatible with your own needs? Do you not like litigious lawyers? Nosy social workers? Alimony prone ex-wives? Misconceived programs for the "good of society"? Why put up with them?

As PT's we can now vote with our feet, but the trip does not have to be irrevocable or permanent. A PT can leave until things get better, then return. A PT gains the world, while giving up nothing except, of course, his rut, and his treadmill.

PT And Politics

PT is merely an arbitrary set of initials we have chosen to identify a certain lifestyle, belief system or whatever you choose to call it. There are no dues to pay, no membership cards and until recently there were no meetings or conventions. However, quite a few PT's exist already, perhaps a million, perhaps as many as ten million. No one will ever know how many PT's there are, because we are all invisible. Many PT's have not heard the initials PT, nor would they use them to describe their lifestyle. Many will never read this report. They are nonetheless PT's, though they have stumbled into our path of enlightenment and freedom on their own.

In terms of politics, the PT may be a supporter of any party or political philosophy. Most likely he is not a registered voter anywhere and never marches in demonstrations. He probably believes in free trade and minimum government. Fascists, democrats, socialists, and communists all end up producing centralized bureaucracies with severe restrictions on personal liberty. Most PT's tend to be individualists of libertarian stripe interested in maximizing their own personal freedom. PT's seek the full and free enjoyment of life without robbing, defrauding, exploiting or leaning on anyone else.

A PT may be religious, but unlike most governments who sponsor official religions he will hopefully not force his views or personal morality down anyone else's throat. A PT may, and certainly should, be moral according to his own lights, but he need not retire at night with gnawing fears that someone somewhere might be enjoying life more than he is.

PT is all about opening up options, avoiding coercion. It is not about cowardice. If you want to fight for some cause, preferably freedom, you can certainly do so, but as a willing volunteer not a draftee to be sacrificed as cannon fodder. Harry Schultz became an honorary commander of a rebel military unit in 1987 at great personal risk to himself, long before the Afghan Freedom Fighters were a popular or winning cause. "Some things we must do, because they are right," says Harry.

All changes wrought by man have beneficiaries and perceived victims. Since PT's are tolerant people who do not impose their will on others, more good than harm will come out of our activities. Cutting loose from a straitjacket, escaping from a life of parochial limitations is a good thing for the individual. It will not harm society at large to have a few more rugged individualists and original thinkers doing their own thing. Not everyone can handle such complete freedom. PT is for an elite minority. One needs inner direction and the ability to operate within reasonable, self-imposed limits.

By exercising reasonable judgment, PT's unlock the best-kept secret of the Big Brother era. Individual sovereignty is a path for all people who merely know and understand its concepts to be truly free from bureaucratic shackles. There is no need to become a hermit or a recluse. You don't need to abandon civilization entirely to eliminate its negative aspects.

The PT Lifestyle

A PT can be any age, gender, color, size, shape, or religion. PT's can be married, attached or single, with family or without. The PT need not work at a conventional job but can and will make infinitely more money than those who do. As already mentioned, without any income taxes or other government deductions, we keep 100 per cent of what we earn from providing others with valuable things. As a result, the PT standard of living and quality of life is stress-free, more healthy, materially richer and literally the best obtainable on earth.

The PT philosophy releases creative souls from the many burdens of coping with Big Brother. Hopefully, once governments realize that they cannot afford to lose their best and most productive citizens, they will become more responsive to the needs of their people. The only historical precedent for individuals going off on their own due to dissatisfaction with government was in Central America. The ancient Mayans of the artisan and productive classes, apparently without any leadership or destination, simply said no to high taxes and the sacrifice of their young virgins. As individuals, they just drifted off into the jungle. A ruling aristocracy was then left without a population to pay its bills. The Mayan Empire disintegrated. Cities with eight-lane boulevards, palaces, and impressive monuments were abandoned.

What If Everyone Becomes A PT?

The reality is that not enough people will become PT's for it to make any significant difference. Paris, Rome, London, and New York with populations in the millions will not become ghost towns. Mass migrations have been going on for thousands of years. If everyone with a taste for travel, an independent income, or a movable job became a PT there would probably be nothing more than temporary exchanges of talented and productive individuals. The best talent, the most productive people are always drawn to places offering peace, prosperity and a suitable climate for creativity. Major cities, economic opportunities, and good weather will continue to attract many non-conformists and individualists. Becoming a PT expands the mind and increases the list of possible destinations.

How To Start

An immediate full-scale PT lifestyle is appropriate only for those who have developed either a sufficient asset base or a source of income that allows them to be mobile and independent from government licenses and a permanent, full-time job in a high tax country. However, there are many exceptions to this. Virtually any individual can become a PT with a few months preparation. Reading this report is the perfect way to begin making preparations.

By adopting the unconventional but consistent and logical set of ideas set forth in this report, you can gain power and freedom. The enviable status of PT is available to all, but few individuals will snatch this prize. Why? Belief systems foisted upon us tend to ensure that most governments will among the many popular injustices perpetuate unnecessary taxes, an aggressive military establishment, and intolerance of minorities and redistribution of wealth by government, i.e., and theft. Who among us has not accepted these falsehoods?

We are told that taxes are inevitable and inescapable and that a powerful and aggressive military establishment is needed for our protection. Never mind that with the end of the cold war even military leaders find it difficult to defend the lunatic policies and military budgets from previous decades gone by. Productive and creative people are needlessly forced to give away the major part of their earnings each year. What happens to this money? It is poured down the toilet, spent on huge bureaucracies that only seem to succeed in creating more and more dependents.

Fortunately, these concepts need not intrude on the PT's world. What is the PT's world? It is an individual person, supreme, unfettered, making his own decisions, leaning on no one and allowing no one to lean upon him. If you travel, it is customary to first visit your doctor for the necessary vaccinations. How many people similarly look for an inoculation pill to avoid being harassed, robbed and possibly incarcerated at the hands of Big Brother? Is there any magic dust or silver bullet that can eliminate all government interference from our lives?

PT will show you the way, but for starters, as the income of most

PT's is immediately doubled and most frustrations of life with Big Brother are instantly eliminated, the logical question is:

"Can you afford not to become a PT?"

Chapter 5

A Novice Becomes A PT

By Dr. "Andre DeBunk"

Don't Wait Till It's Too Late

For much of my career as a MD in the USA, I fought to save patients who "waited too long" to seek help.

They ignored or denied obvious signs and symptoms of serious disease. Had they sought help earlier they might have had a minor corrective surgery and lived in good health, to a ripe old age. As it was, with too much damage done, it was an uphill struggle just to keep them alive and functioning on two cylinders.

It is not surprising that these same kinds of educated and intelligent Americans ignore the clear signs and symptoms of another kind of disease. It is a disease without a name. But until someone comes up with a more catchy name, I shall give it a temporary name: The Anti-Private Property or "Apripo" Syndrome.

In the American hysteria to control "terrorism" and combat "the drug problem" American property rights have melted into oblivion. The courts are a private country club for predatory plaintiff attorneys. Worst of all our own fellow citizens have been so brainwashed that once they get on a jury, they award millions of dollars in compensation and punitive damages to any plaintiff who bothers to show up in court.

A woman who was subjected to a bit of sexual harassment (no injuries) by a dirty old man (Senior Partner) at a law office gets awarded $5,000,000 in punitive damages. No rape victim ever got that much. Any poor slob who gets a grasping contingent fee attorney to represent them against a rich defendant knows that the awards are decided on the basis of who has the deeper pockets. Not guilt or responsibility any more! They (awards) are, more often than not, totally out of proportion to the injuries suffered. This is wealth transference from those who have earned it to the idle and unworthy. In the above case, I do not say that a woman who may have been humiliated to the point of tears should get nothing. But $10,000 or even $20,000 (plus the bad publicity) would make the point.

Pension Plans And Savings Can Be Taken Away

Seeing fellow doctors victimized in malpractice suits, and watching my own malpractice insurance premiums soar to the stratosphere, I was open to any schemes that might protect my invested savings and my retirement nest egg. My retirement money was supposedly immune from creditors' claims and tinkering by the tax people, but as time passed, the IRS did (several times) change the rules of the game: Retirement plans were pried open for the benefit of the tax collectors and for successful plaintiffs in lawsuits.

Who Can I Turn To?

A medical patient can easily schedule a physical examination to determine his state of health and take appropriate remedial action. But where does the doctor turn to assess the state of his financial health? My question was:

How Can I Make Myself Judgment Proof?

You cannot get a good answer to this question from the AMA or your local medical society. They do not have an answer. Local attorneys do not have a clue about going offshore. If they did, they would probably be afraid to advise any client to move assets offshore. They fear they would be prosecuted for "conspiracy." I went to my big city banker. He sent me to see the top salesman at the trust department where they did "asset protection." My question was still the same:

"How can I make myself judgment proof?" The trust department boys came up with all sorts of plans that would give them nice fees for preparing a lot of documents, but as to guaranteed judgment proofing, "That's like asking for a guaranty you'll never die!" Such a thing does not exist according to the bankers. All we can do is make it more difficult for a creditor to collect. You set up a trust for your wife and kids and then keep your fingers crossed that a court will not ignore it.

Nobody brings up the simple solution of moving (and hiding) assets abroad. Within the USA the subject is taboo.

Dawn's Early Light

Let me share with you the joy of discovery and the agonizing frustrations I have known since I began my quest nearly two years ago. Time Magazine, Business Week, and the Wall Street Journal had little to say about moving assets offshore as a strategy for judgment proofing. However, some of their stories about international tycoons, indicated that all of them, without exception, had somehow learned the secret of compartmentalization. In other words, if one country nationalized their local operations or if lawsuits or environmental concerns crippled one segment of their business, they were able to survive. This was accomplished by keeping the properties fully mortgaged (so there was never much to lose) and by keeping them in separate corporations, "compartmentalized," so that if one business or investment was in trouble, it did not topple everything else like a house of cards. I wondered, "Who does the strategy for these tycoons?" What worked for them should work for me. I was all in one compartment: Texas, USA. No US-based advisors would give me a foolproof way to "get my money out of the country before my country got my money out of me."

Could The Answer Be In My Junk Mail?

For the first time I began to peruse the more exotic junk mail that I'd previously discarded without opening. There were all kinds of illegal sounding schemes. Send for a "Family Trust Cook Islands" kit and pay no more taxes. There were invitations to offshore seminars on investments and other topics plus,

Newsletters And More Newsletters

The junk mail described many newsletters. I bought trial subscriptions to all of them:

Expat World (published out of Singapore) is very light hearted, humorous and sexy.

The Harry Schultz International Letter (Monaco) has market and PT advice.

The Freedom Wealth and Privacy Report (Isle of Man) is serious, scholarly and has practical advice about keeping assets abroad, and living abroad yourself.

Larry Abraham's Insider Report (Santiago, Chile) covers investing abroad and from time to time expounds the author's conspiracy theory views.

The Marc Harris Analysis and *Harris Investment News* out of Panama and BVI had good articles about moving assets such as pension plans (that would otherwise be confiscated by taxes) abroad.

[Author's Note: The addresses and a special deal for *Invisible Investor* readers for these newsletters are found in the back of the book — in the Resources Section. But don't peek now. Wait until you finish this report.]

The newsletter writers are all a bunch of characters, but I would not call them lunatics or even lunatic fringe. They say a lot of things that people living inside the States couldn't say. Where tax avoidance is involved, writers and speakers who talk about "offshore" solutions (whether legal or not) will be persecuted by the tax collectors for giving their opinions. Most of the good, independent newsletter writers left the USA because they faced jail or actually served some time for expressing their beliefs. They were the few people who resisted the trend towards Anti-Life, Anti-Liberty, & Anti-Property.

Books

Quite a few books about tax havens and similar subjects were also touted in junk mail offerings. I bought all of them. Most offered a hint or suggestion here and there that I found useful. Until I came across the books of W.G. Hill (Scope International) I didn't find anything that had a coherent useable philosophy that could enable me, by myself to solve all problems, answer all my questions, and move on with my financial planning. Yet although I read the Hill books, I just wasn't quite ready to make the first move. Why? I cannot say exactly. I needed a push. Something to give me confidence to take that step into the abyss — the place on the map that says "Uncharted Territory, Beware of Monsters." Of course, I already knew intellectually that the rest of the world was mostly a very friendly place. All tax and banking havens were and are user-friendlier towards people of property than my own home country is. But inertia or something was holding me back. I knew I had to get out of the country physically to look around.

Leaving The Cocoon Was Not Easy For Me

My previous travels abroad had been to medical conventions and related educational seminars where it was like being in a cocoon. We traveled on United Airlines, or maybe Continental. The programs were always in English. Most participants and speakers came from America. The hotels where we were billeted — usually a Hilton, Marriott or Hyatt. I might just as well have been at home for all the difference in conversations, attitudes, decor, or menu. The only authentic international experience of these trips was the few minutes spent in border formalities at the airport. I never really *lived* abroad. This I determined was part of the reason for my timidity in placing my assets abroad or (heaven forbid?) actually renting an apartment or home in some foreign country.

My Wife — The International Woman

In this respect, I envied my wife who as a student had taken her "Junior Year Abroad" in Florence, Italy. When I first hinted that I'd like to close down my practice, retire completely and move abroad, she eagerly said "Sure, let's go!" as if that was all there was to it. For her, going anywhere, even to Borneo I suppose, was nothing. You just move. Take a course in the local lingo, and presto you settle in, enjoy the local culture, and are right at home. "No problems" according to her. Surely there was more to it. You can't just leave a whole life behind. Or can you? I wanted to make a move, but I needed to stick my toes in the water and wiggle them around. The next step for me was the Offshore Seminars Circuit.

Investment Seminars Abroad

The brochure promised an *authentic offshore experience.* "You will meet with the president of El Salvador, sample native foods and enjoy native dancers. You'll learn how to get in on the ground floor by exploring investment opportunities in real estate, tourism, mining and the expanding telephone industry. Industry representatives will speak to you." The picture of the naked model on the brochure seemed to indicate that we might also have some fun with the local indigenous ladies, but alas, though the pictures were always there, that kind of recreation was never on the official schedule.

I went to a dozen of these seminars. Every speaker was clearly pushing something. It was either "buy stock in my new mining venture," or "buy my books and tapes, subscribe to my newsletter, use me as a consultant," yukketa, yuk. Yet to justify their sales pitch, almost every speaker felt it necessary to present at least some interesting information or useful opinions. Had they not done this, the audience might have walked out. I saw this happen once where a speaker had absolutely nothing worthwhile to offer. Most of the audience just drifted out. This was rare. Generally, you couldn't help but learn *something* from each of the experts who spoke at these seminars. And there was always question and answer time.

CNN — The Same News, Again & Again

The speakers at one advertised seminar were the same basic cast of speakers who regularly appeared at other seminars in the USA and abroad. I began to identify different circuits that various "experts" followed. Star speaker and best selling author, Doug Casey would lecture at his seminar along with his usual invited guests, speakers Adrian Day and Mark Skousen.

Then a few months later the same gang would travel to Larry

Abraham's hometown in Chile where they would all repeat similar lectures. There were a few new faces (speakers) at each lecture. Some, I suspect, were brought in for comic relief. Others were so bad; they must have paid just to get a chance to pitch their products or services to a captive audience.

There were different circuits and different groups of speakers each promoted by a different publishing group. Speakers on one circuit seldom participated in the productions of a rival group. Paying guests were invited to everything. It seems the competing seminar promoters swap or purchase each other's mailing lists. I registered for one seminar as "Loco N. Cabeza" (crazy in the head) and sure enough, in coming months "Dear Mr. Cabeza" was invited as a *specially recommended guest* to buy tickets in the rival's seminar offerings. For a while I went to everything that came down the pike: I enjoyed these gatherings, enhanced my understanding of economic functioning in other countries, and gained an important fringe benefit:

Interaction With Other Seminar Junkies

Most of the paying guests like myself were successful, well off men in there sixties or seventies. They were intelligent professional people, usually retired. These seminars were a form of (tax deductible) recreation. You couldn't afford several thousand dollars to come to one of these seminars (usually with your wife) if you were just getting by on social security. Some of the participants had actually expatriated (moved) out of the USA. Others had established secondary residences abroad and acquired second passports in preparation for the time when circumstances might dictate a permanent move. There were even a few genuine PT's (Perpetual Tourists) who lived in rented accommodations and tended to move on to greener pastures every six months or so. By exchanging views and asking questions of my fellow attendees, I was able to make useful contacts in many countries and for the first time get unbiased advice. What I got from my fellow campers was perhaps more useful than most of the information I got from the people talking at the lectures. Then too, most lecturers offered short consultations at discount rates.

This was an opportunity to ask questions of the "experts" prefacing them with "Don't try to sell me anything." Once I had an idea of what I was looking for, I felt I got some good information and answers in these consultations.

"Take The Plunge" He Said

For almost two years I attended all kinds of meetings but never took any action to implement what I had learned. In a paid consultation one of the speakers asked me if I had as yet opened a small bank account offshore. My answer was, "No."

"What are you waiting for? Take the plunge." My feeling was that once I took the plunge there was no return. I'd have to decide whether to admit to having a foreign account on my tax returns. If I decided to "forget" my foreign account, I'd have passed the point of no return. "Bunk!" You can check the box or you can leave the box blank. Either way, it makes no difference. There is no eye in the sky watching what you do. Nobody cares about you. If your account is under $10,000 there is nothing to file, and if you have over 25 accounts (of any size) there is nothing to file. So, "Take the plunge."

I realized then that I was in grave danger of being like those patients I described in my opening paragraph, They knew they had a problem, but were terrified of taking the necessary steps to resolve a little thing before it became major. Like them I was being irrational. I felt that I was ready to make a move, but I didn't want to make it on my own until I found a GUIDE — a brilliant, honest and experienced PT. The Sufi says that when the student has prepared himself the guide will appear.

It's true! On an impulse, I went to meditate in the Zen Center in Kyoto Japan. While sitting in the lotus position, endlessly repeating the mantra "I need a guru, Oooom" and focusing on the universe, all at once, the skies darkened, a single ray of celestial light focused upon my forehead. The heavens opened up. Lightning and thunder came without rain, and I felt a warm firm hand on my shoulder. Turning around and gazing into the wizened face and blue eyes of an ancient monk clothed in the saffron garb of the sacred Japanese Zen

Order, he said, in perfect English: "I am your Guru, W.G. Hill."

"But old monk," said I, "on very good authority I've heard that W.G. Hill is dead. He died in a canoe on the upper Amazon while in the act of deflorating ["piercing the maidenhood" of] a cannibal chiefs daughter. The chief bammed him with a ram, and they dined on *Ragout of Hill* that night in Cochambamba." The chief knew a good PT when he smelled it. Pretty tasty, he said, with a burp.

The old monk then said with predictable Zen inscrutability, "Yes I have died bammed with a ram, and rammed with a bam. I have died many times: I have died of AIDS for my gay readers, of a broken heart for the few romantic female fans of an old male chauvinist, and I have died for love and the lack of love." Hill rambled on and on and on until I fell asleep.

If you believe that story, anybody can sell you anything. I just made that up and threw it in to see if you were awake and paying attention. I actually met my guru Hill by putting out some feelers in the obvious places — with his most recent publisher. Eventually he contacted me via e-mail. It is true that he enjoys wearing bizarre disguises. One of his favorites is as a Zen Bhuddist Monk. He actually was a monk once. But to meet me he set the place (Sforza Castle Milan, to my wife's delight). There, in the castle courtyard, he sneaked up on us in the less than mystical one-piece jumpsuit of an Italian telephone repairman.

My new guru did not tell me much that I did not already know from his books. He took me by the hand, so to speak, opened my first bank and brokerage accounts in a European city, rented me a house, helped me buy a car, got me a local driving license, and generally set me up. He gave me the push and the confidence I needed to take the plunge. I was reasonably confidant he would not sell me paperwork I didn't need or advise me to do anything stupid.

The net result was I finally made the move, and became internationalized. I am not likely to be the target of any lawsuits or government action because I'm gone! I have few visible assets. If I do or say anything controversial, it will be from a foreign address and in a pen name. I feel very good about my move. After a year as a PT, Junior Grade. I wonder what I was so afraid of.

Is America The Greatest?

Americans are some of the most insular, parochial people in the world. Most Americans have been taught to think that anything "American" is best. The rest of the world is full of smelly, ugh, "Foreigners." Germans and British people are similarly insular and intolerant. The truth is in my opinion [IMO], that people live better and enjoy life more in places like Italy, Greece or France. Maybe it's partly because they don't have our puritan, Protestant work ethic and Boy Scout morality. The "Live and let live" attitudes of my neighbors abroad have been much more agreeable. W.G. Hill once said that the sure recipe for an ulcer was to go to bed full of worry that someone in the world was richer, or having more fun than yourself would.

From cars to medicine, excellence has gone offshore. America may have the most dreaded and efficient tax collectors and hydra-headed government regulatory agencies, but who needs them?

In terms of the right to secure your wealth against arbitrary seizures or baseless lawsuits, "offshore" is the only answer. Personal liberty is much more likely when you live in an offshore country where only real criminals go to jail.

Being able to live very well on your tax savings alone is a wonderful fringe benefit. "Is America the greatest?" No way!

Seminars Within The USA

Although there are financial seminars all over the country, even the most courageous lecturer is intimidated when speaking on hostile soil. Even so, attending seminars in the U.S. can be a starting point for the would-be PT.

You have an opportunity to evaluate the speakers and more importantly to talk with other attendees. Two caveats apply within the USA:

First, remember that the speakers are there for one reason only: to sell you something. Usually what they are hawking is of little or no value.

Second, be very careful what you tell anyone.

The friendly guy next to you could be an IRS undercover agent. Whatever you do, always keep your questions and comments clearly within the boundaries of what is legal. Surprisingly, most of what you will want to accomplish (hiding assets & enjoying life more) is completely legal. Your next step is to attend:

Offshore Conferences

The discussions are more open and you have a better opportunity to learn more specifics.

You should begin your "offshore" move by opening one or more bank accounts. Apply for a credit or debit card that is automatically paid off by your offshore bank. Develop a personal relationship with your bank representative. Open an offshore security trading account.

Read W.G. Hill's book PT and the more recent book Portable Trades & Occupations by his former associate and editor, Peter Trevellian. Hire a guy like Trevellian as your guru-on-retainer if you can afford his $5,000 per year fee.

Yogi Berra, my favorite philosopher, observed that if you do not know where you are going, chances are you won't get there. Thus, you must define your goals:

Turn inward for a few moments and ask yourself,

What Is Important To Me?

Life is not a dress rehearsal. You have to get it right the first time.

Do you have the right stuff to become a PT? How about being a part-time or gradual PT? You don't have to move all your assets overseas, give up your citizenship, and become an expatriate all at once. The trick is to start moving in that direction and be able to leave and resettle abroad — only if you have to! You may choose to only open an offshore bank account, move some "rainy day" assets offshore for protection. You can go on with your life just as it is. You might be lucky and not get trampled by an increasingly obtrusive government.

My own preference is to be conservative and do what is obviously called for: Move your serious money and most of your assets (securities) offshore. Then try to enjoy life by traveling more. If you can afford it, go first class and live first class. There are so many amazing and beautiful places to visit. Even the Third World can be wonderful if you take the five-star route.

Spend a few months on one continent and then follow the summer sunshine to another.

There is much in America to cherish and to enjoy, but you must be prepared for legal confrontations and other unpleasantness. The only way to prepare is to hide your money abroad. With assets in place, you will be comfortable when the time comes for you to go abroad. If you are prepared to leave, you are more likely to never have to leave. Switzerland, a neutral country that was always prepared to defend itself with force, was never invaded. Belgium, a neutral country that trusted others to defend it, was always invaded as the first move in any European war. As a PT, you are prepared thoroughly. You have the option of simply leaving the game (and the country) when you find yourself in a situation where there is no hope.

Cayman, Bermuda, the Bahamas, Liechtenstein, and Panama are only a few of the potential stopover points for the embryonic PT. Once you begin the PT journey you will experience a sense of freedom, of liberation. New opportunities present themselves every step of the way, but only if you take the first step. One final thought.

Few People Are Qualified PT Guides

A lot of the authors and self proclaimed "experts" talk the talk. What you want is the one that walks the walk. Follow the man who practices what he preaches! Hill is semi-retired and will not take on more than one or two new clients per year. We want to put together a list of real PT's like Hill who can offer good counseling and hand holding. Peter Trevellian asks any readers who are real PT's and who would like to help potential PT's (for free or for fees) to write him c/o the publisher. Tell Peter what you have to offer by way of experience or expertise.

Would You Like An Invitation To A PT Convention?

Your author, "Dr. DeBunk," would like to hold an annual meeting in Europe of the sort he sought but never found. A beautiful and inspiring setting where an interesting program, good information, and not too many commercial sales pitches could be found. We realize that some speakers have important things to say, and have useful expertise to sell! Therefore, we won't bar exceptional speakers just because they have consulting services, books or cassettes to sell. In fact, if you know of any products or services of particular interest to PT's, we will give them a few minutes to talk and maybe a booth to display their things. But the emphasis will be on sharing useful information and making contacts with fellow PT's. Making business deals or having social friends is where it's at for me!

If you'd be interested in coming to (or participating in) such a gathering of the PT's (Party Throwers), please send the publisher your name, address (email & fax). Say "Put me on Dr. DeBunk's mailing list for any upcoming PT get-togethers." One of these days, you will get an invitation to an well-organized and interesting PT international convention! I'll be there! My real name is not "DeBunk" by the way. But all we PT's need to have our pseudonyms! What is yours?

Chapter 6

"OFFSHORE" Sounds so good it must be Illegal

*A*FTER reading about Offshore Investing in the last chapter, you've probably decided to move some of your money overseas — if it is legal.

Is it legal?

The answer is **yes**. You can freely and without limits, send all the money you want abroad for deposit to any bank, any brokerage account. You can give (donate) all you want to an offshore charity or foundation. For shoeshine money you can set up a charity or non-profit organization and run it anyway you please. You can buy gold bars, coins, securities, diamonds, antiques, oil paintings or valuable postage stamps, in your home country and ship them abroad without limit or reporting. Or you can send money abroad first and buy your valuables abroad. You can buy real estate, or send money abroad to pay for legal, accounting or any other service. There is no tax consequence, and all these moves are entirely legal. You do not have to report anything to anyone unless you send currency (paper money) or the equivalent of currency — like blank traveler's checks.

Even if you personally carry or send five million-dollar bundles of hundred dollar bills abroad, it is legal. The only problem is that by shipping currency legally and reporting it to the USA treasury you will raise so many red flags that you'll decide sending cash abroad (in cash) wasn't a good idea. The IRS will want to talk with you about the source of the funds and your reasons for taking it out in cash. The postal service (or your courier service) will also have plenty of questions. Finally, at the receiving end, with money laundering laws on every banker's mind, you will have a difficult time depositing large sums of cash abroad — except in oriental countries where cash is the norm. But, assuming you have opened a bank or brokerage account in advance, they will normally accept non-cash deposits of any size from a known customer. Bankers do not like being used as a conduit, where millions of dollars go into a small account at 10:00 a.m. and everything is wire transferred out a few minutes or a few days later. On the other hand, normal banking transactions always involve deposits and quick withdrawals for legitimate purposes. The trick to keep your banker happy is to have a good "average balance."

Tell Your Banker What You Are Up To (If You Can)

When establishing an account, it is wise to tell your new banker about your background, how you acquired your assets and what you intend to do in the banking relationship and why. Not that the story must be true, but it must prepare your banker for any unusual transactions. In this way, he will help you rather than report your account to police for unusual or suspected illegal activities. In every country in the world, including tax havens, there are criminal activities going on. For some categories of suspicious behavior, even the best tax haven banks will freeze your account. Take Liechtenstein for example. I regard the Liechtenstein banks as far more protective of their clients' interests than Swiss Banks, for instance. I have personally done business in Liechtenstein, with all three of the old-line banks there for over thirty years. As might be expected, I know many of the bankers on a personal level. Their motivation? Above all, the employees want to keep their jobs. The banks don't want to be seen as protectors of swindlers or other criminals. If your Liechtenstein banker learns that you are into certain *locally illegal* categories of activity, your welcome mat will be pulled out from under you. What don't they tolerate? Frauds against any bank, pornography, organized crime activities in the USA, or drug dealing. All the above are "no no" activities in Liechtenstein. *At best your account will be closed* and you will be ordered to move your business elsewhere. At worst, the bank pending an investigation by local police in co-operation with Interpol could freeze your account.

What Will Liechtenstein Banks Protect You Against?

Suppose you are involved in a divorce or civil litigation. There is no way that any plaintiff or their lawyers will find out about your balance with a Liechtenstein bank unless you let the cat out of the bag yourself. On the other hand, if your spouse's lawyer shows up in Liechtenstein with a USA (or any) court order to the effect that you owe $50,000 for back child support —together with your exact account number and the name it is held in (corporate or otherwise); it is likely that a Liechtenstein judge would order the bank to turn over funds to your spouse. "We are a civilized country, and in this country a father must always support his family." There is bank secrecy, but if some categories of your enemies learn your account details, your goose is cooked. In Liechtenstein, for instance, last time I looked, your ex-wife would be considered your wife as no divorce was allowed there. Just like in Ireland.

The much vaunted Liechtenstein Foundation or "Anstalt" in German, is no protection if your creditor knows and can prove that the assets are really yours and fully under your control. But the private creditor must come to Liechtenstein with a valid judgment. That judgment cannot be grossly out of line with what a Liechtenstein court would award in a similar case. If Nevada White's money [see Chapter on Nevada White — coming up soon!] was in a Liechtenstein bank rather than a Swiss bank, he might still have his twenty million dollars today.

I mention Liechtenstein only because if I am an expert on anything, is in how Liechtenstein banks will treat you in a crisis situation. The bottom line is that they are far more protective and supportive than Swiss banks that will sell you out in a moment. However, it should also be noted that the oldest and largest "Global Trust Bank in Liechtenstein" now has big branches in New York and London. As a result, it is much more likely to yield to pressure for information about an American or Brit's account than the other banks in the country who have no such branches.

Should You Report Foreign Bank Accounts On Your USA Tax Return?

Once your money or assets are abroad, there is a space on USA income tax returns where you are supposed to check a box if you have any foreign bank accounts. Check the box and you are supposed to file another form with the details of how much and where. However, there are many books by lawyers and others offering creative (legal and illegal) ways to circumvent that requirement. For instance, if you have over 25 such accounts, you do not have to list them.

We always tell our readers to comply fully with all local laws and regulations. As we do not have a death wish nor want our book banned. You will not find any tax evasion encouragement here. We normally cannot even tell you what 'most people do' for informational and amusement purposes only.

That kind of information, i.e. "what you can get away with" has to come from offshore newsletters or an offshore adviser that you talk to personally — outside of your home jurisdiction. Anyone who gives good offshore advice operating domestically is either a government informer or he will not survive too long.

Funny thing is the director of the IRS just gave a talk on this subject. I think we can get away with repeating and paraphrasing a bit of what he said:

"Since we can't catch the taxpayer, let's go after the offshore advisors"

"We suspect that there are millions of foreign accounts owned by Americans and that billions of dollars are involved. But there are no statistics except that offshore deposits in general amount are well over a trillion dollars. We feel that only a tiny portion of this activity (by Americans) is properly reported or accounted for. Once a citizen has moved his money offshore to a location with bank secrecy, we [the tax collection office] cannot usually find out anything about it.

At least half of all taxpayers do not bother to answer the question about foreign accounts. We suspect that up to 99% of such offshore account holders do not file the required reports detailing the names of the banks and amounts held there. This was surprising to me at first because the penalty for non-filing is a $500,000 (per year) fine and five years in prison for each year of failing to answer the question. Maybe juries would be reluctant to convict [in view of such Draconian punishments for simply not making an X in a box] even though they (juries) are not supposed to be told the penalties that will be imposed on tax offenders.

We have had moles [undercover agents] in offshore banks, but as they are violating local criminal laws by reporting to us, this has not proven effective over the long term. Offshore bank officers and financial advisors are now more wary, and it is seldom that we can pick up any information on clients by detaining and searching these people for client lists at border crossings."

"The only way we find out about unreported income or evaded capital gains is if we can intercept bank statements or somehow get original hard copy correspondence within our jurisdiction. Even when our undercover agents get information about such accounts orally from an unhappy spouse or employee, or from phone taps, it is almost impossible for us to prove a tax fraud case without paper evidence.

Paper Trails Don't Always Lead To Convictions

"As banks got more sophisticated, they stopped putting the names of customers and their own [bank name] on statements. This makes it difficult, if not impossible to nail a tax evader who keeps unreported wealth abroad, even in those rare instances where we do uncover bank statements. The reason is that a mere list of securities or deposits and withdrawals means nothing unless it can be positively linked with the offender." Having accounts in the names of corporations or other legal entities makes it more difficult to establish a link."

"The net result is that we catch a few small fry sometimes when they turn red and confess during an audit. However, invisible investors with experience and good advice are able to escape our net. That is why we have initiated "Operation Offshore" in which undercover agents will pose as high net worth individuals seeking advice from offshore financial advisors whom we know or suspect of aiding and abetting tax evasion. By targeting Offshore Advisors, and bringing a few of the most egregious offenders home to face prosecution in the United States, we will exercise a powerful deterrent against practices that have drained our tax base." That is what the boss of the IRS had to say — more or less.

Moral Of The Story

It is legal to have assets offshore, to trade stocks offshore, to do anything offshore that you could do domestically. But while your local bank or broker will withhold taxes and provide the tax collector with full information about your activities domestically, your offshore bank or broker is usually forbidden by law to give such information to anyone. The exception is where, as in Switzerland, there are information and sharing treaties in effect.

It is your obligation to report and pay tax on any interest, dividends, or capital gains you realize abroad. But no one is around to enforce this obligation. Thus, unless [like in our Nevada White story] someone you trust steals your financial statements and gives them to the government, with sworn statements linking you to serious tax frauds, you won't get caught for forgetting to report such things. If there is ever a judgment against you in a place like the States, you are obliged to testify under oath and produce all documentary evidence you can get, relating to your assets. Our guess is that most people in that position would fib and be technically guilty of perjury. Our suggestion: Disappear. Leave the country and do not ever be in the position of having to give false testimony. When there is no body and no assets, there is no case.

Doing It Legally, By The Book

We know that none of our readers would dream of omitting any legal report they are required to file, and we certainly can't imagine any of them wanting to avoid or evade paying their fair share of taxes. Accordingly, we will now explore what can be done legally in terms of moving assets offshore to protect them, not against taxes (which everyone wants to pay) but only against imaginary claims contrived by potential plaintiffs. It should be noted that a huge consultant industry has grown up in the last twenty years, to help people set up corporations, trusts, foundations, captive insurance companies, etc. The purpose of all this paperwork is to make money disappear, but to do it legally (sort of) in such a way as to eliminate all paper trails and obviate any and all filing requirements for the client.

In this author's opinion, if your offshore consultant is located abroad, and if he NEVER GOES BACK TO THE STATES, it might be worthwhile. Some of these operators, like my Panamanian friend, Marc Harris (See Resource List at Back of Book) offer a few cute little gimmicks that help make money flow and grow here, there and everywhere. But if you give up your secrecy and let all of the facts, your intent and the whole story be known to your creditors (or the IRS) all these structures could be ignored by any judge hearing the case. They rely upon secrecy. Wealthy people are often convinced to spend $50,000 per year or more, and to make absolutely terrible investments like "annuities" because they have a Boy Scout Mentality and want to kid themselves by creating the illusion that they have done everything legally. This is why I tell (in another chapter) the sad story of Nevada White. He really believed that his Liechtenstein Foundation was good asset protection. It would have been if no one had spilled the beans. But by the same token, an individual account in a new identity, opened by a foreign citizen would have been just as good, and far less expensive to set up and run.

If the enemies were to find out about assets that held in a false name, they could grab it. If they can penetrate a maze of corporations or other legal structures and find out what's really going down, your goose is cooked. The general rule when you get into court is that any transfers of assets made in an attempt to defraud creditors, spouses, or the tax collector could and will be undone by the courts.

The problem is one of enforcement. Suppose the bailiff or US Marshall cannot find you because you have moved abroad. There is no one to toss in jail for "failure to show cause why he should not be held in contempt of court for not paying the claim of XYZ." The only two ways a court may enforce claims is by taking physical control of either the assets or the body of a defendant. If both are abroad in places unknown to a plaintiff, the whole enforcement system breaks down. Most people do not realize that if they simply move their persona and their posterior out of the jurisdiction where they have a problem, that problem goes away. Extradition is usually not possible for civil matters or for tax matters, but if your whereabouts are unknown and undiscoverable, and the nature and extent of your assets are also unknown, even in a serious criminal fraud case, there is no point in even filing a case. And if no case against you is filed, and you stay low profile until the heat dies down, you are home free — whatever your problem was.

Both the IRS and private creditors have an impossible time trying to claw back assets that have been properly (i.e. no direct paper trail) secreted abroad. But if they somehow find out the exact location and amount — or if they can convince a judge to throw you in jail for contempt of court for failure to tell them where the money went, then your asset protection schemes and dreams come to naught.

Kidnapping

Strangely enough, or maybe not so strangely, American courts have ruled in hundreds of cases, that a defendant who is brought back into the jurisdiction by illegal means, has no right to bring his kidnapping up in court as a defense. The judges have ruled time and time again that fugitives or debtors, once they are physically in a USA court room can't avoid facing the music by claiming that they were beaten, tortured, threatened, chloroformed, or otherwise taken from another country without benefit of legal extradition. This sort of thing (kidnapping) often happens in child custody cases where a child legally in the custody of say a French father, is kidnapped by agents working for an American mother in the USA. It also happens frequently in criminal cases particularly where drugs are involved. In the famous Mark Rich case, where his only offense was a very technical violation of a very short lived rule on crude oil dealings; a multimillion-dollar bounty was placed on his head (to encourage a kidnap) by the US Marshall's service. Switzerland refused to extradite him because his offense was not a violation of Swiss law.

Is Income Tax Fraud A Crime Under Swiss Law?

Most writers and commentators are dead wrong when they say that it is not and therefore, Switzerland won't enforce property claims or extradite anyone for this reason. Take this quote from tax and offshore authority Arnold Goldstein, J.D., LLM, Ph.D. On page 128 of his pretty good book, *OFFSHORE HAVENS,* "Tax violations are not considered criminal under Swiss law so disclosure is never made by the Swiss to the IRS." Goldstein and most other writers have not been around since prehistoric time like me. They have not seen their friends go down the tubes. However, there are at least two major exceptions to the above statement. It is true that if a Swiss has a foreign account and does not report his interest income from that foreign account on his income tax return, there are severe civil penalties, i.e. fines, if he gets caught — but no criminal penalties. However, if a Swiss reports deductions fraudulently (i.e. if he makes up or distorts "facts") on his Swiss income tax return, that is considered criminal tax fraud. The Swiss, by treaty with the USA are obliged to order every bank in Switzerland to turn over all records relating to Mr. XYZ once he is accused of tax fraud, or put into involuntary bankruptcy. Every bank in Switzerland gets half a dozen of these orders every day. The IRS does not have to know the name of the bank. They just allege tax fraud, money laundering, continuing criminal activity, etc. To make matters worse, in the fine print of every Swiss (and Liechtenstein) bank account opening form, the depositor waives his rights to bank secrecy and agrees to "hold harmless" the bank if they decide for any reason, to turn over his account records or assets to any government or claimant.

Liechtenstein Is Not Switzerland

A search and seize order from the Swiss Department of Justice, is not applicable to a Liechtenstein bank. Liechtenstein's legal system does not automatically co-operate with any foreign government, although they will deal harshly with customers found to be in businesses that are not highly regarded in Liechtenstein. Thus, we have these anomalies: An arms dealer whose land mines have crippled millions is well protected, while a distributor of dirty pictures (who has brought joy and relief to millions) forfeits his money and may well be arrested in Liechtenstein.

Are You Protected By A Corporation Holding Your Assets In Switzerland?

Swiss banks are not very secure from USA creditors' or government claims unless assets are not held in your name. Of course the name assets are held under must not be known to your creditors or enemies. Legal entities like Corporations or Foundations no longer give the anonymity they used to. Swiss banks also require that for funds of assets held in corporate names, trusts or otherwise, that they be provided them, (by the client's lawyer) with a statement of who the real party in interest is! Few people know these background facts. They don't suspect that their name is on file, and if someone is looking for assets in their name, their corporate holdings will be revealed.

How To Get Real Protection

If the Swiss bank does not know your real identity, then they can't and won't identify you as the Mr. XYZ whose account has been ordered seized by the IRS, with the co-operation of the Swiss Department of Justice. Better yet, since most people cannot keep a secret, just keep your assets somewhere other than Switzerland. Since it has caved in to Big Brother, it is not as safe as it used to be for Americans.

Safer Than Switzerland

Local banks in some third world tax havens like the smaller islands of the Caribbean, or Vanuatu, Tonga, or Cook Islands, are usually terribly inefficient. Even some of the banks on the Channel Islands leave something to be desired. They can't (from time to time) properly credit a simple deposit without losing it and requiring fifty letters and phone calls to solve the problem. If you have a firm of European or American expats running things in a place like Bermuda or Panama, you will get service just as good as at home — maybe better. For those who want hand-holding, tax return preparation, asset management suggestions, and a fast growing outfit that tries harder, I guess I'd reluctantly have to say my Panama Offshore Service organization is a standout, one-of-a kind outfit. If you can do it yourself, do it, but if you want to be able to call on a lot of experts any time, then use somebody like The Firm of Marc M. Harris, S. A. in Panama or another of The Harris Organisation affiliates worldwide. I have not found anyone who can do the job better. Aside from some of the best-looking and most agreeable women in the world, Panama City is not the greatest vacation spot in the world. Come to think of it, maybe the profusion of pick up bars, beautiful and friendly young women, fabulous restaurants are enough reasons for a visit. But if you bring your own lover once you get out of Panama City, there are some great things to see — like the Panama Canal and the Coral Islands of San Blas. The Caesar Park Hotel in Panama City and the Intercontinental are both very agreeable places at a third of the price of similar deluxe facilities in Europe.

Along with Panamanian banks, Cayman Island banks for the most part are also standouts (for service) among the third world banks. Isle of Man and Monaco are also first rate — in my experience. One observation is that the European bank branches like ABN (Dutch) in the offshore havens are more efficient in comparison with the locals. Outside of Europe, and outside of Switzerland, which no longer has effective bank secrecy, they are much more private. The new Swiss procedures involving circulation of disclosure orders to the IRS does not apply to Swiss or other banks outside of Swiss borders. If you do bank in Europe, the best secrecy is in Austria and Luxembourg. In the smaller tax haven countries, go to Andorra, Gibraltar, Isle of Man, and of course, my favorite, Liechtenstein.

As the public generally knows all of these tax haven locations and banks, I feel that certain other locations may be better for privacy, efficiency, and safety. If I were to mention in this book a certain terribly capable, huge yet user-friendly English speaking bank in a location that is great fun to visit, such popularization would destroy its usefulness to Americans. So, here's what I'll do. You send your request for info on the "S" bank to me c/o my publisher, with $3 or equivalent for postage and handling, and I will send you a printed sheet of information about it. If you have other questions about any subject touched upon in this or any of my other books, send $750 in any form [If a check or MO, make it payable to "Cash"]. I will be happy to call you collect and give you a live phone consultation of about half an hour — or if you prefer and have a lot of questions, I will respond by mail with the information you need, and probably some specific referrals. Your $750 will apply to the $10,000 two-year consultation-retainer if you decide to take it after the first consultation.

Mr. Conforti Moves His Moolah

Let us assume that Mr. Conforti, currently USA citizen and resident is financially comfortable. He wants to stay that way. Net worth? $4 Million plus — all earned legally, and all tax paid. He has been lucky enough to survive a few lawsuits, a divorce, and a few run-ins with the government. Now at age 55 he says he's getting too old to start all over again with nothing. It is time to ensure his financial survival. He has heard that "Offshore" is a good idea. What should he do first?

Make A Plan [Ask The Right Questions & You Get The Right Answers]

It is as easy as falling off a log for me to make a plan for anyone else or myself. I have been offshore personally and asset-wise for the last twenty-five years. I have put many clients, friends, and associates on the right path. Those who got into trouble invariably broke the most important rules. And when I myself got too cocky and careless, I had problems too. We have seen in other chapters what problems result if certain simple rules (set forth in this book at least a dozen times) are ignored. After a few years offshore, you will know the ropes and you will even be able to give objective advice to others. Now as beginners, people like Mr. Conforti and you, dear reader, need all the help you can get.

For a beginner PT who has seen only books by people with a hidden agenda [trying to sell something], it is not so easy to make the right decisions. That is why you bought this book. I believe that I am the only writer who is not trying to peddle terrible "back-end" products like annuities, asset protection plans that do not work, or bank accounts in places like Switzerland. In Switzerland, if I haven't convinced you by now not to use the big Swiss banks, let me use the strongest language I am capable of: Most Swiss bankers are a bunch of strumpets who will sell you out in a minute. They are looking out for number one, and certainly will not warn you of the dangers of dealing with them. The Swiss government is in bed with the IRS. They will roll you over and sell you out without any notice. Don't believe me? Read the Nevada White revelations in this book.

Stay Away From USA — Based Offshore Consultants

There are also authors, advisors, and consultants selling their products from the USA. Some are able to stay in business only because they are registered and often paid informers for Big Brother. General rule is NEVER get your Offshore advice — or any services at all relating to offshore matters from a lawyer, accountant or otherwise based in your home country. Under local rules they must keep records and report any thing QUESTIONABLE you do to the government. In other words, you will get about as much privacy and protection as walking in front of a hail of machine gun bullets dressed in Saran Wrap.

Exploring Your Options

Read up on the subject. Then run your plans by a few self-proclaimed experts. Ask a lot of questions and pay them their standard fees for putting holes in it. Anyone who doesn't charge a fee is probably getting a commission for selling something and as a result, has little objectivity.

Don't Tell 'Em Who You Are

It is not necessary that you reveal your true identity in these encounters, and it is better, in fact, if you don't.

Get A Mail Drop Or Anonymous Communications Center

Before embarking on even the planning phase, consider getting an anonymous mail drop and message service like the Aircraft and Yacht Owners Co-operative. See Resource List at back of book. This is a state of the art operation with all kinds of communication possibilities. They will educate you at a moderate cost of about $150 for a trial period. Once again, I don't want to bring any heat on them, so if you have sent $3 for my report on the S bank, there is no extra charge if you also ask me to put you in touch with AYOC in the same letter. Never pay AYOC or any mail drop with a check or transfer that can be traced back to the real you. And they shouldn't know your home address. You call in or pick up your email from them electronically. I do not get any commissions on any of the stuff I recommend so I can keep my objectivity. Also, as my readers tend to be more of a mutual self-help group who call ourselves "PT's" any suggestions you may have to add to the next edition of this book will be gratefully received. You can have "name credit" and or a free book for any material we use.

One Plan That Fits Everyone?

Sorry! There is no *one right plan* that fits everyone. If there were one, Big Brother would quickly find a way to "close the loophole." The government would like to pass laws to prevent the export of funds. If they could, they would sink every tax haven 20,000 leagues under the sea. Fortunately for us, laws restricting the flow of capital are, for the moment at least, politically unpopular. Our free market Republicans believe that virtually unrestricted capital movement helps create a successful economy. Unfortunately, as the flood of American money (going offshore) drains the economy, we can expect restrictions. In both the European Community and in the USA there are reporting requirements and heavy taxes, but money can be moved about freely — for the moment.

The possibilities of "what do first" are endless. But our suggestion is to ask yourself, **What do I want to accomplish?**

The questions you want to ask include, but are not limited to:

- Asset Protection?
- Tax Avoidance?
- Clean tax free Succession to Your Heirs?
- Establish an International Division for an Existing Business?
- Get Away (Physically) From Relatives or Spouse?
- Escape Creditors?
- Make More Money in A New Career?
- Change Name, Passport, and Country of Citizenship & disappear?
- Start A New Life?
- Do Good by Establishing & Running A Charitable, Education, Religious, Or Research Institution?
- Have More Fun at A Playground Where Your Favorite Pass-Time Is Legal, Accepted, Cheap, and always available?
- Live in a Tax Haven?
- Live Cheaply With A Lot of Servants?
- Have better investment results?
- Escape A Vendetta?
- Avoid Capture, Extradition, or Rendition as a fugitive?
- Live in a place where you can flaunt your wealth?
- Do you plan to leave your home country? Permanently or temporarily?
- Do you want to own a home in the USA?

If I was asked to help you plan a future course of action, the most important question I would ask is this:

"If you didn't have your present problem, and if you had all the money you needed to live anywhere in the world without working, what would you like to do with the rest of your life?"

Obviously, the plan for each person would involve some variations, depending upon input and how much are the assets available for investment. A chap with $250,000 still has to work to earn money. A man with $20 Million doesn't even have to think about the cost of living factor because he can live well on 7% interest, anywhere on Earth.

Let us take the composite character, Mr. Conforti. We shall arbitrarily assign to him the most usual set of answers. What would you tell him to do?

Formulating A 'Typical' Plan

Conforti says, "I'm a retired corporate executive". Goals? I'd like to travel a lot more, exploring different places until I find some country or maybe two or three places that I'd like to retire to and spend most of my time in.

Problems? I have no particular problems except that I hate giving away half my income of $400,000 a year in state and federal taxes. If I can save the time and money I now spend on tax prep and paying, I'd be much happier and could live much better too.

Domestic Relations? I have a 2nd wife whom I'm happy with, and trust completely. She is sane and I do not have to worry about a betrayal, Nevada White styles. [Skip ahead and read that chapter if you can't wait!] She can have everything I own RIGHT NOW if she wants it.

Obligations I would like to escape? It isn't a big priority, but I wouldn't mind getting out of alimony payments to the first one. I suppose if I moved my "ass and assets" I could be in a pretty good position to make a final lump sum settlement with her. I wouldn't want to cut her off with nothing.

Return to the States? My kids are grown, but I'd like to be able to come back to the USA to visit with them and my grandchildren, also, in case I need medical treatment, I'd like to come back to the USA. I don't mind renouncing my citizenship if that would help me save taxes and doesn't interfere with my right to visit here and to come back if I don't find happiness abroad.

How Will I Keep Busy?

I don't want to work or have administrative responsibilities ever again. I am sure of that. But if an opportunity to make a deal comes along, I will take it. I like classical music, culture, theater, and good food.

Where Should I Live?

Want a very urbane, civilized, safe environment. I have lived most of my life in the better suburbs of a big industrial city, Chicago. It has a lousy climate, bad air, high burglary, and violent crime rates. Now I am ready to leave it forever. No more ties in my hometown. Kids are in California. Most of my similar age friends have retired to Florida. A few have gone to the Caribbean, but I don't like either place — too hot and humid for my taste. Oh yes, I have a home worth around $500,000, free and clear bought years ago for $50,000. I have a self-administered pension plan worth another million but as with my house, it will be hard hit with taxes if I liquidate and withdraw funds. Unless you can suggest something better, I would like to move my assets offshore and see if I like living in Europe.

Big Problems At Home?

Your most important question is not applicable to me because I have no big problems. I could stay where I am, but I think I'd like to spend the rest of my life traveling and enjoying life with my wife who is an excellent companion, cultured lady, and speaks several foreign languages. We are both healthy and can live very comfortably on half my present after tax income, but maybe, if I had no taxes at all, I'd splash out a bit more and do a few expensive things: I've always wanted to do something like take some luxury cruises, round the world, go deep sea fishing, and buy a really good violin. I'd like to improve my musical skills, and maybe play in an amateur musical string quartet — just for fun.

A Plan For Mr. Conforti

Like most people, the outline plan emerges rather quickly once the subject formulates a clear idea of what he wants.

Mr. "C" has unwittingly made one very good decision, and that is to "splash out" a bit. If he is unhappy in Chicago (and who wouldn't be in a dirty, polluted, crime ridden city in the rust bowl) the first thing to do is treat himself and his wife to a taste of the good life. A six-month cruise on a luxury liner (for those who enjoy cruises) is an ideal way to enter upon a new life. It is easy to make new friends. After a cruise or two, you will have people of similar ages and interests to visit and hang out with in several countries. There is no domestic staff or garden to worry about. Cruising, you live in a floating hotel suite while visiting many pleasant ports. One of those ports may become a future, more permanent destination.

Why Is It Important To "Splash Out"?

Mainly, start your exodus by treating yourself to good experiences. Many people who move abroad are lonely, disoriented, and homesick. It isn't easy to be away from friends, relatives and familiar surroundings — unless the new life turns out to be a big improvement over what you left. Thus, to make sure your escape gets off to a good start, be sure your first trip or long-stay is in a place you will enjoy. Rent a very nice home or apartment. Splurge on a cruise. If you have a net worth of around $5,000,000, you will earn at least $10,000 a week (tax-free) offshore. Even if you spend even $100,000 each on your round the world cruise boat ticket, you are still going to be well within your budget. For most people, if they do not pay income taxes, their disposable income is immediately doubled.

The biggest sin for a PT is paying retail for anything. Every PT has a big bag of tricks for getting discounts on transport and hotels. Being a *cruise line travel agent* costs little or nothing, but can save 50% on your tickets. Buying leftover top of the line tickets at the last minute is another way to travel top drawer, first class, but at half price or less.

What About Your Old Home? Should You Buy An Expensive New Home Abroad?

Instead of leaving it empty, consider trading the use of it with another retired couple for an equally nice home abroad. Such trades (unlike rentals) are always highly successful and can be arranged through the Vacation Home Exchange Club. People who let you use their comfortable well-furnished home are not going to trash your place and refuse to pay the bills. See back of book, Resource Section for details on trading.

Moving assets like the proceeds of a real estate sale is quite simple. It can be done before you leave — or at some indefinite future time if you plan to go back and occupy your old house. Unless you have creditors or the Revenue breathing down your neck, there is no need to pull up stakes, break all ties and move all assets. In my opinion, if you have a small condo apartment you can simply lock up and leave, don't be in a big hurry to sell. Put it on the market and wait for a good price. However, if you have an expensive home that is too big for you or too much bother to maintain — it is a good idea to sell it before you go abroad. Get rid of the overhead and don't worry about vandalism. Put that money to work for you. Even if your local real estate market is temporarily depressed, having cash in hand and avoiding upkeep costs, burglary and so on makes a sale before physical departure the best option. Generally, it is best not to rush into a new buy for at least several years, and the PT rule is, *unless you can afford to lose it, rent don't buy.* All over the world you can generally rent a first class, furnished home for about 4% of its market value per year. Since you'd lose the return on any capital tied up in a part-time home (investment return should be over 10% on average), you are always better off to rent than to buy. The only exception is in a very depressed market that you think is poised for a real boom.

Let's look at a deal for a theoretical million-dollar house. If you bought it for all cash or with a mortgage, your interest or loss on capital would be around $100,000 per year. Running costs, local taxes and maintenance the landlord usually pays for might be another $10,000. If you'd rent for $4,000 per month or $48,000 (and that's very high) you'd be around $60,000 per year cash ahead by renting.

How To Start Moving Your Assets

You should start the money transfer process by opening several bank accounts abroad in your own name or a variant. Use at least three different countries abroad. Each bank should get relatively small amounts (around $50,000 in each) to open. Explain to the banker that you will be depositing proceeds from the sale of your home (upwards of one million dollars) and will be using the funds to buy a new home in Europe, eventually. This story may not be true, but it will explain why a large deposit will pass through this account. All these "transit" accounts will be kept long term and may be used to pay bills or be accessed by credit card. They are your public accounts or Trojan Horses — the ones you can afford to lose.

Your mother lode will be transferred through these accounts eventually ending up in three or four top-secret depositories. Those funds will be kept in "alternate identity" names or in corporations. No connection to the "old" you. You will never access the mother lode with a credit card, check or do anything with regard to account that leaves a paper trail. The bank will hold all mail and statements are never to be taken out of the bank building itself. Outside of the United States banks and stockbrokers are interchangeable, and so although I say "bank" there are other possibilities. These may be called "Trust Companies," "Financial Managers," or something similar.

These serious money accounts must be absolutely secret. You will not discuss investment policy on the phone nor will you ever make phone calls from your home to the bank. Spending money can be taken out in cash and deposited to another "visible" account where you have a credit card. Then your offshore funds may be accessed from any ATM (Automatic Teller Machine) anywhere in the world.

With a good advisor, you can arrange your affairs and file legally required tax reports in such a way that you do not provide potential future enemies with enough information to seize your offshore money. Eventually, you will become a citizen of a country that does not require any financial reporting from non-residents. That is any country in the world except for the USA. Then you will be free. Free at Last.

And if you can't bear the thought of giving up your USA citizenship, by living abroad with a spouse you get the first $140,000 of annual income tax free (plus housing and expense allowances). There are ways, with corporations and trusts, to shelter any amounts above that.

Chapter 7

Your Own Charitable Foundation – Offshore

*W*E know you will be upset at not contributing your fair share to the taxman, but you will get over it. Why not get rid of your guilt by doing well? Spend your tax savings through a charitable foundation promoting your favorite causes? As it turns out, Americans, if they choose to, can legally divert part of what they used to pay in taxes into a private charity and make money while doing good. A Foundation or non-profit corporation can be involved in education, religion, scientific, cultural, medical, or virtually any activity you choose.

To eliminate government control, a foundation based in a well-selected foreign jurisdiction has the most flexibility. It can pay salaries and expenses, own a comfortable house, collect art works, rent a nice office for its headquarters and devote as much or as little of its assets and income to its good works as the Chairman (you) decides. Are you paying attention? This is one of the best little gems I have buried for you. Cannot say more for the same reasons I have cited many times. For full details send $150, write me c/o the Publisher. Mention "Secret Offshore Foundation Report"

Chapter 8

Taking the Plunge

THE first step on the road towards greater personal security involves so little risk and change that we would liken it in importance to a decision to wear a different color of socks one day a month. Your wife and friends won't notice any difference. You will not look or feel any different. Your investment performance will not change much at first. Nevertheless, there will be a difference. Going offshore? What is it you have to do? More important is, WHY?

Taking the plunge offshore involves nothing more than opening a bank or brokerage account in some jurisdiction that offers banks secrecy. If you live in Florida, Texas or New Orleans your choice may be a bank in the easy-to-reach Cayman Islands, Bahamas or Panama. If you get to Europe a lot, the British Isle of Man or the Channel Islands may be more your cup of tea. For those who like the Orient, Singapore's the spot. Also in Continental Europe, the three banks in Liechtenstein offer more protection and better service than the Swiss. Luxembourg, Gibraltar, and Andorra are also in the running. If you are not Jewish, maybe Israel would be good for you. Why? Nobody would think of looking there for (non-Jewish) money! They have plenty of banks there (in Israel) and foreigners can hold any currency and trade in securities. The best place to hide anything is always the most unlikely! Offshore accounts can be at stockbrokers, foreign mutual fund offices or banks. You might think at this point I'd say, if you are white, put your money in Chad or Senegal (Black Africa). Nope! Stay away from banks in India, Africa, and most third world countries. They are still using manual typewriters and quill pens. That is very inefficient.

There has been a lot said about having no paper trail to your new account. If you truly want your secret account to be secret, you would not simply mail a personal check from your domestic account to "Lloyd's Bank - Isle of Man" to open your first foreign account. On the other hand, if you are a thinking humanoid and plan to *move* money through your first account at Lloyd's into other offshore banks (into accounts owned by a "new" person or company), then there is no harm in opening your first account in such a simple and direct way. Still, a personal check is so easily discovered and traced even twenty years later, that IMO bank drafts or wire transfers from a bank where you don't usually do business are a better way to transfer funds to your first account. I will cover other methods of discreetly moving money, elsewhere in this book. Once funds are transmitted abroad, they have a way of melting into oblivion as far as the rest of the world is concerned.

Abroad, most banks are across between a stockbroker, trust company, and traditional bank, as Americans know it. An offshore bank will manage your money, trade stocks for you, set up corporations and finance your business. An offshore stockbroker will do pretty much the same. An outfit like The Harris Organisation in Panama or its tax haven affiliates goes a bit further and provides a staff of American lawyers to keep their clients on the straight and narrow path of compliance — if that is what they want. They also offer creative solutions to business, marital and tax problems. Most offshore banks will tell you, "we will trade stocks for you or pay you interest and we won't tell anyone. But what you report and whom you report to is strictly your business." Harris goes further and says, "likewise, we won't tell any of your secrets, but if you want to be in 100% compliance with your home country's laws, we will prepare and help you file all the necessary papers."

My advice is that your first deposit to your new offshore account should contain no more than 10% of your assets. In the unlikely event something does go wrong, you can earn it back in a year. Also, your first account should be an opportunity to see how you get along with your offshore service provider. See how things work out. You don't owe anyone lifetime allegiance. You should feel free to move your accounts any time and for any reason. Harry Schultz says: "Close all your accounts every year!" Maybe that's not such a bad idea. But I am not as careful (and paranoid) as Sir Harry.

Some outfits manage money very well and give great performance, but the guy who is supposed to take care of you may be too busy to give you a friendly welcome and a free lunch when you visit. Consider asking for a different customer's rep or changing entirely. Others may be oh so friendly, but lack efficiency. I personally would rather have efficiency and performance, but I have noticed that many of my clients prefer and will stick with charm and the personal touch.

If you have several accounts in several countries, you will have a basis for comparison.

How Do You Get Your Money Home When You Need It?

In prior years, getting your own offshore money back to your home country was the biggest problem. Why? Because a wire transfer or other substantial movement of your own money back to a domestic account could trigger an audit, or worse yet, could be considered the receipt of taxable income. These days, a debit card or ATM card allows one to access funds through an automatic teller machine anywhere in the world. It makes sense that for security and anonymity, your debit card should not be in your own name, but rather a corporation. It also makes sense to separate your account with substantial funds from the account you intend to debit for your consumer needs. In other words, set up two accounts: One for your serious money, and one for your spending money. Do not mix the two. If you are ever apprehended with your visa card, you do not want it to lead directly to your offshore mother lode. For information on a new kind of debit card that has no link to you; see Resource Section and "Plastic Cash Lifeline ™" deal. I have one and am quite pleased with it.

Corporations are very cheap to form in some jurisdictions. I have noticed that if you don't renew them and keep them paid up to date, they are still OK for most purposes. In law, even if a charter has been revoked for non-payment of annual licensing fees, you still have a *de facto* corporation. In my own case, I used a corporation for banking and had its name on my calling card for thirty years after I stopped paying the annual fees to keep it legally alive.

You can form your own corporation without a lawyer by simply seeking out the registrar of corporations, filling out the forms, and paying the fees. IMO, unless you are going into that business (forming corps for others), and want to experience the learning process, it is better to pay a lawyer $100 to $300 for their services. It may also be a good idea to have your spending money account abroad held in a corporate name for privacy. If no signature is required — only a pin code, you may not have "reportable signature control" over any foreign accounts.

When we get more into the "Five Flags" of the PT theory, I will show you how to have accounts in other names by using alternate identity documents. However, for our purposes here in this chapter, this is all you need to know about opening a foreign account.

Why An Offshore Account Is Needed

In the USA, the misnamed *Bank Secrecy Act of 1970* provides that all USA banks shall keep microfilm copies of every check, draft, deposit or collection together with an identification record of the parties involved. These records must be made available to any government official, upon request. Any USA assets, be it bank, or brokerage account may be seized or frozen by government agents or private litigants with minimum formality. In case of mistake, the holder (account owner) will have to go to court to free up his money. This could take many years and the (non-recoverable) attorney's fees needed to fight a seizure are typically more than the amounts involved.

A social security number and any creditor identify every domestic account or government agency can identify all accounts of any individual anywhere in the USA by simply running a computer checking process. Many accounts will be tied up for many years because of errors in similar names or social security numbers.

Offshore Accounts

1. Do not require social security numbers to open them or identification to withdraw funds. They cannot be located by USA based credit reporting agencies. Usually accounts can be held in code names rather than your own (passport) name.
2. Cannot be identified by private creditors.
3. Cannot be identified or revealed to any outside government agents unless you as the owner are proven to be involved in a local crime such as drug dealing or money laundering. Tax evasion is never considered to be a crime in jurisdictions where there are no income taxes!
4. Some offshore accounts pay considerably more interest than you are used to. In this regard we suggest you contact Jyske Bank in Copenhagen Denmark, or Barclay's Finance Co. Isle of Man.

Warning! If your government knows the exact number and the name of your offshore bank it may be able to convince the local government to freeze your money because they (the USA) will claim you are into organized crime, money laundering or child pornography — even if you are not. This is why it is so important that your secret account details be kept secret!

Privacy Tips

If you want privacy, do not use an USA based advisor for any aspect of your offshore dealings. All books and records kept "onshore" in your home country are subject to government burglary, raids, and seizure. The government is very likely to raid any accountant, lawyer, or offshore service provider who operates from within the USA. It is extremely likely that persons using asset protection schemes devised and implemented from within the USA will not get the secrecy they desire. Even worse, they may be drawn into the middle of an unwanted, undesirable criminal investigation just because the "onshore" high profile consultant they worked with is himself getting looked at. Once charged with criminal conspiracy and facing twenty years in Leavenworth Penitentiary, how long do you think it will take before your own lawyer or accountant tries to save his fanny by insisting that it was all your idea. Thirty-two seconds? Nah, not that long.

Never have any bank or brokerage statements mailed to your home country. Never carry them across international borders. Don't even carry such statements out of your bank. Have your broker or bank "hold all mail." Never telephone or fax your bank from your home telephone. Use a public phone. Consider using E-mail and encryption for sensitive communications. In all communications never mention your name or the name of your money manager. Use a code word. "This is Mr. Strawberry Sunday. Is Willie Wonka there?"

Forget Switzerland. They now have information exchange agreements and asset sharing plans (see chapter on "Nevada White") with the USA. The USA government must allege only that a crime was committed. Swiss banks will reveal and turn over any American owned accounts if any USA agent knows just the name the account is held under. They need not know the exact bank. Tax evasion is now a crime under Swiss law if it involves any active "fraud" as opposed to mere "forgetfulness in reporting income." Insider trading and money laundering is a crime, as is participating in organized crime. Numerous environmental crimes are now also recognized under Swiss law.

Bank Secrecy Countries

Consider: Andorra, Austria, Netherlands Antilles, Bahamas, Brazil, Cayman Islands, Channel Islands, Liechtenstein, Isle of Man, Panama, Singapore, Hong Kong, Luxembourg, Macao, Monaco, Uruguay. There are a few others.

The World's Most Ruthless Tax
Collectors In Order Of Badness

Sweden, Norway, Denmark, Finland, USA, Germany, Spain, Switzerland, and France. This list is based upon personal experience of the author and clients. Send in your suggestions and stories for the Baddest tax collectors. "Bad" means that they do midnight raids, they pay informers to lie, grab your assets, and toss you in jail — usually without notice or trial.

No (Income) Tax Countries

Bermuda, Cayman, Sark, Paraguay, Liechtenstein, Monaco, Andorra, Gibraltar (now has a minimum "contribution" for permanent residents).

Countries Where Offshore Income Is Tax Free Or Remittances Can Be Exempted From All Taxes (For Non-Citizens)

Costa Rica, Ireland and Great Britain.

Stay Away From Your Home Country's Branch Banks Or Stockbrokers

If you are an American, even with an account located in one of these suggested bank secrecy havens, and if you have an account abroad with an American company like Citibank, Chase, Merrill Lynch or Schwab; it stands to reason that the home office can be pressured into releasing information and turning over your account's assets. Many computer systems tie in all foreign branches. If your account information can be made to appear on a monitor within the USA, the Supreme Court has said [in US vs. Miller] that account holders in foreign branches of US based institutions have no right to privacy or exemption from legal process. Some people would go so far saying that they would never keep their money in any bank or broker that has an USA branch. That lets out the GT Bank in Liechtenstein, which has a substantial New York City operation. It's competitor, the Private Bank of Liechtenstein has no such exposure.

Jurisdiction!

This is the most important word in this book. Why is it so important? If your assets are totally out of the jurisdiction, they are not subject to any court orders emanating from your home country. If you are out of the jurisdiction, you are not subject to arrest, pressure or detention under a contempt citation. The only exceptions are when the place where you (or your assets) are has a treaty with your home country. Lawyers have written multi-volume sets of books on the subject of extra-territorial jurisdiction, but for your purposes, your investments will be invisible if they are placed abroad in any "off-shore" banking center.

Further, if you are prepared to take a powder in the event of heat, your body is also out of the jurisdiction and thus not subject to any legal process. If you send your assets abroad (just as wealthy Europeans and South Americans have done for centuries) and if you are prepared to go into temporary exile yourself if things get rough, you will always hold on to your offshore property and more importantly your freedom.

All of which brings us to the Five Flag Theory. Most people who have little international experience can readily see the benefits of protecting a nest egg by secreting it abroad. But as they make trips to see their money and realize that there are many places in the world to enjoy life or make money, these trips become longer. A small proportion of our readers decides to become PT's or citizens of the world. What is a PT?

My former associate, W. G. Hill, with my help, developed a whole philosophy. This "bible" was in the form of a famous book titled "PT." Scope books originally published it. PT can be purchased also from our publisher. Fortunately, Hill in his book declared that his writings were "public domain" and could be quoted without limit. As it turns out, we have published here in this book the original version of the PT Theory (before it was edited in a way that Hill felt was detrimental to his original exposition). Accordingly, I have already given you a short chapter from PT. This is the PT basic philosophy in Hill's own uncut, unexpurgated, original words. Let me know if you found it interesting! We have the full book available and for sale. If you ever make contact with Hill, let me know where he is and what he is doing, as we have not seen him lately. Any sightings?

Chapter 9

Capital Preservation Made Simple For Invisible Investors

Estate & Gift Tax Planning

Billions of dollars go into the pockets of lawyers, accountants State & Federal Treasuries *every year* as the result of administration fees, planning costs, and ultimately, no matter what you do domestically, the greater portion of your life savings is flushed down the toilet with estate and gift taxes. Sometimes (as in the famous Dorrance-Campbell Soup Heirs Case) *more than 100% of an estate can be claimed by the various state and federal tax collectors, and lost* to the heirs. How does the Invisible Investor handle these "problems"? There are several ways: Boy Scouts (super honest folks) can transfer assets abroad and set up offshore foundations or charitable trusts to escape all taxes legally. You control the funds during your lifetime, and can use or distribute the funds as you see fit. You let a chosen few run the whole shebang after you die. Like the Nobel Foundation with it's famous "Peace Prize" your name can continue on forever memorialized by your money. No taxes on income or principal, forever and ever and ever... Suppose you want to retire and study the sex life of plants. You could fund a research organization to pay your salary and expenses while you spent the rest of your life working on this project from penthouse suites of various Intercontinental hotels.

A simpler way for those with two citizenship's is to put the money with a financial manager or bank that accepts death instructions, in a place that does not require probate and has no taxes of any kind on foreign owned assets. Upon death, your money or securities can pass in full, directly to the chosen successor(s) or be managed by professional trustees for their benefit. No probate, no lawyers, no accountants, no taxes no costs, and NO ESTATE PLANNING IS NEEDED.

Is Your Money Trapped In A Pension Plan?

Years ago, the government presented gullible citizens with an idea. They said they could set up pension plans to save money for their old age, deduct it from income and let it accumulate tax free until a certain age (usually 59), when they could withdraw accumulated funds and capital gains at reduced tax rates. Too good to be true? At the time in my books issued during the 1970's, I predicted that the government would figure out ways to claw back any taxes saved over the years. I also predicted that such plans would not be truly 100% safe from creditors and plaintiff's lawyers.

To avoid the heavy, double crossing hand of the U-Know-Who, I advised locating the funds and administration of any pension funds abroad. It was legal to do that in the good old days, but this loophole was soon closed for those who had not done it early on.

Just as predicted, nowadays, people who are starting to draw on their appreciated pension funds are finding themselves saddled with regular taxes and special penalty taxes that leave them with as little as 12% of their capital. Would you believe some people who thought they were very lucky and invested their money with great success are hit the worst? An 88% tax bite faces a friend of mine!

Is there a way out? Of course there is! Am I going to publish it here and have this loophole closed? Of course not! But anyone with an IRA or other pension plan who wants to get his money out in full, to use it as he pleases might do well to spend $10,000 on two years of unlimited consultations with me. The answer is simple and will take me about ten minutes to explain. That's $1,000 a minute for my fee. Although if any other questions come up later during the year, you still have me on retainer.

Say you have a $3 Million pension or retirement fund that will be taxed at $2 Million or more. I think $10,000 is a cheap price to pay for a little bit of advice you will not get from your neighborhood tax preparer or lawyer. You will learn of your option to save 100% of what would be taken away from you. $2 Million in our example. "We don't get paid for what we do, but rather, for what we know!"

Judgment Proofing (As In Divorce)

Your author has had more than his share of costly divorce experiences until I learned about the offshore world and became an Invisible Investor for the first time. Good gracious — how time flies. That was thirty years ago! In the divorce of Lady Morgan La Fey, lovingly described in Chapter One claimed (to her lawyer) that I was a multi-millionaire. At first when filing for divorce, she demanded that her lawyer get her Five Big Ones. Five million dollars in settlement.

But as round one began, she had no idea where the money went — if it was ever there. [Where is *there*? "*There* was *there* but its not *there* any longer." As Gertrude Stein might have said.] All I had to do was smell a divorce. This warm body was Prepared Thoroughly. My assets having been sent on ahead, I departed the jurisdiction before being served with process. By the time Morgana's lawyer filed the case, her dear defendant husband and his assets were invisible. I was laying low at the Monte Carlo Beach Hotel & Country Club. But of course she didn't know where I was.

After a futile few months of legal flailing at the wind, dear old Morgan La Fey (predictably) spent her energy, charm, and undeniable sex appeal attracting another rich sucker. When he grabbed the bait & laid a diamond engagement ring on her, she deemed it appropriate to contact my anonymous European mail-drop address and practically beg me for a quick release from the bonds of matrimony. The conversation went like this:

"Honey, I have thought it over, and I don't really want anything from you at all, dearest, I just want you to sign the papers so I can get a quickie divorce and marry "Bruce," heir to the Bruce Fruit & Nut Billions. You don't owe me a thing. Don't stand in the way of my happiness. Just give me my freedom and I'll give you yours."

My answer?

"Morgana dear, you have been such a good faithful companion to me (I was just oozing with sweetness and sarcasm!), I will do as you ask. Just send the papers over to my mail drop in Switzerland along with all the jewelry and those shares of stock that you got from me during the course of our marriage. Then I will be happy to sign and return the signed divorce papers."

Her reply:

"Done!"

Years later, I heard that she took Billionaire Bruce (the fruit & nut guy) for serious dough in her inevitable divorce from him. She has made over a million in settlements on each of her five husbands — so far. I was the exception. The others felt they had no option but to pay. Not me, and not YOU. An Invisible Investor can play with expensive women like Morgana La Fey. With any luck at all, you can play plenty and not have to pay plenty.

If you prefer to negotiate a settlement of any lawsuit on your terms, and not have, Judge Robin Hood and his 12 Generous Jurors give away your money, PT! Protect your Treasure by keeping it hidden and invisible, "offshore."

After I was in the clear with Morgana and she was safely married off, I came back to my old home base with my moneybags intact and started a new construction business. It became a big time success. But as I told you in Chapter One, the government wiped me out a few years later. I had been prepared for Morgana. But in those days, as a good patriotic citizen, I couldn't believe my own government would destroy a good-sized company and put a lot of people on the street over a small disagreement that could have been settled amicably. The government claim was not about money — they wanted to tear down my business and destroy me. A wild ferret is one of the few animals that kill purely for the pleasure of it. They will destroy a hundred gentle, innocent rabbits in a day if put into a borough. I was not allowed to simply pay the IRS claim and settle. The government treated me like some sort of Mafiosi who had to be strangled and dangled. They seized, attached, froze and leined everything until all I had left was the pants I was wearing and a small offshore account I had almost forgotten about.

If I had it to do over again, I'd have kept my USA operations mortgaged to the hilt so that there would be little equity to seize. I would have placed a great deal of emphasis on making deals and investments abroad. I would have compartmentalized my international business activities with corporations, trusts, and foundations so that no single government or creditor could do me any serious damage. You do not need all those artificial "structures" if you are retired and have only passive investments like stocks. But if you are in an active business you are likely to get sued or in a government dispute. Thus, it is a good idea to be able to hide your financial interests behind a facade of foreign corporations, trusts, holding companies, and foundations. They are not absolute protection for domestic assets, but better than nothing, they will serve as a wall to keep the enemy at a distance until you can figure out what to do next.

I didn't think it could happen to me, but I was brought down by a pimple faced new IRS agent who had nothing going for him except the vast powers of a bureaucrat to destroy people more productive and useful to society than he could ever be. Today I know it is a good idea to:

"Get your money out of the country, before your country gets the money out of you!"

Chapter 10

How a Leading Swiss Bank Compromised Their Client

THE SAD BUT TRUE STORY OF NEVADA WHITE

Note: This is purportedly a transcript of a training session for Department of Justice Employees given at Washington DC, in June, of 1996. We obtained it from a known and reliable Internet source where a person who claims to have attended the session leaked it. According to our informant, similar training sessions were given in the United States of America during summer 1996. Names have been changed to protect the identity of our source and for other legal reasons.

Title of Federal Strike Force Training Session:

Seize The Moment! Financial Opportunities For Law Enforcement Officers

Your Instructor: National Strike Force Organizational Supervisor, "Willard Butkis" Rules: No recording is permitted. This session is "off the record".

Mr. Butkis: Our work is getting more exciting and interesting every day. We are finally armed with the powers we need to fight organized and white collar crime. And of special interest to you ladies and gentlemen here today, we will comment about this new era where there are more and more material incentives for individuals. Substantial bonuses can result from seizures and confiscation's you recognize and report, organize or participate in.

Federal Investigative Agencies — Self-Financing Profit Centers

From Biblical times until rather recent history, tax collectors were local warlords who had the power to collect or confiscate what was due the sovereign. These warlords or aristocrats were expected to keep for themselves a generous percentage of all collections or confiscation's. This was necessary to cover costs and provide adequate incentives for the tax collectors (who also served as courts, prosecutors, and police) in maintaining order and quelling revolts. New programs in the United States restore us to the more uncomplicated roles before the unworkable system of constitutional checks and balances were introduced.

Tax and customs collectors of old always had certain duties to their government. They were autonomous, self-financing, and never needed to go hat in hand to a legislative body for money to do their work. Nor would any court second-guess them. I am happy to say we are getting back to that old, more efficient system today. Federal employees are becoming the new aristocrats. Our mission? To protect the government and the citizens from the troublemakers who infest the country and threaten the existing order. The courts, the House and Senate, while not yet publicly espousing this view of our Federal bureaucracy, recognized the necessity of acquiescing on all the important issues. Rather than speaking generally, I will use the Case Study Method to show you all how drastically things have improved for us over the last few years.

Let's Look At The Case Of Nevada White

White reputedly began his career in the 1960s as a jazz musician. For his own sake, he should have stayed in that profession. White was brought to our attention when we received complaints from the Small Business Administration that he was sponsoring a television program, *Free Money*, that caused our brother-agency to be swamped with telephone calls and letters demanding "free money." It appeared that White produced and sponsored a long commercial disguised as a TV interview show. The interviews with successful applicants (who had read White's book of course) made it appear quite easy to get government loans and grants for almost any purpose.

The real purpose of his show was of course to get those watching to send for a $49.95 "kit" which gave information about "thousands of little-known government grant and loan programs." White also ran weekend seminars priced at $300 and up. Those who bought his "kit" could supposedly get further, more detailed instructions on getting government loans and grants at these seminars. Our undercover agents purchased several kits and attended several seminars. They reported that in their opinion, only a small proportion of those attending seminars or buying these kits would ever be successful in their quest for "free money."

Early reports indicated that by the late 1980's White was selling hundreds of thousands of these kits, and making a great deal of money (probably millions of dollars) from his "seminars." His kits were nothing more than legally permitted reprints of government brochures and application forms he had personally obtained over the course of a few months of personal visits to various government agencies, mainly in Washington DC. These brochures were available free upon request from the agencies involved. The loan programs White described did exist but it was never the intention of Congress or the agencies involved that they should become known to and applied for directly by members of the public. Such loans and grants always were, and should remain the province of a small-informed group of specialist attorneys and insiders. The insiders were of course former employees of the agencies concerned who, until White came along, were able to make a comfortable consulting income.

To put information on all the government grant and loan programs directly in the hands of the general public creates an intolerable burden on the government employees involved. Not to mention the loss of income to our brothers who went over to the other side of the fence after putting in many years of loyal service. When the agencies involved might have had none, or only one or two applications per week to cope with, they now had hundreds, sometimes thousands of applications to deal with. Naturally supervisors at the Federal Housing Authority, the Veteran's Administration, the Small Business Administration and various art, social work and educational bureaucracies were very disturbed with White. They asked us at Justice to do something about him. Basically, they wanted him shut down.

We at the Department of Justice saw the need to preserve order, and to prevent Mr. White from making obscene profits from government programs certainly not designed to benefit the likes of him. We quickly identified Mr. White as the sort of vermin that must be eradicated. He was a clear and present threat to the orderly functioning of bureaucracy. Our strategy with all such criminals is to burn them alive, to barbecue them, in Government Speak, to give them the KABBOB treatment:

KA) KONFISCATE THEIR ASSETS
BB) Put Them Behind Bars
OB) PUT THEM OUT OF BUSINESS

To this end, we unleashed a Strike Force on White. As you, all know the Strike Force is assembled for top priority cases and involves assembling and assigning an interdisciplinary group from the various agencies. The people involved will later be involved in prosecutions, confiscations, licensing matters, and tax collections. Their main purpose is to investigate, and to put together a list of crimes committed by the strike force target. In this case White was proved to be an exemplary target.

The strike force is used against high profile enemies of government who espouse ideas repugnant to the bureaucracy. This word, "repugnant," pretty well describes Nevada White. Once a strike force is unleashed, we always come up with several dozen crimes, and the evidence and witnesses to prosecute these creeps effectively.

In recent years, another purpose of the Strike Force has been to identify assets for seizure and to sequester such assets. *This program has been growing at an exponential rate for the past five years. Seizures and collections under it are providing billions of dollars in revenues for the Treasury, plus magnificent personal wealth enhancement opportunities for individual law enforcement officers. Finally, we have a situation where the good guys have a chance to enrich themselves at the expense of the bad guys.* We will go into more detail on this interesting topic, but first, let us look at what is expected of you when you get involved in such a case:

Do Not Limit Investigation To Immediate Past Or Present Business Affairs

Because White had been a musician ten years before our investigation began, and as we know that all musicians are involved with drugs we felt that Drug Enforcement Administration personnel should be made part of the strike force to investigate White's undoubted links to drug. Especially, users and drug traffickers from his days on stage where he worked with many South American black musicians and singers who used drugs.

"Michael Smernov" of the DEA was assigned to investigate all past contacts and to assign other agents to work undercover in the matter. To infiltrate White's office with one or more of our operatives was also given priority. When selecting Potential Government Witnesses, Undercover Agents and Informants, agents should remember during investigations that we have in excess of 3 million Federal prisoners currently in jail and on parole. One out of every four black men has a criminal record. Any of these who have had prior contact of any sort with a target (or who form future ties as an undercover agent) are potential government witnesses.

Mere association with underworld characters, drug users and admitted felons is often sufficient to taint any defendant in the eyes of a jury. **To get very damaging testimony from our criminal element, we have to do little more than suggest that immunity will be granted, their existing sentence will be reduced, or pending charges will be dropped. We rarely need to script or invent any testimony. Usually it is enough to ask a leading question like "When did the subject last sell you illegal drugs?"**

The potential witness seldom fails to rise to the bait especially if can be released from incarceration and in appropriate cases, be given such treasures as financial support and a new identity immediately under a witness program. Selling drugs is of course only one of the possible offenses to suggest. Merely discussing or giving advice about any questionable matter is the crime of "conspiracy." Any discussion or actions regarding money can be crafted into a case of money laundering." Any use of the mails or advertising mediums can be construed as fraud. Every investigation suggests many possibilities of the target being tangentially involved in an illegal enterprise.

The fact that the subject enjoyed playing cards for money is clear evidence that the target was engaged in organized crime, i.e. gambling. If target provided his cronies with marijuana or untaxed liquor while playing poker, such actions are very serious felonies known as "continuing criminal activity" **under the RICO Act and the penalty can be confiscation of the home or building where the gambling took place.** At the very least, new environmental laws give us the option of initiating confiscations or criminal prosecutions in connection with the improper storage of waste materials, over-use of utilities, excessive size of home or office windows, and improper use of motor vehicles such as White's Rolls Royce motor car with a grievous emissions problem.

Finally, if all else fails, accusations regarding abuse of children (especially target's own children) are easy to make, easy to corroborate, and very effective at tainting any target.

The Preliminary Investigation Of Nevada White

As a first step, even before the active investigation began, our agents compared the names on the target's 300,000-name customer mailing list (surreptitiously acquired from his mailing list broker). These names, together with the names of all persons he telephoned or who telephoned him in the past ten years were correlated against the names of all prisoners, drug users, suspects, known criminals, and past offenders in our database. We came up with a goodly number of matches — approximately 3,675 potential witnesses against White.

Criminal associations of one to two per cent of any target's customer list and personal address book are common for any "legitimate" business. The criminal element is very susceptible to the use of the carrot and the stick. Thus, the threat of prosecution or cancellation of parole, or merely pressing charges with a few hundred well-selected witnesses will cause a squealing and singing to warm your hearts. Another trick we use for retail stores is to test cash for minute quantities of contraband drugs on currency.

Positive chemical analysis and the possession of tainted money justify seizure of all cash and the business itself. Unfortunately, White dealt mainly in checks and credit cards. Special Agents of the Internal Revenue Service arranged for a mail intercept, as they always do. Eventually, all cash and incoming checks were photocopied for five years to see if every single one of these items were deposited to White' customer accounts and reported as taxable income.

We later learned that some cash items not reported as income had never been received by White because they were pocketed by dishonest IRS agents who were in the team that monitored his mail. These agents were quietly dismissed. There was no reason for us to reduce the proof of White's income by the amounts stolen. The law is that such funds are income, whether received or not. Our indisputable evidence was IRS record of cash sent in by customers and not reported as taxable income by White. Mail intercepts can be very useful for other reasons. They pick up such items as foreign bank account statements, and correspondence relating to foreign assets we can later identify and seize. Plus, we find loves letters and discovers many other secrets that can be used as the basis for criminal charges against the subject.

In the Martin Luther King case, such letters were very effectively used to discredit King and his Communist fellow travelers. Regarding White, from all sources we expect to have over 400 different criminal charges to choose from in the White case. Admittedly, none of them separately amounted to a hill of beans, but taken all together the evidence will paint a picture of an irresponsible member of society who, for instance, seldom bothered to use his recycling containers. He failed to renew his automobile safety sticker for three months after it had expired because he wanted to pollute. He cheated on his wife with Laura, the undercover agent we sent in.

Correspondence with his tax lawyers and accountants proved to be very useful in getting those professionals to give evidence against their client or face loss of their own licenses. As we all know, proof of an intention to reduce taxes legally is now sufficient to cause the loss of any tax benefits. In many cases "tax planning" itself may be a crime. White spent a great deal of time on minimizing his taxes with offshore vehicles that the courts let people like California attorney Margulies and his clients get away with. But times have changed from the days of "Operation Haven" and we have ways of avoiding judicial review. **Scoundrels like White can be reduced to poverty and forced to plea bargain because the weight and variety of charges we lay on them would cost far more to defend than any private citizen could afford.** But if we can seize all of the target assets during an investigation, he can't even afford to confer with any defense lawyers.

The Trap Snaps Shut

Our inter-agency strike force raid was extremely useful with regard to our objectives for White. No charges had been brought after five years of surveillance and investigation. We didn't feel absolutely confident that we could win a court case. In the old movies the crooks could say "You ain't got nothing on me." If they were right, we had to back off. But not any more. We were going to shut this culprit down!

A full scale raid, with guns drawn and doors kicked down is an excellent way to put most operators like White out of business immediately. No warrant or court permission is needed any more. It is an administrative decision. In his case, the several hundred attendees at the White's Free Money weekend seminar we raided were told to go home and on their way out, we instructed them to ask for refunds. We knew that half the cash generated by the seminar had already been spent on promotion, the meeting rooms, salaries, refreshments, and guest speakers. Thus, having to fork out nearly $900,000 at one crack would be a considerable financial blow to White. Advance notification to the news media on our raid of a seminar created bad publicity to scare away future attendees. At the raid we confiscated all or most of White' supplies of books, tapes, scripts, projectors, films, computers, and so on.

Nothing puts a lecturer out of business more quickly than a raid. It destroys his credibility, grabs his cash, and confiscates needed props. But this was only the beginning. We were also able to confiscate from White's person several checkbooks, and his US passport; in addition, his legally obtained foreign passport. We confiscated the cash in all of his personal and company bank accounts the same day on the grounds that they were the proceeds of money laundering. Were we correct? He made the money with advertising fraud (more about this later) and thus it was tainted money - just as if it had been speckled with cocaine powder.

We also got from one of White's safe deposit boxes a third passport from a Central American country (with a different name on it). Bribery or fraud must have obtained this document. This single item alone could be the basis of several felony charges with a total of six four-year jail terms.

Now for the advertising fraud charges: Our associates at the Federal Trade Commission examined old tapes of White TV programs. They determined there were several possible counts of advertising fraud involved. Nothing in the programs indicated that it was advertising. Yet the program was today what would be called an "infomercial." This is advertising, pure and simple, yet described in the program itself as "educational." Unfortunately, as White was the first to present a national infomercial, the laws were not entirely clear. The FTC sent White a registered letter (a few days before the raid) informing him that past and future programs would be deemed fraudulent advertising unless they were clearly labeled as "Paid commercial messages."

White did something else that was clearly fraudulent advertising however, and each act was a serious crime with a five-year jail term possible for each act under both past and present laws. He offered an additional "free book" on some related subject to the first 100 callers. When thousands of callers rang up his toll-free "800" number to order his $49.95 Government Loan & Grant Kit, the operators were instructed to congratulate all callers (not just the first 100) that they had won a free book. In the supposed resulting euphoria, the order-takers then solicited the customer to purchase still another $25 book, which over half of all callers did. The Federal Trade Commission labeled this procedure clear consumer fraud. With the strike force coordinator's approval, instructed the target (White) that the FTC would at his expense send out an apology to every single past customers and offer them a full refund plus interest and postage costs, without the need for returning any of the books or merchandise.

There had been no prior complaints to the TV stations or the Federal Trade Commission from the public, but this was only because he cleverly avoided trouble with his customers by giving a full refund to any customers who asked for them. The giving away of these free books meant that White could be charged with some 800,000 felonies calling for his imprisonment for five years on each offense. Or four million years give or take a hundred thousand years. [Laughter].

After our letter offering them a refund has been circulated and publicized, over two per cent of all of White's 800,000 customers demanded their refund. [Author's note: When a similar letter was sent to 1 million purchasers of Levi's blue jeans whom we felt had been defrauded in a similar scheme, there were 2 million refund requests, over twice as many refund requests as Levi's had been sold during the period in question.]

We Can Finally Do Our Work Effectively, And Profitably!

As you recall from our introductory remarks, one of our primary goals is to put criminals like White out of business. These days, we are able to do that by means of raids, seizures, and refund orders like the above — without the need for inconvenient trials or judicial review. If there is a judicial review, administrative bodies and strike force work is undone or criticized in fewer than two per cent of all cases. American courts have correctly recognized that the end justifies the means. As a result, old constitutional restrictions have slipped away. Illegally obtained evidence can now be admitted. In tax cases and many others, a target can no longer refuse to give us documents and evidence we can use to convict him. If we entrap a target into committing a crime, he can no longer get away with it by showing he would not have done it if we hadn't lured him into it.

The case of Mayor Marion Barry of Washington DC illustrates how we successfully hired the ex-girlfriend of the mayor to invite him to a hotel room offering him drugs (supplied by us) and sex, supplied by her at our request. [Laughter]. We videotaped the whole set-up and got him a nice long jail term for drug possession. Unfortunately, the stupid people of Washington reelected Barry after his jail term. Our next action will be to take away the vote of the undeserving people of Washington DC to insure that responsible, appointed city managers run the town, not the convicted felons they elect. If a target like White dares to flee abroad, we don't have to extradite any more, we just kidnap. The courts have ruled that kidnaps or even murders outside of our borders by government agents are not criminal offenses for which the agents can be charged. Bringing in a suspect from abroad with illegal force is no reason to free the suspect. But here's the important thing!

Confiscations! Our Most Important New Tool

For the past five years we have been able to confiscate (without inconvenient court proceedings) any assets found in this country. Even if the target is / was never found guilty of any criminal charges we could keep the money or *tainted* property. There was and is no clear rule about how we have to identify or deal with such money and it can certainly be kept or distributed within the department. Any assets can be seized upon suspicion that they are tainted in any way. With White, his background as a musician alone was sufficient to assure us that any money he earned or saved would be tainted money. But fraudulently giving away some 800,000 in free books sealed his fate.

Now (Some) Assets Abroad Can Also Be Seized

We can now confiscate any assets of the target that we locate abroad in some of the most important countries because of **mutual assistance treaties**. The most profitable one for us has been with Switzerland. No trial or legal proceedings in the "offshore" country are usually necessary. In White's case, we were able to use our new powers to the fullest. But this is only the beginning of White's nightmare and our triumph. The best is yet to come. You recall that we placed an undercover agent in White office. This woman was an experienced embezzler and thief, who also had worked part-time as a prostitute and exotic dancer. She proved to be an excellent operative for us at no cost! "Laura" was out on bail for pending charges. We agreed to give her a pass and complete immunity if she could come up with anything useful on White for us. A natural-born criminal, she produced results beyond our expectations.

Our undercover operative, Laura was able to get White involved in an adulterous affair with her, and also to participate with her in tax evasion activities. That his new "tax planning" activities were new for him and inspired by our agent is no longer a defense. With letters of recommendation we had produced for her, and by using all her charms Laura was hired and she quickly became White's personal secretary and mistress. She suggested to White that as long as he was under a lot of heat, he should start skimming cash and depositing this to a secret account that she would set up as his nest egg. Laura did in fact set up an account to which $350,000 in cash receipts were eventually diverted.

With our permission, Laura took this money for herself, putting it in her own foreign bank account. Laura concealed the theft from White by, from time to time, showing him her own foreign bank statements with the growing cash balance. She told White the name and she removed address of the depositor and the bank for "security purposes." Of course, the statements were for her own personal account to which the White' skim money had been transferred. Her testimony about his skimming at any trial; will clearly show that he diverted these unaccounted for sums intending to use the money to pay his attorneys or to live on after he escaped the jurisdiction. The matter of her theft is not admissible, and we have agreed not to prosecute her or demand any tax on the funds.

She certainly deserves them for her excellent services. [Laughter].

Laura came up with the additional information that White had transferred a "mother lode" of about $20 million in fully taxed profits to a bank in Switzerland over the years. However, she was not able to pry the exact location and account number out of him despite valiant efforts. [Laughter].

Searching For The Mother Lode

Our mail opening and wire taps in the year before the raid also yielded some indication that White had substantial funds abroad, probably in Switzerland, because he regularly visited Zurich. Yet there were at first substantial problems in front of us if we were to seize funds on deposit in Switzerland. Under the old rules of the game (pre-1996), as per our treaty of mutual assistance and exchange of information with Switzerland, we had to identify the holder **by the name he used in Switzerland**. We had to identify the **exact bank and branch**, we had to convince the Swiss Department of Justice that the funds were the **proceeds of a crime that was also a crime under Swiss law**.

In 1995, we came to an agreement that money laundering would be made a crime in Switzerland. Money laundering is any activity regarding tainted money. Now, if we knew only the name of a suspected criminal like White (and not exactly, where the assets were), the Swiss Department of Justice would circulate that name to all banks in Switzerland. In the event of a possible client account match, the info in our USA file copy of the passport, plus the passport copy on file with the bank would be compared. In the event of a positive match, the account would be frozen. The Swiss account would be turned over to the US Treasury if and when the target was convicted of any crime in the USA.

These Swiss rules made it theoretically possible, but extremely difficult for us to actually gain control over an account.

To apply pressure on the Swiss Banks the Department of Justice began seizing all the USA dollar deposits [Note: All US Dollar accounts
are held in USA banks and every Swiss bank has many US Dollar
accounts whether they have any branch operations in the USA or
not] of any Swiss banks where identified accounts we wanted to seize
were held. This resulted, as might be expected, in a good deal of
screaming in pain by the Swiss bankers. A compromise was then
reached.

Swiss Bankers Will Sell Out Clients — The New Secret Accord

**This highly profitable deal, gentlemen, is to be kept secret as long
as possible. We always knew the Swiss banks were harlots who
would sell out to the highest bidders.** Their public relations image
was to pretend that their much vaunted bank secrecy was put in force
IN 1941 to protect Jews who were being persecuted in Nazi Germany. The fact is that any non-legally-resident endangered Jews
were shipped right out of Switzerland during the war into the hands
of the Nazi Gestapo. Even though the Swiss officials knew concentration camps and eventual murder was to be their fate. The banks
were then; very happy to transfer the dormant Jewish accounts to
their own capital. So much for the good intentions of the Swiss.

When any Jews (wealthy or otherwise) wanted short-term sanctuary,
the Swiss said, "The boat is full!" Big accounts protected by bank
secrecy against victorious allies were not Jewish, but were Nazi accounts. Like the secret list of the Nazi owners of the massive I. G.
Farben Trust, these names were never to this day released. Many
fugitives Nazis in South America have lived off stolen money in Swiss
banks all these years. Yet I digress. The deal that we should all
know about was the one we negotiated to cover the White case and a
dozen or so similar cases where the amounts involved come to over
$200 Million in aggregate.

From now on, *we can seize and have transferred to New York City,
any known accounts owned by Americans in Switzerland with no
trial, and no proof of anything. It will be almost as informal and
easy as grabbing an American-based account.* We fill out a standard
form and presto, the account is "arrested." There was a price to pay,

but considering the benefits, we think it is a fair price. Here's the deal: Today, we give the Swiss Department of Justice the name of the miscreant whom we believe to have a Swiss account with either cash or securities in it.

Every offshore account of every American citizen involves money laundering, insider trading, or some kind of fraud, as far as we are concerned. Our laws clearly require the detailed reported of all assets. Failure to report an offshore account is felony tax fraud and money laundering - at the very least. There is no good reason for any honest, patriotic American citizen to have *any* assets abroad. Even safe deposit boxes are covered by the new agreement. The Swiss will circulate the name and freezes any accounts or boxes in any name we give them. After (not before the seizure) there will be a cursory check with the owner to make sure our colleagues are not arresting a totally unrelated account from a similarly named but uninvolved individual. After the seizure the account is then divided up three ways.

Dividing The Spoils

The bank gets to keep a third. The Swiss Department of Justice gets to keep a third. And the US Treasury gets the last third. So as you can see, the Swiss banks have a real incentive now to help us with cases like White. With them being able to keep a third of the account, they would give up their own mother without a fight. The target can't do much to fight us. Even if a criminal like White has fled the jurisdiction, he cannot go to court in Switzerland to claim the old traditional defense that he did no crime under Swiss Law. That would have been a complete defense against seizure in Switzerland up till last year, but now, under our agreement, any defendant who shows up in a Swiss Court and is not a legal Swiss resident *will simply be delivered to a waiting US Marshall without benefit of extradition hearing.* Just like the unwanted Jews of World War II, our accused criminals will be placed (without trial) on the next plane to the USA. This police-friendly procedure is called "rendition."

As part of the deal whereby they keep two-thirds of the money, the

Swiss have agreed that *anybody we want is somebody they don't want* in their country — regardless of how good a bank customer they might have been. So, in the procedure technically called "rendition" Swiss police and our US Marshall escort the unwanted deadbeat, having been stripped of his assets by the Swiss, to the airport. He is forcibly placed on the next plane to us. If he yells and screams enough to disrupt the flight, we will inject him full of Thorozine™ and put him (unconscious) on a military plane.

How Swiss Concerns And Misgivings Were Satisfied

The *touching concern* of the Swiss authorities *for human rights* where foreigners are concerned is illustrated by our discussions with them about the implementation of the new accords. The Swiss Department of Justice people asked us: "What if after we take our third, and the banks get their third, and the depositor's government takes a third — what if, against all odds, the depositor manages to overturn any convictions and he emerges "lily white" with a court order in his home country that all funds must be returned to him, with costs? Under international law, wouldn't a Swiss court be obliged to order the Swiss government and the bank involved to return the depositor's money, and wouldn't we be then out a lot of money for our trouble?" **The Swiss "win-win" solution was to pass regulations that in such cases, the "innocent victim" of government mistakes, false arrest and perjury would not be able to recover any damages in Switzerland, and further, the government and banks involved may, before making restitution, deduct all their costs and lawyers' fees.**

This arrangement gives the USA government everything that we want: If it ever turns out that we have seized money wrongly (according to a USA court) there will be so many costs and fees deducted that the depositor won't get anything back, even if he wins! The Swiss government gets to keep their blood money, win or lose! Because Switzerland is not a member of the European Union, there is no appeal to the European Court of Human Rights. In the case of White and others like him, I am sure you agree they should have no rights! With bankers' fees only about one per cent per year, it would take 33 years for the Swiss bankers to earn what they get in one day under our deal.

For public relations purposes, the Swiss banks will no doubt downplay the fact that they are selling out their customers. We can expect to see them make reassuring noises, telling other customers that only drug dealers and serious criminals are affected. However, as you see from the White case, under the old rules we could never have attacked his money. Why? Because giving away free books on television and not reporting a foreign bank account is definitely no crime in Switzerland. The Swiss don't protect their consumers as the US Government does and that is their business. But consumer fraud here is enough for any American to lose their freedom and their money. And that is as it should be. Aside from the consumer fraud, the rest of the stuff we have on White is either petty or stuff that used to be called entrapment. Nevertheless, we in Justice know that if we were able to get a person to commit a crime, he would have committed a similar crime eventually anyway. Thus, we need entrapment as a crime prevention tool. White is unquestionably guilty as hell: For disrupting our entire grant and loan programs he deserves at least the 20 years in Club Fed that we are going to impose on him when we get him back here. And mark my words, we will get him back here, one way or another. But for White and his ilk, for the first time, in this breakthrough, the Swiss are with us instead of against us.

As I said at the outset, it is really sweet when the customer's whore finally comes in out of the cold and becomes a government agent. The Swiss, having tasted the easy money to be made from confiscation programs will no doubt be rushing to make similar deals with the French, Italians, and Germans. *And that will be the end of the myth of bank secrecy in Switzerland!* Now let us go back to the story of White. Let us say we didn't have his assets in hand yet. If we had him in custody, we now have legally sanctioned ways to get an inmate not only to spill the beans about any secret offshore accounts they may have, but also we can get him to sign it over to us. Our methods are no big secret. We throw the bastards into a metal box without any windows — without any food, water, or toilet facilities. We tell them to signal only when they are ready to co-operate. And then we "throw the key away" and forget all about them. We get co-operation or else they are dead. Our statistics are roughly 100 per cent co-operation within five days. [Laughter].

We Need The European System

In White's case, we could not arrest him in the past because preparation for our criminal case wasn't complete. In every case, when we throw someone in the can, here in the USA we still have to bring charges within a few days. Of course what we need is the continental European system where *suspects are held (no bail!) indefinitely in prison without trial*. But for the moment, we don't have this system. We still have to convince a jury that the guy has committed enough crimes to warrant a jail sentence. Our 99 per cent conviction rate means we are doing our job very well.

Fortunately, an American jury cannot be told whether their conviction verdict carries a one-year sentence or 20 years. They might refuse to convict a guy like White if they knew we'd send him away for the rest of his life for *giving away books*. Part of the case against White will be proof that he controlled $20 million on deposit in Switzerland. Being rich isn't *ipso facto* always a crime of course, but as we saw in the famous Leona Helmsly case, of a few years back, anyone with serious money in cash is an automatic guilty verdict — unless they are perceived as a great philanthropist. We know from much trial experience, the American Common Man, (and Woman) on a jury will always sock it to a philandering male millionaire. That is why we must choose our targets carefully and create the facts and circumstances that guaranty a conviction. The new long mandatory jail sentence laws do the rest. White will get forty years or more in the slammer when, not if, we get him. [Applause]

Turning The Wife

With White, a key objective in our case was to turn his wife against him: We were able to do this very effectively in this case. White's wife was shown a video taken surreptitiously by one of our investigators clearly showing that he was having sex with his secretary Laura. This screening at our offices was met with a "so what" attitude on the part of Mrs. White. But we know from bugs in their home, that there was a very furious row about it that night. We also know from taps on the White's home phone, fax and E-mail that within days, White's wife was cruising the Internet, looking for dates, presumably to give him a *dose of his own medicine*. With our inside information, we were able to arrange for her to be complimented, courted, and eventually invited to move in (with her two kids). Her lover was to be one of our own people, that famous Romeo, "Kevin Wooster." And at this point after a 15-minute re-freshment and toilet break, I'll let Kevin take over the floor and tell you how to make a government witness out of a broken-hearted woman.

The Seduction Of Iris White

Mr. Kevin Wooster:

I'm "Kevin, "Rooster" Wooster" [not real name]." Formerly a FBI agent, I am now specializing in undercover work as a freelance pri-vate detective. I work only for government agencies. I am hired as a last resort when serious matters are involved and when the reliabil-ity and credibility of the undercover agent might be a big issue — if there is a trial. With my FBI background I am much more effective as a witness for the prosecution is than the zonked out freaks that get out of our penal institutions. Too often these convicted felons are pathological liars who couldn't tell the truth if their life depended upon it. Such scumbags often fall apart under cross-examination. And then we at Justice don't look good. Courts have always found me to be a "credible witness." There are no surprises when I testify for the government. I don't get emotionally involved with my tar-gets, and I always get the job done.

Butkis came to me with this White situation: The fraudster White was believed to have moved his entire net worth of something between ten and forty million bucks outside the jurisdiction. He was in con-tact with a lawyer in Liechtenstein and another in Switzerland. Preliminary investigation with our moles in Zurich indicated that if he had any accounts with the banks favored by Americans, they were not in his own name. Maybe he used another name (for which he'd have to have a passport) and maybe he had his money in some sort of corporate or trust set up. If I was able to find the details of his account, under the new accord with the Swiss it could be seized. Better yet, if Mrs. White had signature authority over the account, I might be able to convince her to transfer it to the USA where it would be seized immediately, without the need to give up a substantial portion to the Swiss.

My deal was up to 20 per cent of any net recovery to myself as a personal bonus, plus all expenses and $1000 a day while working on the case.

The weak link in the case for White as it is for almost any man, was of course Mrs. White. Could we turn her? As you see, I am a well-developed male, in my early 40's. She was about 40. Butkis had found out she was very vulnerable. I was the kind of guy who could conceivably be attracted to her. After seeing our feature film of her husband having sexual relations with our undercover agent Laura, we knew she was contacting chat groups on the Internet, sending out provocative messages. These clearly indicated she was looking for either short-term sex, or a "relationship."

My experience has been that most wives of long duration know all the secrets of their husbands. If I can get them into bed, most wives are eager to inflict maximum damage and happy to tell every nasty secret they have on their cheating husband. Before I ever contacted or met Mrs. White whom I'll call Iris from now on, I had my assignment and a game plan in mind. The main object was to get a balance sheet out of Iris and to discover the exact location and identity of her husband's secret accounts abroad. Of course my personal object was to end up with a possible 20 per cent of $40 million bonus, or $8 million for my trouble. As it turns out my bonus will be quite a bit less, but still in the million plus range, not bad pay for two weeks' work — if you can call it that.

I tuned into the encounter group — chat lines that Iris was known to frequent and sent her an informal E-mail letter, portraying myself as a lonely single guy who liked kids and was anxious to meet someone attractive like her, with good breasts and around forty. I was tipped earlier that Iris had a boob lift and was proud of her new breasts. After a few E-mail letters, I volunteered to visit her in her town, then Las Vegas. On our first date, after a good dinner she was in my motel room. Then she visited me at my home in a nearby town in California.

Iris apparently enjoyed the sex, the first in 20 years not with her husband. Obese at the time, he was no longer attractive to her. She was still good looking and had an excellent figure. Naturally, I did not press her for financial information during our first two dates because I knew that sooner or later everything she knew would be coming out. Of course, it all worked out according to my plan. On her second weekend visit to my home she told me all her complaints and confided that she would love to get a divorce and send her husband away for a long stretch in prison if she only had an alternative place to go with her two kids.

For the wife of a very wealthy man, she was not thinking rationally. She was looking for revenge and another man to support her. I suggested that she might get a cash settlement from her husband. Like so many middle-aged housewives anxious to "find themselves" and dump a husband who took care of all their material needs for years; she was blissfully unaware of the difficulties of supporting herself and her two kids by getting a job. Without any work experience, she would be slinging hamburgers at minimum wage. Yet, she insisted she did not want a penny from White. She conveyed her thought that I would be there to take care of her. Fat chance!

"Move In With Me"

My line was that I didn't like to carry on with married women, but if she did in fact get a divorce (and could then as you all know, be compelled by Justice; if needed to testify against her ex-husband). I would invite her to live with me — along with her two kids. She took the bait, and did in fact move in with me, bringing her two kids, ages 8 and 12. She filed for divorce and began child custody proceedings. The kids hated me and wanted to stay with their father.

Iris was not in control of herself from the moment she moved in with me. Even if I did not have other motivations, she'd have been an impossible woman to live with. She was often hysterical, crying, and flailing herself around senselessly — like a chicken with its head cut off. When her husband contested child custody, he brought in witnesses and experts to testify she was emotionally unstable and unable to care for her children properly. That's the American system: Whoever has the money for the best lawyers wins the case! Consequently, Nevada won the divorce and an interim custody order for him to keep his kids with him.

Iris Co-Operates!

At this point Mrs. White lost the little coherency, sanity and self-control she had left, screaming at the divorce hearing that she wanted to crucify her ex-husband. Back alone with me she had wild ideas like hiring a mob hit man for $50,000 to cut off his hands, feet, and testicles. "Hell hath no fury like a woman scorned." Naturally, I wondered about my own safety when this nut case found out the truth about me. But then if you expect to earn $8 million for a few weeks of bonking, there has to be some risk (Laughter).

Once Nevada White gained custody of their kids; Iris gave me every bit of damaging information she had on him. The most important bit was that [after we began our strike force activities,] Nevada had sworn under oath to his own lawyer that he was insolvent. His lawyer, using this false oath, represented that there was no point in sending out 800,000 notifications of entitlement to refund since his client did not have the resources to meet such claims. The truth, according to Iris, was that Nevada was far from insolvent. He had a net worth of over $20 million at the time. He had stashed his money abroad in a Liechtenstein "family trust" or foundation.

Technically he did not control the foundation's money — a board of directors had the signing power. But the reality and understanding (as it had been explained to Iris when they were on good terms) was that Mr. White called the shots. The Foundation Board did whatever he told them to do. This meant that White was guilty of perjury, obstruction of justice, and unlawful concealment of assets. He didn't list the foundation's income as his income on his tax returns. and for the purposes of his insolvency statement, he "forgot" about his $20 million altogether. These lapses of memory as documented by Iris, would be worth some 55 years in jail and several million in fines for Nevada White. Iris came through for me by going back to Nevada for a weekend visit with him and her kids, pretending she was returning to him for good.

During this reconciliation visit she swiped Nevada's most secret papers. These included all his offshore bank account statements. The Foundation accounts did not have his name on them, just an account number. However, as she had broken open his well-hidden attaché case and had given us an affidavit that she knew these were his secret funds, we now had the ammunition to go after White's main stash. The KABBOB was ready to roast.

Striking It Rich — The Mother Lode Uncovered

The big prize in this case was what Iris referred to as the "Mother Lode." It turned out to be $18 million dollars in securities and cash on deposit with the "B" Bank of Zurich in the name of a Liechtenstein Anstalt or Foundation. Although the assets were registered to a foundation, the papers that established the foundation (which Iris provided) indicated that the person in control was none other than her husband who was identified as an American citizen. This was important because as you will note, our deal with Swiss Justice clearly covers Americans who use Swiss accounts to conceal assets. White had legally obtained a foreign passport in a different name. However, fortunately for us, he didn't refer to his foreign citizenship when setting up his foundation or the bank accounts that it controlled. The "B" Bank account might have given us a bit more trouble to seize of it were "Foreign owned." Maybe we would have been able to seize White's money anyway, but USA-owned private funds are clearly within the agreement.

Our seizure agreement with the Swiss banks only covers American citizens at present. Possibly, dual-citizens are included, but this was not an issue here. Iris gave me the exact name and number and agreed to personally deliver this information (in the form of bank statements she had snatched) to the IRS (criminal tax evasion division). Ostensibly, to help Iris get her revenge, I arranged for her appointment with Department of Justice prosecutors. They worked quickly and two months later were able to initiate the seizure of White's account in Zurich. To this day, Iris does not know I am neither an undercover agent nor what my real purpose was in wooing her. Nevertheless, Iris betrayed her husband big time that day.

Essentially she made a gift of her husband's $18 million to the Federal Government. In one way, part of me understands that she wanted to hurt her husband, but with any sense she would have also protected her own interests. Her children and she herself were the beneficiaries of the foundation! Under the marital property laws of her state, half that money was legally hers and the other half would her children inherit one day. Had she told her own lawyer about this account, it might have been frozen for her benefit. Had she told White about giving this information to us, he could have moved the money. But she didn't tell him over the next 60 days and he didn't have a clue that he was about to be KABBOBed. I guess he thought the foundation's money was well protected and she, well she just wasn't thinking at all.

Breaking A Liechtenstein Foundation

In case you don't know it, a Liechtenstein Foundation is sort of a private trust established only to conceal the true owner's name from tax authorities. All instructions regarding asset management and withdrawals must come from a "Board of Directors", usually a firm of lawyers. These Swiss lawyers, usually with two signatures, are the only ones empowered to give orders to the bank. In this case, without the information of Iris, we would not have been able to identify this account because even the bank didn't know it belonged to White. All they had was the name of the "Kid's Foundation." Once Iris went to the IRS with me, we quickly put in place the mechanisms to raid White's personal home, his office, his USA banks and stockbrokers, seizing all his personal assets and the company cars. Most important was the mother lode in Zurich.

We knew he would not get any warning and a chance to move his assets if the raid on everything came the same day. It took over two months to make all the arrangements for the raid and seizures. It was important to keep our plans secret and to seize all of White' assets on one day. If we hadn't been able to do this, he might have been able to afford a high-priced dream team of lawyers that could have applied for court injunctions prevented the seizure of his Swiss money, and also beaten the criminal rap he was eventually going to be convicted of. But White went on giving seminars and made no effort to move the mother lode even though he was now involved in bringing criminal charges against Laura for theft. The stupid oaf had to know that his wife was no longer his trustworthy best friend.

The Feds do not ever want an O. J. Simpson case. We used to win 98 per cent of all cases a few years ago. If we are able to prevent a defendant from having a good lawyer, by tying up his assets before trial, we will be batting 100 per cent. Even if White was able to beg, borrow, or steal for lawyer's fees, in money laundering cases like this, we can claw back those lawyers' fees as tainted money. Asset seizure is one of the most effective prosecutorial tools available. The second most important thing after getting enough evidence to make a case to a jury is making sure the defendant doesn't have a pot to piss in. (Laughter) That's why it is important to cut off his income stream by putting him out of business. When we KABBOB some-one, we do it right. What does KABBOB stand for?

Audience response:

KA, Konfiscate Assets!
BB, Behind Bars!
OB, Out of Business!
[Applause & Laughter]

"We Win All The Chips"

The raid and the seizures went off like a charm. The money at "B" Bank was "arrested" as the proceeds of crime, and moved to the "B" Bank's branch in New York City. Eventually, if White does not come to the USA to defend, or if he is convicted, it will be transferred to Treasury. Without any lawyer and without any money, White is now powerless. He is in no position to negotiate anything, I feel he has no choice but to cop a plea and spend around 14 years serving out a 20-year sentence. We will not settle for anything less than a guilty plea bargain and a 20-year incarceration. If he defends with an incompetent lawyer, he is likely to get 40 years.

At his age, 50, that means he will be 80 before he sees the light of day again. His other alternative is to flee the country and spend the rest of his life as a fugitive. If he does that, he will never see his kids, friends, or relatives again. As we have his three passports, flight abroad may not even be possible for him. Being a fugitive certainly cannot be pleasant life for a man who is penniless.

If he is somehow able to get a lawyer in Switzerland, he won't be able to defend his claims to the mother lode in a Swiss court because we have a deal with the local police to ship him back to us without any trial or hearing as an undesirable. Our financial arrangements with the Swiss police put the cooler on any judicial review in Switzerland: If he shows up there to defend his phony foundation, we get his ass. We predict White will straggle in to beg for mercy during the next few years. He will try to work out a deal and take his medicine. He cannot stay afloat long without money and he cannot work in the States or get a work permit or legal residence abroad.

As a fugitive, he can never again take a high profile and do the only things he knows how to do — playing jazz or peddling his worthless products on television.

White is history.

He is a KABBOB!

Question? What Happened To Iris?

Well, once we had the needed information, I picked an argument with her. This wasn't hard as she was hysterical and running around like a freshly killed chicken most of the time I knew her. I told her we could not go on with her emotional state and said that after seeing how she treated her last husband, I was fearful she'd do the same hatchet job on me some day. This was met by a lot of screaming and a physical assault on me—as was usual with her. The next time I had the opportunity, when she was out of my house, I piled her luggage and the kids' stuff on the street and changed my locks. I bolted the shutters and then left for a week. Never saw them again.

I will probably move out of my old place. Who knows what she might be capable of when she learns the truth about me? I heard that after I threw her out she moved back in with White—even though they were divorced by this time. He was foolish enough to take her back. But I guess he didn't want his kids on the street. Of course, she didn't mention spilling the beans on his Zurich account and all the other stuff. He was a sitting duck when we grabbed all his books, papers, files, computers, bank accounts, safe deposit boxes, and the Swiss mother lode!

Once the raid took place, White disappeared, leaving the family home. Iris was evicted for non-payment of the mortgage soon after. The kids were abandoned and will become street kids, I suppose. His 12-year-old daughter has already been arrested several times for shoplifting and drug offenses. A 12-year-old pretty girl on the streets of Las Vegas does not have a bright future, but that is what happens when you choose a criminal for a father. His boy is eight. He sleeps at a youth shelter. The White kids will both end up in a juvenile detention home. We are keeping them under surveillance just in case White tries to contact them. I foresee Iris White being a bag lady. She is too crazy to hold down any job and care for herself, much less her children.

Where Is Nevada White Today?

We believe White is floating around Mexico somewhere. At this writing, we have not filed any criminal (or any civil) charges against him. The beauty of it all is that we have put him out of business and we have seized all his assets. White the criminal has been turned into a cringing, hiding dog with his tail between his legs by the mighty and magnificent force of Justice. Maybe, if he doesn't turn up, we won't do anything and he can just dangle in the wind for the rest of his life! Questions? Does White have any money left? At one time, we thought he had upwards of forty million stashed away. We have uncovered around 21 mil. In my opinion, he is broke, down and out for the final count.

Now, to answer the question you have been waiting for: How does a Federal Agent (or ex-Federal Agent like me) make money in these confiscation deals?

The Well-Deserved Reward Of Rooster Wooster?

How much will I personally make out of this all? It looks like the total seizure of assets uncovered by me will amount to $20 million. After giving two-thirds to the banks and the Swiss government, I personally could net up to 20 per cent of the remaining $7 million or $1.4 million. But Iris, in the unlikely event she can snap out of her irrational mode long enough to hire a contingent fee lawyer, may be able to claim a ten per cent finders fee. [In the worst case scenario for us, she could go after all the assets in the Foundation.] However, assuming she just claimed the standard IRS finder's fee for informants, that would reduce my take by ten per cent.

I stand to make over a million personally. Then too, those agents who seized cars, furniture, files, computers, books and other things out of safe deposit boxes get to use them for undercover work and such. Our somewhat loose procedure for seized cash and assets from our targets does provide for individual agents holding on to them as sort of incentive awards. For example: I got Nevada's $40,000 Rolex watch as a gift from Iris and I'm keeping it of course. It is all legal. This sort of gift is duly reported and possession worked out in meetings between the agents involved and their supervisors. Of course, a lot of things just "disappear" these days. Especially creeps like "KABBOB" White and their ill-gotten gains! [Laughter] End of session. [Applause].

Publisher's Note: Any person may republish or copy this chapter in whole or in part without any permission from the publisher. In the public interest, the Nevada White story had been gifted into the public domain.

To verify the story, this publisher was able to contact the "real" Nevada White who contributed the following Chapter 11: "Don't Make My Mistakes."

Nevada White's Response: "Don't Make My Mistakes!"

*R*EADERS who think they are immune from unexpected, arbitrary prosecution by the State can benefit from my experience. Though spilt milk can never be made sweet again; you don't have to make the same mistakes. My mistakes involved what I thought were minor decisions at the time, but they cost me big bucks — twenty million dollars to be exact. In a few short months I lost my family, and suffered more anguish than I hope you'll ever experience in a lifetime.

More important, after reading the government report, you may think, "He got what he deserved." You believe it could never happen to you. You are "good," or "smarter", are you really? Have another think! Re-read this whole story carefully. I used to think I was smart. Now I've had a good dose of humble pie. Twenty million in the bank (that you've made all by yourself) makes you think you are a lot smarter than the next guy is. You're not. As my old mentor used to say, "Intelligence varies inversely with the amount of money most people have the richer they are, the dumber they are." That was his little joke to put both himself and me down. The element of truth in his aphorism is that *successful people too often think they are infallible* and expert in all subjects. They disregard good advice. *Don't you do it!*

I knew all the "PT" rules, but in my asset protection plan, I made a few fatal misjudgments. You'll see what I did, why I did it and the sad results. But first:

My Version Of The Truth

The government has painted me as a con man, philanderer, money launderer, and all-around dangerous criminal. You know from the "Butkiss Report" on catching guys like me how they have broken up my family, traumatized my two young children, drove me into hiding, and caused my wife to become a raving lunatic. Let's not forget the money either.

Without any justification that I can fathom, they destroyed my business, put dozens of people [my employees, associates and those who depended upon them] out of work and redistributed my money to the "needy": Lawyers and government investigators. Until I obtained and read the previous government document, I did not fully understand what was behind everything that happened to me.

All my assets both domestic and "offshore" were confiscated — without any hearing or trial. If they did it to me, they can do it to you — if you are not careful and if you don't have as your advisor a rational, informed person to keep you from making obvious mistakes. I had such an advisor. To my great regret, I disregarded much of his good advice. More about that later. Now, back to my "crime." Remember: I have never been arrested nor indicted in my life. [Sorry, I have had a couple of speeding tickets, but that is the extent of it.] I have no criminal record. Even at this moment, there are no warrants out for my arrest and no criminal charges of any sort have ever been filed against me.

What Was My Crime? Giving Away Free Books!

As a loyal patriotic and law abiding American, a few years ago I would have thought that what was done to me (and what you read about in the government report preceding) was unconstitutional and illegal — in a word, impossible. Yet now I understand that what happened to me is an every-day routine matter. More than that, my fate is the *destiny* of almost anyone who has a high profile in the

United States. Anyone who makes good financially will probably be a target at some time in his life — more likely, several times. The latest fad in American bureaucracy today is confiscating assets on one pretext or another. If you have substantial assets [over a million dollars], some local or national agency will try to steal from you. Getting your assets offshore (as I did) is a good move, but it may not be enough to save your ass, I mean assets. You have to do it right!

Since my own troubles began, I have discovered that there is hardly one successful author, media celebrity, mail order merchant, pop musician or political activist who has not a similar story to tell. Someone should put all these stories together between two covers, to serve as a warning of government excesses. The closest thing to it at this moment is "The Hall of Frame" in the PT book. Everyone should know how the government targets, taints and tears successful people to shreds.

Nevada White: Who Am I?

Here's my life story (short version). You decide if I am such a bad guy — a dangerous criminal. Should the government have put so much time, planning and effort into putting me out of business?

Born in 1948 in Baltimore, Maryland. Grew up with an ordinary, poor, honest, and working class family. My widowed mother raised two children, my brother, and myself. After high school, my brother and I went our separate ways, both becoming moderately successful professional musicians. He was into classical music, I into jazz.

As a jazz musician, I went on many tours all over the world and performed for many years with The Charlie Byrd Trio. Then Stan Kenton. There were many other bands I worked with — and countless one night stands. The US Government paid for many of our shows. Some of our government-sponsored shows were meant to inspire good will towards America in trouble spots like South America and Southeast Asia. During 1976, the US State Department sponsored my Trio as part of the American Bicentennial and performed all over Central and South America for months promoting America. In those days, I was a true red, white & blue patriotic American who proudly represented the "Land of the Free." After about ten years in show business, when I was nearly 30, I realized that I'd had a wonderful time and a good life. However, like most musicians, there was nothing in the bank to show for a decade of travel, discomfort, and hard work. By this time I had a new wife, Iris, a lovely girl whom I'd met at one of our concerts. Her brother was the bass player in one of the countless bands I had formed. Iris and I were very much in love and wanted to start a family. We both agreed that show business did not provide the stability needed for us to have a real home, roots, and steady income.

My First Profitable Real Estate Deals

Looking for a new career, I attended several seminars: Bob Allen's HOW TO BUY PROPERTY FOR NOTHING DOWN, plus THINK LIKE A TYCOON, and another one on HOW TO MAKE A FORTUNE IN MAIL ORDER. As a result of what I learned, we (my sweet wife and myself) tried out the ideas and decided that our best opportunity to earn serious money was by creating low income housing with government financing. In 1977, anyone could find run down housing in the Baltimore — Washington, D.C. area, and get substantial low interest rate government loans and free grants to restore these often abandoned slum dwelling units. Developers, such as my wife and I became, were then obligated to rent the refurbished units out to low-income tenants. Rent was paid or subsidized by the government welfare system.

After a few years, because the tenants were usually unemployed, destructive slobs, with a very bad attitude about property maintenance, the units were slums again. The government programs provided that the "urban renewal" process could then be repeated. There was more time spent on red tape than on construction work, but once into my first project, I learned the ropes. Soon I was providing the government with hundreds of approved federally subsidized dwelling units. It turned out that my wife and I were managing and marketing them more successfully than my competitors. We were finally earning serious money: Profits? Close to half a million a year, net after taxes. Not bad for a former jazz drummer who barely graduated from high school. My income taxes were low to non-existent because government rebates and tax credits for those engaged in this sort of fairly unpleasant work were granted considerable tax relief. It was nice to be earning this kind of money. Especially nice that it was tax sheltered. If the government was giving me all this money in the forms of grants and loans, and if they were letting me keep more than most people could via a special tax break, I figured my great and wonderful country must be appreciative of the work I was doing. I was providing decent housing for the needy. Could I show others how to do the same thing?

The Money Was Good But I Wasn't Entirely Happy

Why? The people I had to deal with in government and my tenants/employees were not nearly as stimulating as my associates from the world of music. I liked the money, but hated the job. Because I had attended a seminar that exposed me to this new opportunity. I decided to teach my new trade (opportunities in government loans and grants) by means of a weekend seminar in the Baltimore area, where I was operating. It was a way to get back "on stage," tell a few of my favorite jokes; make interesting friends. Once again I enjoyed applause and audience adulation.

OK, I am an egotist. But as Zsa Zsa Gabor said when asked if she slept with perfect strangers: "Nobody is perfect." Giving seminars was a lot more fun than running construction crews and collecting rents. It provided me with interesting new business associates. Being a lecturer and author enhanced my stature as an "expert," with the government housing bureaucrats I worked with. In fact, many of them were guest speakers at my early seminars.

It is surprising to hear at this late date that the government wanted to keep these programs secret! I always understood that the grant and loan programs were underexposed because the government lacked PR skills and funds to promote them. I thought they welcomed chaps like me who would popularize them and bring in "customers." Today, as we know, many HUD officials from those days (early 1980's) were indicted and sent to jail for self-dealing as a result of the HUD

(Housing & Urban Development Department) scandals. Now I understand why they didn't want me to focus attention on these giveaways' programs. They did not want anyone except their cronies and themselves to get the giveaway goodies. The same thing has gone on for years at the Small Business Administration. My prediction? It is just a matter of time before some investigative reporter uncovers the (bureau) rats in the cheese at SBA.

In any event, to get people to buy tickets to my weekend seminars, I did radio and TV talk-shows, and gave a free public four hour "preview." At my preview I promised in my ads to give away a free book to the first thirty people who arrived, but then to eliminate hard feelings, I gave away free books to all who came and signed up for my course. Strange as it may seem, the offer of a free $25 book was a big inducement for people to sign up.

At the end of my free talk, I would invite my attendees to my Govt. Grant and Loan Program, a $349.95 weekend seminar. A quarter of the freebie people came and probably a third to a half of my early seminar attendees actually went into some aspect of the business and did well at it. Why is this fact important? Because if you think back to the government accusations, my program was a "complete, worthless fraud" and nobody benefited but me. That just wasn't so.

As might be expected, there were those who did not make any effort, I called them "seminar junkies." Because they seemed to be people who just liked to go to various seminars and night school classes for social or other reasons. They were lookers, not doers. Some admitted they were on a never-ending quest for the Holy Grail: What Holy Grail? A perfect business: No work, no effort, no investment, and no risk. Just cascades of cash falling down on them from heaven for reading a book or attending a seminar. The seminar junkies took my course, were told they could make a million — but that successfully running a construction outfit could be a fourteen hour a day, stressful job. Then they decided that their "Holy Grail" was somewhere else. Even so, I offered a refund (at the end of the weekend) to anyone who was not happy with my seminar for any reason.

A Standard Of Success That No Teacher Can Guarantee

The government claims that my program was some kind of fraud because 100% of my graduates didn't have success. I ask, does everyone who reads a diet book lose weight? Of course not. *They have to do what the book advises* — and that is usually to cut down on intake and exercise a bit. Some people, maybe the majority, can't hack it. My course was the same. If you took my prescription to heart and actually did it, you couldn't help but succeed. If you sat on your fanny and waited for a magic cascade of cash to blow through the nearest keyhole, nothing happened.

Some of those seminar junkies from the 1980's will no doubt make a life-changing career move sooner or later. Everyone finds a niche somewhere. But while I usually heard from my successful graduates, I could not determine what happened to those who did not persevere with my business start-up government loan and grant program. Like someone who teaches diet and exercise, I can educate and motivate, but not everyone who takes my course or any course will follow through. But the U.S.A. Federal Trade Commission insisted that I offer every single person who ever took my course a full refund! Does Harvard Law School have to give a lifetime refund offer of tuition? Seventy per cent of the Harvard grads do not end up practicing law? Is Harvard Law School a fraud? I think not.

That's Show Biz

Back to my life on the seminar circuit before Big Brother came into my life and put an end to it:

As time passed, I noticed that I had a lot more fun *talking* about my old deals than I experienced doing them. Enthusiastic audiences laughed at my stories. The applause gave me a rush. It was great to be back on stage — in show business again. I turned over my real estate mini-empire and actual construction business (by then a corporation) to others and decided to spend most of my time touring the USA giving more seminars. For a long while, I was having fun and making good money — a few thousand dollars a day. For around five years after I left the old business, income kept rolling in from my rental units and those low income rental projects, even without me at the helm. Thus, my seminar income was insulated from tax by all those low-income housing tax shelters I owned. The seminar business itself became quite profitable. Only a few years after quitting music, I was a multi-millionaire.

My relationship with my wife was excellent. We acquired a comfortable, upper middle-class home, and a new baby daughter, then another child. It was too good to last. I didn't know I was under surveillance having been targeted by a Federal Strike Force for prosecution. I later realized that just about everyone who made it big on the seminar circuit was cut down by the government. Just as with Al Capone, agents were diligently fishing around to discover some federal crimes they could pin on me. The process took almost ten years. The tenacious Feds always look very hard, not stopping until they can fit some offense to the facts. If they don't find exactly what they need, they create the needed "facts." To help the process along, they send in their people to infiltrate and entrap. Once they get someone in their sights, that someone can be as innocent as a lamb, but they'll get their target.

At that time, in my life I had no reason to believe my fate to become a disgraced, bankrupt fugitive had already been decided in Washington. My thoughts, before the Feds gave me the hook and threw the book at me, were on improving my seminars.

A New Idea — The TV Infomercial!

When you are in show business, the audience is always demanding new material. Old material is stolen by less talented imitators. The same was true of my low income-housing seminar. I started out by explaining how low income housing, a tiny segment of the trillion-dollar real estate market worked. Later I broadened the seminar to cover other investments. Few people were interested in going into unglamorous low-income housing (regardless of how good it was financially), but almost everyone was interested in at least buying or fixing their own home or condominium with government sponsored zero, or three percent interest rate loans and free grants. I tried out a lot of different ideas and material in order to come up with new seminars, plus book and cassette tape "products" that could be successfully marketed. Some ideas worked, and some fell flat. My seminar *"FUNERAL HOMES FOR FUN AND PROFIT"* was an opening night flop. Nobody showed up. People just do not want to hear about certain topics.

Replication And TV Exposure — My Ticket To Serious Money

Doing live seminars every weekend was fun, but putting educational material on video or cassette tapes and in books was, I felt, going to be my future. Replicating myself mechanically would be less strenuous than all those personal appearances. I knew that a best selling recording or book would make me as much or more money than running a thousand low rent tenement apartments. There would be less grief and no exposure to drug-crazed tenants with guns who despised landlords. I dumped the real estate business by giving it to my brother. I had tired of endless travel and stays in hotel rooms to put on my weekly live seminars. A one-shot correspondence course would be cheaper and better for the buyer because a live seminar was $350 and I could put the same material in a mail order "kit" and sell it for $50. The tapes could be played or viewed over and over. It would certainly get to more people than my performing live.

After several years on the road with my seminars I wanted to spend more time at home with my family and no longer needed the "show biz razzmatazz". My first real estate home study courses were not particularly good sellers. Why? There was too much similar material on the market at that time. Also, government changes in the tax laws had made real estate far less attractive. With prices of property free falling as a result of the law changes, nobody showed up for real estate oriented seminars nor did they buy my books and tapes. I looked at the more successful mail order books on the market and zeroed in on a few winners that seemed to be selling well:

How To Do Your Own Divorce,
Published By: Nolo Press.

How To Do Your Own Will Or Set Up A Trust Without Lawyers,

By: Norbert Dacey.

How To Set Up Your Own Corporation For Under $100 Without A Lawyer,
By: Ted Nicholas.

The big selling point for each of these popular books or courses seemed to be giving the common man the "secrets" of how to do something technical without paying lawyers, accountants or other experts. Their ads always offered a free bonus something-or-other "if you act now." From my own experience, a free offer of some sort always cinched the sale for many of the otherwise undecided. Nobody but anybody ever considered this fraudulent advertising. Because of my experience with low-income housing, low interest rate loans and free grants, I was aware of how some government loans and grants could be obtained.

I made it my business to find out about other government loan and grant programs. To understand them better, I applied for some of business development and other grants for myself. They worked. I made good money with those grants and low interest loans. Then I gave a few live seminars on the subject, pointed my students in the right direction, and worked with those first men and women until they did in fact get substantial loans or grants. Then, we made a very interesting video documentary of interviews with these ex-students, government officials, employees and others. The documentary showed, how ordinary people were able to work with the government and get very substantial funds out of the public teat by simply filling in a few forms. We poked a little fun at the government's programs — saying it was like a giveaway lottery — with one important difference: The chances of winning a grant were perhaps 90% (i.e. 9 out of 10 applicants were winners) — instead of 1 in a million. The entry costs were nil. It was an interesting and informative program.

I got a local TV station to play my documentary in a late night spot.

They needed filler material that didn't cost the station anything. A local station was happy to give me sixty seconds to promote my $50 *"How to Get Government Loans & Grants"* kit at the end of a thirty-minute educational show. It never occurred to me that my low budget documentary would be the "crime" the government was waiting to pin on me.

Public Enemy Number One

My documentary did get me in deep trouble. As it turned out, I had made the world's first "infomercial." TV stations all over the USA were soon running my programs on the same basis (free educational material in exchange for a free commercial at the end). It was a miracle. Like a hit record or box office breaking movie, orders for my kit poured in. I grossed over $40 Million on them in just seven months. This was more money than I had ever dreamed of. Then a dozen imitators came out with similar material and TV presentations. The party was over. Sales fell to a trickle.

Ready To Retire When The FTC Struck

The party was already over and I was ready to quit and go on to something new when an "injunction to protect the public from my fraudulent advertising" from the Federal Trade Commission was served on me. It was a bolt out of the blue, without any warning. In this court paper, I was accused of deceptive advertising and mail fraud; ordered to have a printed message on any future videos to the effect that the entire half-hour was a paid commercial message. In my opinion it was a pretty good inspirational program. Only thirty seconds was a commercial.

Worst of all, the FTC said they were going to send all my customers a letter at my expense, telling them that they had been defrauded. The fraud was that I offered the first hundred people who ordered my book a free gift book, but as the government correctly pointed out, "in reality the defendant Nevada White, *fraudulently* gave away the free book to everyone."

A letter with this statement in it was sent to all my past customers. It contained an invitation to request a full refund. Regardless of how long ago they had taken my seminars or what their personal results had been. Under the terms of the FTC "offer" to give away my money, customers did not have to return the merchandise or show any evidence that they had paid for it. Just file a claim and good old Nevada White would pay you. Without any trial, hearing or anything resembling due process, I was ordered to pay for the entire (refund offer) mailing — a several hundred thousand dollar project — and to stand by — ready to pay out on whatever requests for refunds came in.

Officials at the San Francisco FTC office were particularly harsh and dictatorial. I had always offered a thirty day "no questions asked, iron clad" refund, but an unlimited, open ended refund offer without even any need to return the material was going to bankrupt me, I thought. The experience was very upsetting. The FTC people threatened me with millions in fines if I didn't go along with their offer. [Off the record to my attorney, he was asked to pass on the threat of a long jail term if I didn't play ball according to their rules. The FTC officials who made these threats perjured themselves in later testimony denying this.] I read in the newspapers that Levi-Strauss of Blue-Jean fame had to make a similar refund that offer because of a promotion they did years earlier. During the period they sold about 2 million pairs of Jeans at $80 per pair. But the number of refund requests that came in, and which they were forced to pay, amounted to 8 million — Four times the amount of pants they had sold. I knew I'd be reduced to poverty. So I spirited away a few million bucks in an account abroad. Then it turned out I didn't have to squirrel away my little nest egg.

After many months and (no kidding!) a couple *million* dollars in legal fees, the conflict ended as unexpectedly as it started. My lawyers worked out a compromise. They settled this *civil* case. With no admission of guilt. I agreed to pay a non-crippling fine and to insert in any future TV Show a notice that the entire program was "a paid commercial" for the product I was selling. This was not true in my view, but I couldn't afford to spend another two million in attorney fees fighting with government guys who had an unlimited budget and formidable enforcement powers.

Since the refund requests from the FTC mailing were minimal, less than 1%, I paid off on them and thought it was back to business as usual. All I had to do was think up a new product to recoup my losses. Oh, one little thing, as part of the settlement, my lawyers submitted a signed affidavit by me that my personal net worth was (then) well under a million dollars. Keep this in mind because it becomes important later in this tale.

Why I Went "Offshore"

In view of possible future problems with the government and my being told that the Feds had new programs to seize your money first and take you to court later, my lawyer suggested (after the injunction had been filed) that I protect my family by moving my money out of the country. We did this legally. I established a Liechtenstein Family Foundation run by a bank in Switzerland. The deal was that I "gave" most of my money to some trustees who were to manage it at their discretion, and pay out income to my family as long as we lived. Any balance when the family died off was to be used for medical research. I was told that this arrangement meant I could sign an affidavit for my own US lawyer's use — to the effect that I had divested myself of most of my worldly goods. My US and Swiss lawyer assured me that this arrangement would keep my assets protected against any creditors who materialized after the trust was started.

Unfortunately It Did Not Work Out As Planned

I did not know that after my FTC settlement I was targeted as an enemy of the state. Until I read the government report [How A Swiss Bank betrayed its Client] released over the Internet, I was unaware that they had me under surveillance for nearly 10 years looking to create "crimes" that I could be prosecuted for. It was from the government report (reprinted just before this — in this book) that I first discovered that a sexy female government agent had wormed her way into my staff as my personal secretary. She had seduced me at a weak moment during the FTC proceedings, by giving me tea and sympathy, (as well as some skillfully administered copulation).

At the time of my serious problems my wife was more interested in her boob lifts, fanny fillers and other cosmetic surgery. She couldn't be bothered to give me any understanding or affection. Laura (the government undercover agent sent out to seduce me) pretended to sympathize with my problems. With her connivance, the government had secretly taken movies of our trysts in her apartment. These porn flics starring taxpayer funded Laura, and I (both naked as a JayBird) were shown by federal agents to my wife in an effort to turn her against me. They were successful. My wife Iris, after betraying me by giving them my Liechtenstein Foundation bank statements, lied to me that she had refused their request to tell them where our money was. She still tells me that she was not the source of this information. Maybe she believes it. I guess she is still in denial.

She certainly spilled the beans, to her government-sponsored lover, Mr. "Rooster Wooster," giving him and the agents who showed her the film of Laura and I fornicating in my office. In return for their exhibiting this porn flic to a one person audience (my wife), the Feds got from her all the details of our Liechtenstein Foundation arrangements. It was incredibly stupid of my wife Iris to give them this information because the $20 Million of Foundation money in Switzerland was half hers and *all for her and the kids* when I passed on. But as William Shakespeare said, "Hell hath no fury like a woman who sees a movie of her husband *in flagrante,* bonking a lady IRS agent." I just made that up, but a Shakespeare character said something like that, much more elegantly I'm sure.

The undercover agent, Laura of B. J. fame, during the course of her employment with me, actually stole $450,000 to $500,000 from me, not just the $350,000 admitted by the Feds in the previous document. I guess she needed the extra $150,000 cash she stole in order to pay her income tax bill on the money they authorized her to steal from me. Naturally I sued her and tried to have her arrested, but all to no avail. She was protected as a government witness (against me) by the government. Was this unusual? Not at all, I discovered. There are literally thousands of criminals on the loose, with phony references provided by the government, preying upon innocent victims. After their crimes are discovered the Government Witness Protection Program gives them immunity from arrest or lawsuits.

My wife began acting very hysterical and irrational early on — after my troubles with the government began. Instead of us sticking together as a family, she dumped me and ran off (taking our two kids) to live with "Rooster" a strange guy she met on a computer chat forum. I just now learned from the secret Butkiss Report, that in addition to my lover Laura, a government agent also seduced my wife. Maybe everyone I knew or worked with was also a government undercover agent. That sort of thing can drive you nuts.

A lot of people in my employ turned against me, stole, and ran off with whatever they could. It was incomprehensible that my wife gave away trust money that was to support us both in our old age — divorced or not. She gave away the nest egg that was to put the kids through college and give them a good start in life. The Liechtenstein Foundation was half hers. Why give it to the government? She had so much hatred and resentment against me getting a few BJ's from Laura, that her own future and the security of the kids was a distant second to her need for revenge. Irrationally, she cut off her nose to spite her face.

Betrayed By My Bankers

It was another surprise that my Swiss bankers sold me out by turning my money over without any legal resistance. I couldn't understand why. Now it has been revealed: They (the banks) stand to gain a third of any client's account by giving up one third to Big Brother and one third to their own department of justice! Surely, the cruelest blow of all was Iris — my wife of twenty years — betraying me, taking the confidential information on our Foundation to give to the government and filing for divorce and child custody. A fine how-do-you-do after twenty years of marriage! I thought it was karma when "Rooster," her new boyfriend threw her (and my kids) out on the street after an argument. Little did I know it was all part of the government's plan to have a second go at me.

Why Iris And My Kids Came Back After The Divorce

I did not want my children to be out on the street or to think badly of their Mom or me. This was after the divorce. I was granted full custody because she ranted and raved incoherently in court about castrating me and sending my penis aloft with helium inflated balloon. The lady judge wasn't impressed with Iris' ability to be an ideal mother under the circumstances. But remember I still loved her, and all women get a little crazy from time to time. Even though we were divorced, as soon as possible, I set Iris up in a new (separate) house so she could live across the street from me and still help raise our kids. I didn't suspect she had already sold me out! She had in effect given the government information they would use to seize all our assets. The money in my Foundation was half hers and would have ultimately gone to our two kids. The government guy who seduced her and got her to give up the family fortune must be very pleased with himself. No doubt he will get a medal and a promotion besides his finder's fee.

Soon after Iris came back my house, books and records, my computers, furniture, and Federal agents seized all my petty cash money in a raid. I didn't know fully how or why it happened or what the story behind all this was until friends gave the previous article to me. They said they got it off the Internet. I never dreamed in my wildest dreams that a former drummer, turned entrepreneur, could warrant the government investigating me for 10 years. What was the social imperative that made it so important to sink a guy whose main crime was *giving away books* to everyone who called instead of just the first hundred.

All Of This Brings Us To The Present Time

Now I am flat broke, stuck in a rotten hot and humid place because, I was given a free house to take care off by an old friend. I'm unable to afford the lawyers needed to get that day in court I am entitled to. Contingent fee lawyers don't seem to be interested in taking my case even if I offer them 99% of any collection. They are immediately intimidated by threats (from the other side) of having their own finances and tax situation investigated if they touch my case. They are told that my "money is tainted," and if they get any of it they can't keep it in any event. My nutty ex-wife doesn't speak to me. She seems to be living on a different planet — oblivious to reality and convinced that I am plotting against her. The kids are having problems. The government doesn't care what they do to families. They would probably like to see my kids homeless and on the street without supervision. Hopefully, it will not come to that. But my two little children don't know where their fugitive father is. Obviously, their quality of life has changed drastically. I can't reveal my whereabouts to my children nor anyone from my past life — especially now that I know the government wants to "put me away for at least 40 years."

Often, I'm not in such a clear thinking mental state myself any more due to so many trusted people in my life betraying me. Losing your family, twenty years of savings, and having your entire life flushed down the toilet isn't so easy to accept with calm resignation. And now, from the Internet, I learn that if I show my face, I'll be indicted and clapped in jail. I don't know whether there are any warrants out for my arrest, but there probably are. I wonder if giving away free books on TV qualifies me for the "Ten Most Wanted" list. The American cops probably consider me a fugitive.

Am I paranoid? Just because I think they're out to get me doesn't mean they're not. I am in hiding and expected to stay in that mode until the situation clarifies. Maybe the government will tell me what else they want from me at this point to settle the case. "Suicide" is probably the answer they will give. From the previous document, my situation and that of my family doesn't look very promising. Having escaped from the land of the free and home of the brave, I regret that I didn't follow my guru's advice. I could have compartmentalized my assets offshore in several places so that they didn't get everything in one swoop. It would have been impossible for Big Brother to get everything if I'd followed the good advice of my advisors. I could have divided my money in several accounts in several different countries. If different entities or names were involved, and if the deposits were spread out among several banks and brokers, they couldn't have seized all my assets. *I'd have had some warning and could have done some damage control.*

I Was Greedy

The bank in Zurich I used to manage my money was making me over 20% a year. Also I wanted to keep things simple and not have too many accounts to worry about. Trouble is if your mother lode is all in one place, and if your enemies discover it, you can be wiped out, just as I was. But I always thought that a top secret Liechtenstein Anstalt or foundation was the most secure way assets could be held. Wrong! If your enemies (in this case, my ex-wife and personal secretary) know the exact account numbers and have copies of all the papers setting up a trust, foundation or otherwise, your goose is cooked. Your assets are going to be lost! If there are copies of these papers anywhere in your home country, you are at risk.

My Biggest Mistake:

What was it? Trusting my wife with financial secrets. Who could have thought that she would essentially give away what was half hers (and all hers, if I died). I regret that my wife knew too much. My lawyer and another advisor warned me that wives, lovers and disgruntled employees were the cause of more legal distress than any other factor. She had access to all the information: Foundation agreement, balances, account numbers, the works. She was so angry or out of her head that a skillful undercover agent gained control of her head. The money is gone!

Was I A Bad Guy? A Criminal?

I don't regret anything I did in business. Why? Because I do not think of myself as some kind of villain: I never hurt anyone, I never defrauded, nor conned anyone. Sure, I was entrapped into cheating on my wife. But some women when they hit forty or so and realize their good looks are going begin to go crazy and do irrational things. In my case, my wife simply cut me off sexually and then running off with a government agent, she tossed the family treasure down the toilet. She gave no thought to the impact that throwing away twenty million dollars would have on her children, or herself. I should never have put her in the position to be able to destroy our family as she did.

Here Come The Violins

Is *giving away free books* such a crime that I should have the punishment I got? I was a good husband and good father. As far as I know, I never broke any laws. Although nowadays there are so many laws. I guess everyone has enough theoretical violations so the government can select a few criminal offenses and pin them on anyone they choose. You may never have heard of the law they use against you, but if they make you a target they will find a crime to fit.

Giving away free books was my initial "crime." The affidavit (that they claim is false) — about my net worth being under a million, was another crime. The offshore trust was something I was pushed into by circumstances and my expert lawyer's advice. There is no reason it wouldn't have stayed quietly in place and been an excellent retirement fund — if my wife hadn't blabbed. Even now, it seems to me, my statement was truthful because I did give my money to a Foundation. But I would not take my chances in front of a jury on that one. The exposure by my wife? It was made possible by my bad judgment in telling her where I hid the money. I knew she was mentally unstable when I told her about the offshore trust money in the foundation. The lawyers and my guru said "don't tell her." "Keep your mouth shut." But I guess I wanted her to know that she and the kids were taken care of, no matter what. As a result, she knew enough to cook my goose.

Regarding my seminars and tapes — I was one of the very few who actually had successfully done what I was teaching. I personally used many government loans and grant programs and thousands of my students did too. My program was not a fraud. It worked. Perhaps it worked too well. To stain me even more, the Feds have accused me of being a hop headed dope fiend. The truth? Like our President, I smoked but never inhaled. And that was thirty years ago when I was doing a show in Morocco where puffing on a hubble-bubble between the acts was legal. I'm trying to make light of it — but the dope accusation and much of the government's case against *you* will be that sort of smear that has nothing to do with reality. It is just to turn a judge or jury against you, and unfortunately, it works.

In a private lawsuit, you can dig up dirt against the other party, but most people selected for jury duty believe (wrongly of course) that the Department of Justice is Lily White, blameless, and is there only to protect them. Each juror sees himself as *Horatio at the Gate.* They are conned into believing they are doing a public service by putting defendants away. But at a trial they can't be told that long (and often undeserved) terms in prison at taxpayer expense are what they are passing out.

The End?

This whole experience has been nothing less than a nightmare. It was as bad as any fiction dreamed up by Khafka or Stephen King. What will happen next? Don't ask me. Right now, I'm depressed. If you have any suggestions to cheer me up, pass them on to my publisher. He doesn't know where I am, but I'll visit a cyber-café and send for any messages now & then. I hope you've learned something from my story! Learn from my mistakes. Not only do you have to get your money out of the country, you have to keep its location and the name it's in a secret from your spouse and other potential turncoats. And based on my experience if you still think of Switzerland as the best banking haven there is, you'd better go back and re-read Chapter 10.

Nevada White
(Not my real name)
Late 1997
Somewhere in Belize

Chapter 12

Chew Off Your Leash

*T*HE United States tries to keep its citizens on a short leash by threatening not to renew the passports of those who have not filed tax returns. But with a $70,000 exemption of earned income and no way to check on what is really being earned abroad. It is possible to file income tax returns, earn under $70,000 ($140,000 plus living expenses for a couple), pay no taxes, and remain in good standing. It is also now legal for USA citizens to carry a second foreign passport. There is no pressing reason to renounce USA citizenship unless you are sure you will never return there. The government threatens to toss in the poky Americans who keep their citizenship but don't file tax returns when they return. Are they figuring that all Americans will someday want to go home to Uncle. Such arrogance! My experience has been that after a few years abroad, the trips back become fewer and fewer. Most people soon realize that the sun doesn't rise and set in their hometown. They become comfortable in their new life.

Billions of dollars and millions of people have left former homelands in Russia, China, Poland, India, Ireland, and South Africa to make their homes elsewhere. Most people like to return and visit their native lands, but if the old country is going to put them in jail or levy a fine, it does not take a college degree to figure out that few, if any, emigrants are going to go back.

Patriotism — Have You Been Conned?

It is helpful in this context to clear the mind of useless bogus concepts that have been foisted upon us. Old fashioned patriotism, for instance. How childish to feel that any one flag is better than another. A few hundred years ago, in much of Europe, countries were often no bigger than a few acres. A local prince, or in many cases a democratic government, constantly went to war with the guys who owned the hill next door. Every now and then some distant warlord, such as Genghis Khan or Charlemagne, would sweep over everything, taking the good looking women as love-slaves and stealing the best toys. They left their favorite generals behind to replace the former local king. This is how political boundaries came about in Europe — by brute force.

What about democracy? Is it so wonderful that there are two brutal, ignorant mobs in a country? Does it make any sense that the one with the most members gets to push the others around? Hitler was democratically elected and was supported by the vast majority of his populace — until it became certain that he would not win World War II. The majority in a democracy prescribes how all people must respect their authority. But what if you're not in the majority? What if you march to the beat of a different drum? Then, the PT concept becomes very important.

When times are economically good, almost everyone is happy to stay put and be comfortable among familiar faces, laws, language, and customs. When one is starving or feels politically oppressed, one can and should vote with his feet. Why not anticipate rough times and try out new places early?

The American middle class has been oppressed and squeezed. Why stay behind and put up with it all? We should not continue to be patriotic about our country when a self-serving group of bureaucrats have seized power. Only a country with maximum levels of personal freedom deserves our patronage. Blind loyalty and patriotism have no place in civilized society.

If we think of government as only a management group running a hotel or chain of hotels, it can do wonders for our perspective. Each group of managers has a different style. Some of them, just like people who have become political leaders, can be self-destructive and irrational. Politicians and hotel managers have a lot of other things in common. One of them is that they control some desirable and some not so desirable chunks of property. Both of these managers need paying guests. For us as PT's, there is no shortage of choice.

Becoming A Priority Thinker (Basic PT Theory)

Once you leave your encrusted rut and become a Perpetual Tourist, old-thinking patterns will change. Big Brother's intrusive control over every aspect of your life and finances will no longer exist. Once you have made the mental switch to become a PT, choosing your government will be like choosing a hotel. PT's look for location, service and price. Expressed another way, once you leave the jurisdiction and control of your old home country, that country no longer has any power to restrict, control, draft, tax or jail you. If a government has neither the power to put you in jail or to confiscate your assets, then they have no way of controlling you or making you their subject. That makes you a PT: *Prior Taxpayer*.

Nonetheless, as somebody controls every square centimeter of habitable space on earth, you will have to do business with one of these innkeepers. You will have to sleep somewhere. You will have to keep your stuff somewhere, meaning that your bed and possessions will have to be located within some political administration. The difference with the PT philosophy is that no government will have the power to own you any more.

Hence, the PT has formulated his plan of action. One key element is that his passport will be from a different government than the place where he actually lives. Furthermore, the place where he lives must be different from the place where he keeps his serious money. Finally, the place where he invests actively and visibly in real estate or a going business is in still another place. The locations of all these mini-centers of his diversified activities are decided purely on the basis of which country, which innkeeper, offers the lowest costs, best deal, most fun and best climate. Who offers the greatest advantages for those particular activities that you find most desirable?

Each innkeeper offers certain advantages and usually a few minuses as well. Nonetheless, at the planning stage, the PT must be ready to divide up his business, financial and personal life into several categories. They are:

1. How and where should you conduct your active and visible investment and business activities?
2. What passport should you carry?
3. Where should you be resident and domiciled?
4. What country's banks and financial institutions should you use?

How And Where To Conduct Your Active, Visible Business Activities?

The answer is, probably back at square one. The best place to make money for most people is their home country, the place they know best. But just as often, the same business that is being conducted successfully at home could be left in the safe hands of others. Taxes should be paid and regulatory problems dealt with. While you, for expansion purposes and PT freedom, open other branches in other countries, creating a fully diversified operation. When this is done benefits and profits can be multiplied enormously. Not only are you personally a PT, you control a multinational business as well. You generate profits where they can be accumulated and enjoyed tax-free.

Since every country where you are considered a foreign investor knows your enterprise can sprout wings and depart for greener pastures, they all, like innkeepers, compete actively for your business. Certain basic rules like having all fixed assets heavily mortgaged can be your insurance that the worst confiscation that Big Brother can come up with will amount to only a minor and temporary inconvenience. You should be in a position to say "Bye Bye" to Big Brother if any country makes it unpleasant or unprofitable for you to operate your business there.

Another possibility for professional people who want to become PT's (doctors, dentists, lawyers, engineers) is to hire themselves out to international agencies and multinational companies. With the right skills and in order to be assigned to any place you want to visit, arrangements can be made. With the correct passports and financial arrangements, one is effectively beyond the control of Big Brother.

What Passport Should You Carry?

First and foremost, you want the passport of a country that does not burden its citizen's abroad with any unpleasant obligations. One such possibility is compulsory military service. If you are of military age, which can range from 17 to 55, you may want to be wary of Switzerland, Israel, Italy, Mexico, and many third world countries. In these countries, if you do not complete your required active and annual summer camp duties, you will either have to pay a fine (Switzerland), go to jail (the Middle East) or even lose your citizenship (Mexico or Paraguay). At least the US, about which I usually have something nasty to say, gets passing grades in the military department, for the moment. Compulsory military service was abolished three decades ago in the States.

The World's Most Useless Passports

Then there is the question of travel restrictions. For the most part, travel documents from a stable first world country allow for a much greater amount of visa-free travel than most others. As would be expected, these are also often the most difficult passports to acquire. Travel documents from poor countries that produce large numbers of immigrants tend to invite intense scrutiny at border posts. This makes travel documents issued by Bangladesh, Black Africa or Haiti less than ideal. The Philippines is a step up but Filipinos, too, are given a hard time. How about Lebanon or Syria? Due to several decades of terrorism and mischief, a passport from most Arab countries subjects the holder to excessive scrutiny and search. Give them all a pass.

Don't Bother To Get A Pariah Passport

Then there is the problem of the political pariah country. For example, entry restrictions imposed by other countries used to make a South African passport about as useful for international travel as a visible case of leprosy. With recent developments in South Africa, this situation has changed, but beware of countries that practice policies, which attract almost universal condemnation. Taiwan, due to the fact that its government insists it is the rightful government for all of China, does not offer a very good travel document. Hong Kong passports are better now, after the much-discussed hand over to Mainland China has taken place.

Have At Least Two Passports

Depending upon the time and circumstances, even if it is a good passport, like that of the UK can be a ticket to harassment or even jail. For instance, during the British-Argentine mini-war over the Falkland Islands, British travelers were given a very hard time in South America. Cases of beatings and jailing were common. Thus, a second or even a third spare passport from a neutral country for easy traveling is always a good idea.

Learn To Lie

Sometimes a stupid bureaucrat can give a perfectly good passport. Recently a friend with a British passport applied for a visa to visit Australia. Australia is one of the few countries in the world that requires every single visitor (except New Zealanders) to have a visa. The long application form asks a lot of questions. One of them is "Were you ever arrested?" There is a space to explain. My friend (with stupid honesty) stated that he had been arrested in Argentina during the war — just because he was British — and he was held a week or so, until the short Falkland Islands war was over. The result was that Australia denied his visa request. A stamp indicating this visa denial was placed in his British passport. Now when passing through any border, he is detained and questioned as to the reason why he was denied entrance to Australia. Moral of the story: Learn to lie when necessary. *A visa can and will normally be denied to anyone who admits having been arrested for any reason.* It might be possible, after years of litigation, to get such a decision reversed. But in my friend's case, it would have made his life much simpler if he had answered every question on the visa application with exactly what the bureaucrat wanted to hear: No arrests, no venereal diseases, no criminal record, no bad stuff.

Unattainable Passports

Nonetheless, choosing a passport is a lot easier to do than choosing a playground, only because when the unattainable and undesirable passports of the world are eliminated, there is not a heck of a lot of choice! In the unattainable passport bin we can put almost all of the tax havens, including Switzerland where a twelve-year physical residence plus military service is required. There are some possibilities for getting a passport from tax havens that are or were part of the British Empire, but obtaining the passport of any tax haven is not easy.

Easy Passports

Desirable, neutral countries are usually expensive and/or their passports are hard to obtain. The time needed involves fairly long residence periods as well. What's left? A few Caribbean islands (Barbuda, St Kitts), Canada (three year residence), Australia (three years), Belize, Germany, Israel (if you are Jewish or convert), Uruguay, Argentina, Paraguay, Ireland, Sweden, New Zealand and a few others. For an exhaustive review and update on this subject, consult *The Passport Report*, now in its tenth edition. See the back pages of this report for more information on how to obtain it.

Where Should You Be Resident And Domiciled?

Some PT's do not bother to become officially resident or domiciled anywhere. They operate according to the principle that the less government knows about them the better. Hence, they feel that going through the bother of filling out forms, being fingerprinted and registering with local police is really not justified by whatever benefits residence may have to offer. Instead, they operate according to low profile principles and are genuine Perpetual Tourists. No government on the planet considers them to be even remotely linked with it on a permanent basis. This means no government can claim them as their own. No taxes, no military service, and no interface with bureaucrats.

Do You Need An Official Tax Haven Residence? Maybe Not!

High profile PT's probably should establish an official residence and domicile in a tax haven. Do you want to drive a Lamborghini, have a pet ocelot, and drip diamonds from every pore? Then Monaco (where 5% of the population are cops devoted to protecting your right of conspicuous consumption) is the place for you. Some PT's may need an official residence because (like sports and entertainment figures) they are too high profile to just blend in. Or perhaps because they just feel more secure knowing that everything is officially on the up and up. They fear that simple low profile techniques may not be enough protection. Residence and domicile are complicated legal concepts that can have serious implications for tax liabilities. In high profile cases, residence and domicile should be established in an official tax haven — a place where you are a registered resident. The Bahamas, Bermuda, the Cayman Islands, the Channel Islands, Costa Rica, Monaco, St Kitts and Nevis or Turks and Caicos are among the many options. The path that you choose concerning this area of the PT philosophy is entirely up to you. But the reality is that the whole world is a PT's tax haven. As long as you rent (don't own) and stay out of serious trouble, you can stay anywhere you want for as long as you want, technically a "tourist." To do this all you need is a passport from a country that doesn't care about you (or tax you) once you leave. The best passport is any passport from any country except for the USA.

What Country's Banks And Financial Institutions Should You Use?

The fact that Singapore is full of palm trees and warm beaches does not enter into my decision about banking there. As PT's, we look at governments as service providers. Since we use them only part-time and can give parts of our business to more than one, we should match the qualities we need with what each country has to offer. In matters of finance, most governments will not let a citizen legally earn a free market interest rate in the currency of his choice. In Singapore, the government is most accommodating. One can have an interest-bearing checking account or a high interest, fiduciary savings account in any currency. Dealing in large amounts of cash is the favorite sport of everyone in Singapore. Singapore is certainly not the only place where this can be done, but it is one of several spots affording a high degree of choice and flexibility in asset management. Depositing or removing large amounts of cash is not something that generates a need for reports to the government. In fact the government facilitates large cash transactions by issuing $10,000 notes that are worth about $7,500 in USA dollars. This makes a Singapore $10,000 note the largest value banknote in common circulation. With these notes, twenty million dollars can be transported in a small attaché case. Comes in handy for those occasional nights out on the town.

Foreigners Get The 'Edge'

Did you ever hear of the Edge Act?

France, Italy, and the US are far more restrictive of the financial freedom of locals in comparison to foreigners. Almost any country other than your homeland can be a tax haven for your money. In the USA, under the provisions of the "Edge Act," *foreigners* are told that they can have secret numbered accounts *in the USA* with a guaranty of no reports of any kind to any government and no income tax withholding. These accounts are touted as being secret and claimed to be secure against creditor seizure. [But I wouldn't trust the perfidious Americans. Look what they did to Marcos!] Obviously, American citizens can't get the benefits of an "Edge Act" account. In most countries, even where their own citizens get no privacy and where interest income is taxed at source, foreign depositors get a special deal. Example: I once arrived at Dublin airport where all kinds of signs and brochures invited me to open an ultra-private tax-free special account at the Bank of Ireland. The secret accounts were announced to be especially for the needs of our 'Irish American' Visitors. The Irish themselves are taxed until they are pipsqueaks, but visitors have privileges. What did I tell you? Be a foreigner! Be a foreigner in your own country if you want — by providing them with the proper paperwork. The most important document in this regard is a second (foreign) passport.

The Government Treats People Like Mushrooms: "Keep 'Em In The Dark & Cover Them With Manure

The average person does not know of the opportunities for profit and safety of capital provided by accounts in foreign currencies. A typical American never conceives of the possibility of telling his local bank to put half the cash in his saving account into yen. It just isn't encouraged. Although the regulations have been changed so that American banks would be permitted to advertise and accept deposits in foreign currencies. I feel that foreign currency is best held discreetly in a foreign country. No doubt politicians will (whenever they need a new scapegoat) call the American holders of foreign currency accounts unpatriotic and without faith in the dollar. Special taxes will probably be applied to these domestic foreign currency accounts — especially when the time comes that they show a spectacular profit against the dollar. You can be sure of this: If legal foreign currency accounts in the USA become "obscenely profitable" special taxes will wipe out any currency gains on those accounts within the US. They'd like to tax foreign exchange account gains too, but they know that nobody would pay them.

The Russian PT In Malta

Japan, Italy, Russia, and many other countries (most countries!) have rules to keep their citizens in ignorance. These rules are intended to force them to endure confiscatory taxation, domestic inflation, and regular currency devaluations without any options. It is in fact illegal for approximately ninety per cent of the population of the world to own unreported foreign accounts. In Russia today, a Russian can still (theoretically) be shot for owning a foreign bank account. But he can legally own all the shares of a corporation that owns a foreign account. As a result, Russians are big users of offshore service providers in Malta, which has become their favorite tax haven. Malta is one of the few countries where a wealthy Russian can go without a visa. The Russian entrepreneur brings his foreign currency to Malta in cash, acquires a few corporations and passports, and presto, he's a PT — without ever reading a book like this.

Your Asset Management Base

It is important to choose as a management-base for your assets, a country that has a free market in financial services. Most tax havens can offer good offshore asset management services and objective advice. Domestically, in Russia or in the USA there is a real fear that the adviser will be branded a criminal or just unpatriotic. Advising a client to "Get your money out of the country before your country gets the money out of you," might be good advice but it's also PT: Potentially Treason!

The Worst Place For Your Money: Inside Your Own Country

Once again, as with the list of desirable passports, the list of desirable places from which assets can be managed effectively can be counted on your toes! Put political stability, honesty, efficiency, secrecy, and reasonable charges on your wish list. You also want competence and good communications. If you are not German, British, or American respectively, then Frankfurt, London or New York are very good bets. Put another way, an American who wants confidentiality can get it in Germany or London but not in New York. A German should keep his assets in London or New York but out of Germany! The word "offshore" in finance applies to quite a number of financial service centers, all of them pretty good in smaller countries offering tax havens and secrecy. Some of the places from which you can effectively run your money include Andorra, Austria, the Bahamas, Bermuda, Hong Kong, Liechtenstein, Luxembourg, Panama, and Singapore. Switzerland is pretty good for non-Americans, though its banks have the highest service charges in the world. But for the money, you get good efficient and discreet service in Switzerland — most of the time. But not always:

How A Major Swiss Bank Blackmailed Me!

Once upon a time a few years back, my major bank, (one of the big three Swiss Banks), received a clear, unequivocal currency trade (Forex) order from me to sell all my Sterling (£). They failed to execute. A week later, after a major devaluation, which I'd anticipated, when I expected my account statement to reflect a US $50,000

profit, there was none. I was told by my usual "procurist" or customer rep that the trader who should have executed my order took
his vacation a day earlier than expected, and that was the reason for
my problem.

"My problem?" I repeated, "It is your problem. I think the bank
should offer to make up all or at least a part of the loss."

I also learned that on the same day, as my order should have gone
through, the bank made *a similar transaction for its own account.* I
suspected that I was getting screwed because they booked for themselves a very profitable trade that should have been done for my
account!

After seeing various bank officials about "my problem," and not getting so much as an apology, or offer of lunch, I mentioned to the
manager of the branch that I might consider a lawsuit. To my great
surprise, the banker said "In such cases, the public release of all your
financial records to your Embassy by us would surely end up costing
you more than the $50,000 involved." In those days I was so shocked
by the obvious blackmail threat I said "I'll just close my account and
you won't see me again around here." The next day I received a
check for most of my balance, less $40,000! To add injury to injury.
I had been subjected to a 4% "closing charge." I was later told that
when a customer closed his account in a huff and was expected not
to do any further business with that particular bank, an arbitrary "closing charge" was made.

As soon as the check cleared, I called the branch manager involved
and promised him that for the rest of my life, in every book I wrote or
published, I would always tell this story, and mention his bank. His
response was "We don't need your business nor the business of anyone who reads your books." The arrogance of this prig and the similar general attitude of the "Big Three" Swiss banks have ever since
kept me and any clients I advise out of their orbit. But I will never
forget the time I was ripped off by a major Swiss Bank. As far as I
am concerned, all of the Big Three Swiss banks share a similar attitude. "Let the customer be damned!" and I wouldn't do business
with any of them.

Where To Spend Your Time After Expatriation?

For a place to live most of us want to be able to buy fresh, healthy food at a clean, well-stocked local grocery store. We would like a maximum degree of personal safety, no violent crime on the streets and no fear that our homes will be burgled. Agreeable weather is also necessary. If we have kids, we want high standards of education and, for their benefit, a moral climate of a certain type, i.e., no heroin dealers in the schoolyards. The intellectual stimulation of creative local people and live theater (in languages you can understand) may also be a factor. Depending upon personal financial circumstances, the cost of living may or may not be still another factor to consider.

Unlike most stay-at-homes who may change cities once in a life-time, moving around and figuring out where pleasurably and profit-ably to spend the next season, that is a regular factor in the life of a PT. Changing addresses annually will frequently be the modus oper-andi for most PT's until the perfect spot to settle in is finally discov-ered. The whole idea of being a PT is that you have the freedom to do anything and everything you want to do. If traveling is not your style, then you can certainly put down some permanent roots. You should start by planting yourself in a tax haven such as Andorra, Bermuda, Campione, Monaco, The Isle of Man or one of the many other gorgeous little tax-free paradise islands of the world.

Your Very Own Plan

This is a good time for you to bring out a blank sheet of paper. Start your own destination plan by making up a list of what is important to you. One of the nicest parts of being offshore is the annual or semi-annual review of what the world has to offer, followed by a decision on what to try next as you match the possibilities with your aspirations and goals. "Ain't it grand," you'll say to yourself, "to have no problem more serious than deciding what wonderful place to go to next!" You can get a free subscription to various expatriate newspapers and magazines to help make your decisions. See the Resource List at the end of this report for their addresses. And don't forget I am available (for a fee) too!

Just in case this chapter sounds a bit familiar to material in other books, like Beethoven, I like to put old themes into new works — when they fit. Do you like to hear my familiar old tunes — or do they bore you? Let me know. For anyone going offshore either in person or by way of investment, *PT* by Hill, and my other book *Portable Trades & Occupations* are essential reading, IMO [In My Opinion].

Most important, consider yourself part of a mutual-help club. To keep my special reports timely I need your support. I need you to tell me when I'm wrong or my information is out of date. I need you to contribute information you feel might be useful (or even just amusing) for your fellow PT's. The fact that you buy my books now and then and tell your friends to do so is important. I can't go on publishing them if most copies in circulation have been illegally pirated and copied for free. If you are wealthy enough to afford to hire me with a $10,000, two year retainer (or to offer me something worth that in trade), go ahead and splurge. All of my clients are very happy with the information, services, and general ambiance of having me as a friend in need.

Chapter 13

Five Flags Unfurled

[Author's note: this is the original, previously unpublished Peter Trevellian original draft version of "Five Flags Unfurled," a chapter from W.G. Hill's seminal classic *PT*, The PT / 5 flag concept was created back in 1985. It has since become the philosophy of hundreds of thousands of "Perpetual Tourists." A current edition of this timeless work of practical philosophy inspired by Sir Harry Schultz, is available from the publisher — see back pages].

Today, millions of the wealthiest and most productive people on the planet take advantage of the best that each country has to offer. Governments are viewed, as providers of facilities and services, like hotelkeepers. If they offer good accommodation and make you feel comfortable and prosperous, you stay. If your government becomes too demanding or too nosy, or if a competitor offers a better deal, you can move on. Economic opportunities, financial privacy, taxes, extradition treaties, social values, military obligations, quality of passport, stability of government, medical standards, respect for property rights, personal safety and freedom of travel, thought and action — these factors are all taken into consideration when choosing legal residence and citizenship.

People of intelligence and wealth owe it to themselves and their descendants to have more than one flag. No one with common sense should give all their assets or allegiance to just one country, one flag. Why? No country or government has ever survived more than a few generations without totally annihilating itself or its own middle and upper classes. Even in that last bastion of capitalism, the US, people of property have been thrice pushed out of the country. In 1780, the entire middle and ruling class was forced to move to Canada, these were the Tories who supported England in the American Revolution or War of Independence. In 1865, it happened again. All large land-owners that supported the Confederacy in the Civil War migrated to Mexico, Europe or South America. In the post 1917 period, prohibi-tion, compulsory military service, confiscatory income taxes, and suffocating government regulations once again caused many independent-minded Americans and their European counterparts to seek new flags. They made the *amazing discovery that as expatri-ates or tax-exiles abroad; they need not belong to any particular country nor participate in its senseless policies.* Ernest Hemingway and Gertrude Stein might be considered PT's (Proto-Types).

The PT's relationship with (or divorce from) government is a matter of choice. It is an option. *The passport you hold and the country where you live need not be a burden that you were born to and will be saddled with forever.* No government can be trusted to control your money. They will not take your best interests to heart. Politi-cians are interested in redistributing wealth. In the end, they will only succeed in redistributing taxpayers. The major portion of all liquid private wealth, the smart money, has already been anonymously registered offshore. It has been re-flagged.

Individuals can remove themselves from the control and jurisdiction of any government by acquiring dual-citizenship, investing interna-tionally and becoming human multinationals. Departing physically and permanently is not required. A PT can live where he wants, leave when he wants. The secret is paperwork to effect a change of legal status. Many wondrous benefits can be achieved by merely wrapping yourself and your assets in a new flag.

Your Five Flags Unfurled

In order to accomplish this miracle, you merely have to re-arrange, relocate, and re-title your possessions and persona according to this simple outline. Your five flags:

Flag 1. Passport And Citizenship

These should be from a country unconcerned about its offshore citizens and what they do outside its borders. There must be no tax or military requirement for non-residents. Passports must be available to foreigners.

Dual or multiple nationality is one of the cornerstones of the PT philosophy. The PT should strive to have several passports regardless of original nationality. A second passport always comes in handy and has often saved the skin of many an individual during times of war, persecution, and political upheaval.

Flag 2. Business Base

These are the places where you make your money. They must be different from the place where you legally reside, meaning your personal fiscal domicile. They should also be places that give free land, grant interest-free loans and offer a tax holiday to your business without subjecting you to over-regulation. Good access to markets, a cooperative workforce, and needed materials are also important. London, Tokyo, and New York are the big apples for finance and insurance. Zurich, Milan, Singapore, and Frankfurt are among the good second-rank contenders. Even oppressive regimes like present day Chin a will offer interesting concessions to the PT interested in manufacturing, assembling or distribution.

Flag 3. Residence And Domicile

These should generally be in a tax haven with good communication systems. A place where wealthy, productive people can be creative, live, relax, prosper and enjoy themselves, preferably with bank secrecy and no threat of war or revolution. Monaco, the Channel Islands, Campione, Andorra, Bermuda, and the Bahamas are all recommended.

Flag 4. Asset Management

This should be a place from which assets, proxy can manage securities and business affairs. Requirements are the availability of highly competent financial managers, confidential banking and the lack of taxation of non-residents or non-citizens. One of the best places in which to plant your fourth flag is Panama. Other possibilities are Austria, Luxembourg, Liechtenstein, New York, and London.

Flag 5. Play Grounds

These are the places where you actually physically spend your time. Quality of life is top priority. Normally, because of legal restrictions on how long one may stay without being considered resident for tax purposes, it is necessary to have from two to four playgrounds, although other arrangements can be made if you want to spend all of your time in one playground. However, for the most part, the PT should try to avoid spending more than 90 days per year in any particular country.

My personal recommendations. For no nukes and good fishing: New Zealand. For the most interesting sex life imaginable: Thailand, Costa Rica or the Philippines. [Note: Since writing the unforgettable classic, *Sex Havens for Tax Fiends*, we have discovered Boca Chica Beach, Dominican Republic and give it our top score]. For a superb year round climate: San Diego, California, USA, nearby Cabo San Lucas at Baja California (Mexico) or Queensland, Australia. For the gourmet in you: the French Riviera or Hong Kong. For stimulating parties and an active social life: Paris, London or San Francisco. For the best things at the cheapest prices: Singapore, Taiwan and Hong Kong (for consumer goods), Denmark (for cars), Ireland (a summer home), Punta Del Este, Uruguay (winter home).

Consider The Following Five Flag Scenarios:

Flag 1: A second passport from Canada, Brazil, Italy or Australia. *Flag 2: A* business or source of income in New York, London or Singapore. *Flag 3: A* legal or fiscal address in Monaco, a Channel Island or Andorra. *Flag 4: Bank* accounts or other assets registered anonymously in either Panama, Luxembourg or through Liechtenstein holding companies, trusts or foundations. *Flag 5: Friends* and fun in Paris, Bangkok, Manila, Buenos Aires, Sydney and San Francisco.

Every PT should know and understand that governments only have power, i.e., jurisdiction, over their citizens within their home territory or colonies. For this reason, the PT should generally stay out of the country on whose passport he travels. His major assets should be invisible and far away from the country in which he actually lives. His lifestyle should be as humble as possible.

By using the PT theory, you too can get the most out of life. Once you have at least your emergency passport and enough money 'to survive at your destination, you can feel secure and prepare for a plunge into previously uncharted areas that will enrich your life. Five flags are better than two. Two are better than one.

What To Consider In Choosing A Flag

When formulating your own approach to freedom through individual sovereignty, remember to consider countries in the same manner that you consider competing companies offering you a service. When you come right down to it that's all they are.

What country gives you personally the best deal? Your occupation and interests should be given special consideration.

Where, in an unfree world, will you receive the maximum freedom? In other words, where can you do the things that you like to do without breaking any laws or upsetting the locals?

What travel documents or other papers are most suited for living unmolested in those places where you would like to spend your time? You only want to live in a country that welcomes people from the country for which you hold a passport.

What passport and domicile combination will offer you maximum safety from high crime rates, wars, pollution, industrial accidents, and terrorists while also offering freedom from taxation? Yes, you can have your cake and eat it too.

Where are the greatest business or professional opportunities available to you? You may discover that this is back home, where you are already established, or in some unforeseen area where a person with your experience and wealth is welcomed into a host of new opportunities.

Is safety in the event of a nuclear war or contamination a consideration? If so, you may want to at least consider a part-time residence in New Zealand, the most clean and green place on earth.

It will also be necessary to constantly evaluate your specific formula once it has been established. If at some future date, your government looks as if it will become too oppressive or your personal situation looks as if it may suddenly turn dangerous, consider voting with your feet. This time honored expression simply means that you can get out while the going is good. Consider the situations in South Africa, Hong Kong, Eastern Europe, and much of the Middle East. Even in relatively stable Japan and California, economic or natural cataclysms, such as the recent earthquakes, could cause life to become extremely unpleasant for local inhabitants.

Preclude Tyranny

Keep enough money or assets abroad so that if unjustly accused of anything or if faced with a crippling law-court judgment, you can get a fresh start somewhere else. Protect your treasures by keeping them out of the grubby reach of potential enemies. Buy or rent a small place abroad. Do the paperwork so that you have the permission in advance, i.e., and a residence permit, to live in a safe haven on the other side of the world. Keep a spare passport outside of your country but where you can reach it without a passport or make an arrangement.whereby your spare passport will be delivered to you in case of emergency. Try to obtain a second passport from a second country as well as a duplicate passport from your native country. Obtaining alternate nationalities is the best way to opt out of the unwanted burdens of an undesirable citizenship.

There was a time when a passport symbolized one's loyalty and patriotism. Today, losing or renouncing citizenship for the sake of possible future moves or tax avoidance should be practiced as a strictly logical business proposition. After too many wars to end all wars, PT's have come to see that patriotism is something invented and exploited by politicians to keep people's minds off local problems such as unemployment and confiscator taxes. "Let's have a little war so we can declare a national emergency and arrest and imprison for treason anybody who opposes the present regime." That seems to be what the politicians call creative thinking.

Constant worrying and petty disputations over borders and religions went on for hundreds of years in Europe. Finally these countries grew up and accepted economic integration. The United States of Europe is becoming a reality. Today in the EU everybody has the same maroon passport, that of the "European Union". After millions of lives went down the drain for *Le Gloire* de France, *Deutchland Uber Alles* and British Imperialism, the EU is one community, with neither borders nor customs. It's about time! And the people love it. The Frenchman, German, Briton, and Spaniard can all move, work, and travel in a much-expanded area. The EU passport is a better document than any of its constituents were. It allows for more visa-free travel and reduces government hassle. For a terrific passport, get one from the EU if you can. If you already are an EU citizen, it's a good idea to acquire one from any neutral country outside the EU, like Canada or Argentina, for instance. The Harris Organisation in Panama and its international affiliates offers a few interesting residence and citizenship programs.

Prepare Thoroughly

PT's must take the steps to gain at least two or three of the five flags referred to. Even ordinary working people, by making contacts over the next border or two, could have a warm, safe and cozy home waiting for them. Too often when leaving becomes an urgent priority their feet are bare. Those unprepared feet must cross barren wastelands. Can you picture yourself starving while snipers shoot and aircraft strafe? All this may be too dramatic for you to accept as your possible fate, but think about it.

One out of every ten people in the western world has been displaced in our generation. With a historical chance of ten per cent, or even five per cent, shouldn't you protect yourself against the eventuality of your country becoming involved in a war, revolution or unexpected political convulsion or health hazard? I am not saying that such a situation is inevitable or even likely. The chance of you being forced out of your comfortable rut is statistically small, perhaps the same as having a flat tire in a lonely and dangerous swamp. Do you carry a spare in your trunk?

The reality is that it is easier to prepare in advance than to get out of a swamp full of alligators or any other potentially dangerous situation. Don't wait until the alligators have you between their jaws. Too often we become vulnerable exposed to rape, robbery, poverty, imprisonment, industrial poisoning, riots and all other kinds of degradation and exploitation, perhaps even military attacks or torture in concentration camps. The plight of a detained, innocent refugee today in Lebanon, Thailand, Pakistan, Central America or Ethiopia is worse than the regimen of a criminal in many prisons. If you accept the possibility that some day you may have to navigate through a treacherous stretch of space and time, it is only sensible to equip yourself now with essential survival equipment rather than wait until the need arises. Even if you never make use of your precautions, being Prepared Thoroughly is a sensible course of action. Indeed, PT works best if you have the foresight to prepare before your problem becomes critical.

Partially Transparent

PT's can be hermits or have legions of friends and an active international social life. We can be conventionally middle class or wildly eccentric. The key is to be what we are or would like to be in a place where we blend in best. Nothing offers better protection than living a low profile existence calling only minimal attention to you. Darwin noted that the most effective life forms evolved to blend in with their environment. Animals camouflaged by nature became invisible to predators. They adapted, survived, and multiplied. Living low profile, or Partially Transparent, is essential. Conspicuous consumption and public display, such as ostentatious cars, expensive jewelry, spectacular homes, glamorous mistresses, and journalist profiles should, for the most part, be avoided. I have found that this task proves to be more difficult for young people who often have some sort of a psychological need to flaunt their financial success to their contemporaries. Such high profile activity is a huge mistake in most parts of the world. Government tax officials, thieves and hungry lawyers will soon be sprouting from the woodwork.

The beauty of PT is that with care, countless varieties of lifestyle are possible. In a Rio *favela* (slum) it would be unwise to park your white Rolls Royce with a solid gold hood ornament and stroll about flashing like Diamond Jim Brady. Yet in Monte Carlo, no one would give Diamond Jim a second glance. Vienna and London tolerate original dress and immoral lifestyles that would be dangerous to one's health in rural Ireland. In Switzerland, the "people who matter" would shun a playboy who does not do what they feel is productive, solid work. In other places, like Cascais, Portugal or Palm Beach, Florida, someone who is simply a connoisseur of fine wines and racehorses would receive red carpet treatment.

The key is to fit in with those around you. The only places to spend money like a drunken sailor, if you must, are resort areas or gambling establishments, not your habitual hangouts. Try not to make enemies or create jealousies. Insofar as possible, let no government or even any private business list your real name or home address on any of their computers. Live comfortably but not ostentatiously. Do not flaunt your lack of regard for local morality wherever you are. Fit in!

In short, do not give anyone cause to consider you vain or disrespectful. You can do your unconventional thing, but do it quietly and only in places where it is not considered scandalous, illegal or immoral. Those who violate this rule, as the brilliant homosexual playwright Oscar Wilde did a century ago, may shine brightly for a while, but will always be broken by society in the end. Oscar Wilde spent his final years in jail on moral charges. People who are too far out front, those who seek confrontations with the establishment are almost always ruined. Never seek publicity. Don't be a hero. Don't engage in head on confrontations with anyone, particularly government agencies. Keep yourself in a position whereby you can retire gracefully from any dispute. Don't allow yourself to become a target. Low profile and genteel poverty are the most reliable protective measures available to the PT.

Possibility Thinker

Some intelligent readers may not want to break out at once or become a PT at all. They are just familiar with the lessons taught by history and want to be aware of their possibilities and prepared to modify their lifestyles in the event of a crisis. Knowledge will make you a PT, a Possibility Thinker who is ready for whatever crisis tomorrow may or may not bring. The Possibility Thinker is someone who also wants to explore, wants to know exactly what the options are that life has to offer.

Even if after making the necessary preparations and exploring all of your PT possibilities you decide that there really is no place like home and no routine quite as nice as your own, nothing will prevent you from continuing with life as you know it. Furthermore, due to your new knowledge and experiences, you will be able to garnish even more satisfaction from your lifestyle than those participating in similar activities around you will. You have seen and explored the grass on the other side of hill and know that in fact it's greener right over here, on your side.

Private Transactions

You can and should get your mail and phone calls in a private way. If you do not already have a post-office box, get one in a common pen name for all sensitive or financial correspondence. Consider getting such services abroad if appropriate in your case. These days you can get an electronic office on the other side of the earth where mail and phone messages can be held for you until you call for them from a public phone. See back pages of this report for more information.

Self-protection can also be accomplished by simply using pen names for different activities. If you subscribe to a magazine or newspaper, have the mail sent to a private mail receiving office, i.e., a mail drop. Address it to an innocuous name like "Acme Rental Services". If you have a credit card, it should be from a distant foreign bank with bank secrecy. Bills should be paid directly by your bank. It is not a bad idea to also establish one credit card in a pen name like Joe Smith. Furthermore, presenting yourself as an employee of a small business is always preferable to being Director of European Operations or Executive Vice President. Why should you want a prestige title on your business or credit card? Who will be robbed, kidnapped or burgled first, Mr. Nobody or Mr. Tycoon? Whose credit card would be stolen first? Who will the corrupt cop hit for a bribe?

Your government and other potential enemies should never know or be able to find out the details of your offshore business or financial operations. This does not require cumbersome arrangements or any great expense. You can get by with just a cheap studio apartment in Monte Carlo, if you are not French, or Miami, if you are not American. Your rent checks can be automatically deposited and transferred to a third country, which is neither where you live nor where you own property. The cost of making such arrangements is peanuts. Peanuts! But if you run into troubles, a war, a civil disturbance, a divorce battle, or other litigation, you will be thankful beyond your wildest dreams. There are hundreds of reasons you should place a nest egg abroad and then visit it now and again. Only when you feel comfortable with the idea of using your option to move abroad will it be a viable proposition. If you could arrange to be a silent partner in some business abroad, this could help solve initial passport and visa problems and also support you (financially) offshore if things were to go wrong at your primary home.

Chapter 14

Your Invisible World

*T*HE year was 1948. Postwar U.S.A. The most popular song of the era was *"Ding-Dong Daddy of Cable Car Number 9."* It turned out that the subject of this ballad, a certain trolley car operator in San Francisco had two wives and two families. The deception was that discovered on the day both wives decided to have a free ride on ding-dong daddy's cable car. As the media ran stories about the man they dubbed *ding-dong daddy*, a third wife and yet another family materialized. The Ding-Dong Daddy's invisible world was shattered. Today, he'd make a million on the books, tapes, and his lecture series — but in 1948, he served a short jail term for bigamy, then went back to ringing the ding dong bell on car Number 9. His two worlds (and three wives) collided uncomfortably. Yours won't — if you are careful.

There is no reason that your private world of offshore assets should ever be revealed. Let's suppose you decide not to become a PT, but only to keep a good chunk of your assets abroad — out of harm's way. How can you do it in such a way that there are no links between you and your invisible assets?

Shipping The Assets Out

As there are no USA laws or rules against exporting your capital, and no filing requirements or other red tape to be dealt with in connection with sending assets abroad, you just do it. The bank that wires transfers your money to the Bank of Luxembourg (or?) provides an electronic computer report to Treasury. Unless your name is on their special little list of narco-traffickers, no particular notice is taken. There are millions of money transfers abroad every single day. They are all logged electronically, ignored electronically, and forgotten electronically. It doesn't matter if you dribble your money out little by little, or if you make one wire transfer of $20 million. What's the best way? My opinion is that it is best to test with a small transfer first. Say $5,000. Make sure the newly opened account abroad will receive your funds without glitches. If everything is handled well, then IMO, ship out the big money and get it over with fast. Your worry with dribbling is that some of the transfers will go into the wrong account or be accounted for wrongly. If you do 51 transfers, there is 51 times more likelihood of a screw up than on one. You don't lose your money and such mistakes can always be corrected. But you waste a lot of time and burn up the telephone and fax lines of communication. This means much more chance of attracting unfavorable attention. Naturally, there will (for many years) be a retrievable electronic record of to whom (what account) your money was sent. Any creditor or government agent will be able to find out that on a certain date, you sent $X out for deposit to your account abroad. Logic indicates that you must have had $X on deposit at a certain bank abroad — if the transfer was from Jake Tinker of Texas and destined for the account of the same Jake Tinker in Andorra. If the money transfer went to a corporate account (not known to be associated with you), then your creditors or a government agent can't assume that the money was still yours once it reached the foreign shores. Perhaps you bought a house in France and "Newcorp Offshore Holdings, Ltd." a Panamanian Corporation (who got the money in Andorra) was the seller. Or the first stop for your dough in Europe could have been a trust account in the name of an accommodating lawyer, or a so called "transit account" set up by your Panamanian banker or broker to do nothing but receive and transmit money somewhere else.

It doesn't matter very much where your money pauses on its first stop in the free atmosphere "Offshore." But if you want privacy and invisibility, the first stop (certainly if it is an account in the same name you used at home) can be only a transit point. Don't leave it there.

Should You Close Account Number One After Your Money Has Passed Through It?

Don't close the account. It may be useful for you in several ways. For instance, a year after the big money has passed through, you can ask (and you will normally be told) if any official inquiries have been made (after the fact) about you or your money. Leave $5,000 behind in it so you are still considered a customer. This account can be in your public world. It can be the foreign account you dutifully report on your income tax returns. Also, a transit account is a useful thing to have for future movement of funds. It is getting harder and harder to open a simple bank account. Most banks now require references, holding periods, and confirmations of street addresses. With an old account where your banker "holds all mail" your bank may have as your official registered address a place you rented briefly and left five years earlier. This can be a useful circumstance if someone from your past is looking for you. Your first stop account may be the account supporting a foreign debit or credit card in your own birth name.

Never mix your public accounts and your invisible accounts. When you add money to account number one, your public transit account — if it comes from your offshore funds, do it in cash. If the addition comes from your domestic funds, it doesn't matter how you do it.

Transferring Your Lolly After The First Stop

For people in international businesses, or with contact's abroad, it may be possible to "buy" certain PHANTOM goods or services. The proceeds from the fictional transaction go into your new secret account. Example: When you move the money your instructions say "Remit Swedish Kroner 1 Million to account of Hans Brinker in payment for thirteen thousand pairs of silver skates." As the funds are routed through a third party, it is unlikely that an investigator who discovers this transfer instruction years later will assume that Han's

Brinker's account ever belonged to you. There is no fraud involved because you are not trying to save any taxes by this maneuver. No one is being swindled out of any money. You are doing a pretty good job of disguising the destination of your own money, however.

If the original destination account (First Stop) is in a place with bank secrecy, and if the funds are soon moved to other banks in other countries — also with bank secrecy, then the trail is broken insofar as any private investigators are concerned. Some governments can pry open bank secrecy, once or even twice — with great difficulty. To do this they must allege criminal activities. They normally need court orders. Your banker, if he (unlike the Swiss) is any good, will tip you off about any activities early enough so that you can move your money. Governments have had very little luck pursuing funds once they have moved beyond the first stop. If you opened an account in London (where there is a degree of bank secrecy) and then moved it to the Isle of Man, thence Gibraltar, and if your mother lode ultimately ended up in Liechtenstein, you could be pretty sure the paper trail would be broken. It just can't be followed — as a practical matter. There is a trail, but unless you were number-one on the "Ten Most Wanted" list, no cop, and certainly no private investigator could afford to spend the time and money to trace the funds.

How To Be Super Sure Of Breaking A Paper Trail

Once upon a time, when I was feeling very paranoid, I simply told my offshore banker (Bank X) in Zurich to use the assets in my account to buy me gold bars. I took physical delivery of the gold bars and carried them by taxi (in several trips — because they were very heavy) to a jumbo sized safe deposit box I had rented in a savings institution used solely by local (not international) customers. I left the gold bars all alone for a few years, hoping they would rise in price. They didn't.

Eventually, I opened a new account at bank Y on the basis of "alternate identity." I brought in my gold bars in three installments, had them sell, and convert the proceeds into investments in Luxembourg based mutual funds. I could be sure in my own mind that there was absolutely no connection between my deposit at Bank X and my new holdings at bank Y.

Where's The Money Honey?

A friend recently told me he would not have an account in Panama or the Bahamas because it was too likely that some thug would take power and seize all bank assets to line his personal pockets. *This line of reasoning shows a fundamental misunderstanding of how the offshore banking industry operates. The money (aside from small change) is never in the "offshore country."* If it is dollars, it is on deposit in a major bank in New York. If it is Deutschmarks it is in Frankfurt. Yen is in Tokyo. Banks themselves have been PT's for years. Their "offshore" branches merely facilitate transactions and earn fees, which for the bank are tax deferred. Let me explain further. If a large German (or American) bank were to make a billion Mark loan to Mercedes Benz to expand its Mexican factory, it would have to pay a substantial tax on all interest received. Plus there would be national income taxes due on the many other charges (appraisals, environmental impact reports) tacked on by the bank in the course of making a loan. By booking the loan through their branch office in a low tax or no tax jurisdiction like Panama, the bank escapes all or most taxes. They can save enough tax money on one single deal to build a skyscraper in Panama. Instead of bringing profits home where they are taxed, banks do plough tax haven profits back into expensive office buildings and other investments in the offshore center. That is why a place like Panama City looks like Manhattan.

Why do most governments allow banks to escape taxes by booking business and profits in offshore tax haven branches? Simple, because every country wants strong banks. If all the other banks could book offshore business tax-free and banks of say the USA always had 50% of every profit taxed away; they would become smaller and non-competitive. Another obvious reason is that banks and insurance companies have good lobbyists banks with offshore branches make a lot of donations to be sure the government understands and is sympathetic to their point of view.

Political Risk

Banks are well aware of political risk. At the outbreak of World War Two, Swiss banks physically transferred all their gold and non-Swiss currency holdings to New York City. The offshore banks of Panama, Gibraltar or anywhere else have their serious money far away from any political risk. If a thug like Noriega does come back to power in a place like Panama, the banks will simply turn off the lights and. leave for the duration. All customers are referred to the home offices of the banks or other branches that might be convenient for them. Customers don't lose a thing because the parent unconditionally guarantees all accounts. If the parent bank is the Bank of Crooks, Con men and Idiots (BCCI) then a client can lose. There is little one can do about crooks except to apply the smell test. If there are lots of nasty rumors going around and if the bank's reputation is not sterling then don't use them. Period!

Trevellian Of Arabia And The Bomb Blast

One personal story: Many years ago, I had an account of about £150,000 with the British Bank of The Middle East. There was a revolution going on at the time. One month my monthly statement said, "Due to the fact that our bank has been blown up, we will not send out monthly statements until further notice. Neither can we process any transactions. We regret any inconvenience this may cause." As you might guess, I was a very worried. At the time the amount involved was a substantial portion of my net worth. I also needed it to live on. I bought a ticket to London and pretending I didn't know about the dynamite, I went into the customer service desk of the BBME with my checkbook and last accurate statement. I asked them to transfer my £150,000 to London branch and give me £10,000 in cash. I had to wait about an hour, but they did it, and apologized for the delay. Whew! As you see, troubles at a foreign offshore branch don't seem to bother the placid folks at main branch. Of course the Big Three Swiss bankers try to weasel out of their obligations at every opportunity. I wouldn't trust them with fifty bucks. Which brings us to a Swiss Banker joke: "If you see your Swiss Banker go to the top floor of a tall building and jump out of the window, what should you do?

Answer: Follow him and jump too. Why?

Answer: A Swiss Banker doesn't do anything unless there's a sure profit in it. [Well, we thought it was funny the first time.] In contrast, British banks tend to be more honorable. That opinion is based on my personal experiences.

Super High Level Secrecy

If you are ever going to be charged with criminal money laundering, or bank robbery, you need to break the paper trail completely. Why? Banks tend to co-operate informally to nab scam artists who have defrauded them or their colleagues. Obviously none of our readers are into criminal activity, but the mere accusation may be enough to get some offshore banks (especially the Swiss) to squeal. This is a risk that our readers would rarely if ever face. To keep a proper perspective, an account in the USA might as well be a public record. In the offshore world, only one file in a hundred thousand will ever be "unsealed," — and in such cases, the bank violating their own bank secrecy provisions will need a very good reason. One example:

Years ago, a lady who had fraudulently obtained a passport in the name of "Helga Hughes" opened an account in a Swiss bank in the name of "H. Hughes." Later, her boyfriend received a check intended for the late, secretive billionaire Howard Hughes. The money was deposited to the H. Hughes account. After Howard denied receiving the money, in the face of worldwide publicity that they were protecting a crook, the Swiss bank "in the interests of the public good" said that the money had been deposited to the account of a Swedish lady named "Helga Hughes." As it seems to be a clear case of fraud, the Swiss bank froze the account without interest until the USA courts determined ownership of the money. It eventually went back to a publishing company that had paid for an autobiography but had received a work of clever fiction.

Bearer Securities — If You Have A Serious Problem

Here's still another tip: In addition to the conversion of wealth into gold bars, in Europe and Latin America there is another option: Bearer

Securities. You can buy stocks or bonds that are unregistered. They have no name on them and belong to the bearer. These securities can be kept in a safe deposit box or in your home strong box, or anywhere you think they will be secure. Like paper money, if they are stolen, you lose out.

What If You Lose Bearer Securities Or They're Destroyed?

Although most people don't know this little secret, when you buy a bearer security, you get a receipt. Always make a photocopy of the bearer security. Keep it separate from the real one. If the original is lost in a fire or even stolen, you can pay a fee of about 5% of the value involved. With a copy of the receipt, proper identity documents, and a surety agreement, you can get a "Lost instrument surety bond." This replaces the lost or stolen certificate. The issuing company has a note that the (old) securities in question are no longer valid. If the thief tries to sell it, he will get the cuffs. That is why most crooks that traffic in stolen bearer securities just borrow against the stolen security by pledging them at a bank. They let the lending bank take the loss years later when they don't repay. Just in case this gives you the idea to pretend to lose bearer securities and then go out and get a loan on the "lost" securities, and maybe on the new ones too, this is pretty hard to do. The insurance company issuing the lost security bond will do an in depth investigation of your past, and will check with police to see if you have ever been involved in any fraud. They will want financial information in order to chase you if it turns out you actually sold the bearer bonds or got a loan on them. They may even insist upon a 5 year recorded *lein* on property you own. The loss ratio on these lost certificate replacements is almost nil, so IMO there are better ways to earn a dollar.

Rare Coins, Stamps, Diamonds, Antique Collections

I once had some high quality oriental rugs. A friend told me that if I auctioned them off through Sotheby's in London, I would get more money than via a local sale where I lived. Although the auction house charged outrageous commissions I still came out marginally ahead of the net I could have sold the same rugs for at my hometown.

I believe I paid 20% and the buyer paid 10% over the bid price. But there was a lot of hassle and delay. I wouldn't want to go through it again. In general, because of high dealer mark up, unless you are a dealer or expert, it doesn't pay to convert your assets to "collectibles" just for the purpose of exporting or moving your capital. Neither is this a good way to store wealth unless, as I said, you are an expert and can buy paintings (or whatever) at $100 each and sell them regularly for $10,000. Not many of us have that talent. If you truly enjoy collecting or accumulating things, unless they are small and portable, you run the risk of becoming a slave to your possessions. You need to worry about a place to keep them guards, insurance, deterioration, and so on. Dealers make profits. "Collectors" are usually suckers who overpaid and were conned.

The Heartbreak Of Parting With Possessions

Many people in this world do collect and, as I once did, they derive great pleasure from owning certain things. To me, I got tired of any piece of fine art that I owned, and after a few years, I didn't even notice it any more. But I always traded for new things and I enjoyed having fine things around me. Eventually the time came when I had to move in a hurry. Try liquidating a museum quality collection of antique furniture, oriental rugs, classic cars — not to mention a first class wine cellar, library of autographed first editions,, pedigreed dogs, horses and even doves Koy Carp worth up to $10,000 each. A quick sale is a major frustration. If you know what you are doing and can buy, trade and sell at leisure, collecting is a pleasure. You deal with wealthy people of similar tastes and interests. It is social. It is fun.

Bye-Bye, Toys

When a government agency or creditor is breathing down your neck and your best pieces go out the door at auction for five cents on the dollar, it can break your heart.

These days, the only things I want to own are useful computer programs and money. I access these possessions with a computer, fax or telephone when I need them. They are stored in my invisible world.

Everything else is rented. A PT should keep visible wealth at a minimum. Even the car I drive is a five year old, common-as-dirt model.

Tax Free, Probate Free Succession

This is one of the best things about an offshore account. Instead of long delays, administration costs, inheritance taxes and estate taxes, when the main owner dies, funds pass to the control of whoever is designated as successor. No probate, no will, no estate or inheritance taxes. Talk to any offshore banker to learn how to make it happen. If they don't know, change banks, brokers or send me a message and I will set you right. Also, get an outside consultant or person (a third party) you trust. Why? To be aware of the situation in a general way. Perhaps your trustworthy PT (Protector of Treasure) should have the name of your money manager and account balance in a sealed envelope to be opened only in the event of your death. The envelope should also have a copy of your "disposition directive." There have been many stories of banks failing to notify heirs and simply keeping the money indefinitely. In fact, a big source of profit for banks are dormant or abandoned accounts. With a little care however, your mother lode on deposit abroad can pass seamlessly to any persons, group, (or charity) you name. If you are a dirty old man with a little *boca chica* that your family doesn't know about, your girlfriend, and thence your kids with her can be provided for without a scandal. No messy litigation, everything is done quietly.

What If Your Kids Are Worthless Losers?

If the person you want to have your money is an irresponsible, druggie, spendthrift, or nut, arrangements can be made to pay them an allowance with the right of responsible trustees you name to increase or decrease the payout. You can also have a clause in your trust agreement that if any heir contests the arrangements made by you in any court, they lose everything. As with all offshore funds placed in a good banking haven with secrecy, your money is beyond the reach and jurisdiction of any creditor, ex-spouse, court, government agency, or even any family members who don't like the arrangements you made. The arrangements you make to dispose of your offshore holdings after you go to the happy hunting grounds will stick. Unlike arrangements made "at home" where your family will blow the little bit left after taxes by fighting with each other over their respective shares.

A Place Where Murphy's Law Doesn't Apply

Your invisible world can be a world that you control. Where you can sleep peacefully knowing that whatever could possibly go wrong, probably won't happen. This is in contrast to your onshore world where "Murphy's Law" applies and anything that could possibly go wrong, will go wrong!"

Chapter 15

The Kiss Of Life For Corporations

By Marc Harris, CEO, La Firma de Marc M Harris, Republic of Panama,
Corporate Services & Financial Planning & Asset Management
Mail: P O. Box 6-1097, El Dorado, Panama HQ: Balboa Plaza Building
Telephone: 507-263-6900 Fax. 263-6964, E-mail· directors@marc-harris.com

*F*ORMING a corporation is like giving birth. A new "individual" is created. *But the baby has no real life or existence until people get involved and breathe life into it.* All too often, in perhaps 95% of all cases, a new corporate charter is handed to a client. It is stuck in a drawer, and nothing more happens. Sometimes the new corporation never even gets it's own bank account. A year later, the first annual renewal fee becomes due, and it is never paid. The registrar, in due course, send out a notice to the last known address of the corporation. The notice says, "The Corporation is Dead" for non-payment of annual fees.

Although most corporations die this way, without ever taking a breath, our specialty at the Firm of Marc Harris, is creating a corporation, and then making it a useful, functioning, *living* thing. It may not sing and dance, but these days we can give it a personality, and yes, we can even make it sing and dance. How? By giving the corporation a Web Site and E-mail address of its own through our own Internet Provider Service. Anyone in the world can contact your corporation, find out what it does, and do business with it. If appropriate, your corporation can be programmed to sing jingles, take credit cards, and sell any products or services. Of course it can hold bank accounts and trade stocks.

My company, The Firm of Marc M. Harris is the world's largest independent financial service provider. We are also; an offshore discount stockbroker with a large group of audited and internationally registered in-house investment funds. We have been around for over ten years and currently have a staff of over two hundred. Our efficient back office operation (accounting, controls, and trading) is second to none.

We Are The Only Full Service
Offshore Financial Service Center

Everyone else in the financial service business steps out of the picture once a corporate charter is handed over. The client (who usually has no offshore experience) is left holding a piece of paper without a clue as to what to do next.

Years ago I decided to offer the client a service so that his offshore corporation would have substance and reality. The first step was to have relationships with banks all over the world so that corporate bank accounts could be opened for our clients. Then for customers, who already have a domestic business, we can assign staff to handle offshore sourcing (buying needed materials) product sales (exports), invoicing and collections. For the staff, the corporation is very "real." It pays their salaries and gives them daily tasks to perform.

Naturally all this profit producing activity has to be funded (at first) by the client — but my clients from the beginning, understood that with Marc Harris, they weren't forming "sham" corporations just to avoid taxes. Our offshore corporations are in business to make money — and they do just that!

We Form And Manage Offshore Commercial Enterprises

A mere shell corporation wouldn't serve any genuine economic needs. Most of the corporations formed by me had (and have) a sound business purpose and most of them make money. Take banks for instance. A gentleman in the USA has made a fortune by selling bank incorporation charters. But most of these "banks" never do anything but print up letterheads, certificates of deposit and letters of credit. Then the promoters or people, who formed the bank, proceed to flog (sell) this worthless paper at a discount. Truth is, they could have done the same swindle without any $35,000 bank corporate charter. The famous Bank of Sark scandal involved a *non-existent bank*. They took deposits promising double the usual interest rates. The man behind it was the invisible Dr. No. It was a scam and would have been funny except for the fact that many innocent people were swindled out of their savings. More recently, Harvey Penguino and his bank of Melchezidek in Anarctica pulled of the same scam.

Why Should Anyone Start His Or Her Own Bank?

A more legitimate use for a bank is to take advantage of the USA law that allows real, BONA-FIDE banks, and real insurance companies owned by American stockholders to accumulate profits abroad, untaxed.

The reason that US citizen owned banks and insurance companies have this privilege is that if American owned offshore banks had to turn over half their profits to the government, they would not grow as fast as foreign, untaxed banks. Accordingly, companies actually engaged in the banking or insurance business get a tax break. Naturally, the sellers of bank charters advertise the tax implications. Bank charters were sold at around $35,000 each to wealthy people who want to trade in securities offshore and not pay taxes on their gains. Trouble was the government said, "You're not a real bank, you're just a tax dodge Do not pass go. Pay a fine."

A real bank usually has more than one stockholder. It has a lot of depositors. It makes real loans. It has an office and a staff. Unless your Bank walks like a bank, talks like a bank, swims like a bank and looks like a bank, your "bank" is not a bank. Your bank is a turkey. That's what the IRS says.

Forming offshore banks (and similarly privileged "captive" insurance companies) was another opportunity for me to administer my kiss of life! Instead of forming a bank for just one client, I was able to consolidate several clients. This of course reduced costs and overhead to each client. Our new bank (or insurance company) then hired staff, rented space, and accepted deposits (or premiums) from unrelated corporations we were running. Our Bank put out the word that we were well funded and eager to joint-venture or participate in all banking ventures like underwriting, lending and so on. The net result was that our clients by pooling their interests, got to be stockholders in their own bank that was clearly and definitely a "real" bona-fide bank, with all the tax deferment benefits. The extra dividend is that our "real" bank made more money than a mere personal holding company, and could eventually be sold off to an even bigger traditional bank at great profit.

We Make Serious Money For Our Clients

The fun we have and the vast profits we generate for our clients comes from the fact that I don't want the Firm of Marc Harris to be just another mechanical operation. I like to see synergy between our clients — take advantage of new opportunities in mining, tourism, and keep my eyes open for new opportunities. Our clients are wealthy, successful individuals who are always presenting us with opportunities for joint ventures. We introduce our clients to each other, provide facilities, and watch the sparks fly.

We don't bat 1000 on every deal, but we have enough big winners so that our clients are very happy with the performance of their "offshore" holdings. Our in house mutual funds also do very well. Ask for details!

Sure, tax considerations are important, and we have a staff of very straight, conservative lawyers who used to work on the other side. Our lawyers prepare tax returns (both corporate and personal) and are in regular contact with the regulators. Unlike stateside lawyers and accountants, we are not government sub-agents and our books and financial accounts are not open for fishing expeditions. We take advantage of the fact that we are offshore, but we try not to rely only upon secrecy. Our deals stand up to scrutiny and are not tax motivated. We try to make money, or in the case of our foundations, to really benefit the people we are set up to educate, treat medically, or otherwise help. As a Panamanian operation we have certain independence and need not roll over and play dead when a foreign government agency makes threatening noises. At such time (if it ever comes) that Panama caves in and insists we sell out our clients (as Switzerland did). We will no doubt relocate. Having said that, we reaffirm that we are into legal tax planning, not in the tax evasion business. We want to help our clients comply with all laws that apply to them, and we certainly don't seek confrontation with the USA or any of its agencies.

Frankly, I know of no other financial service organization or bank in the entire world taking this approach. We give corporations, foundations, banks, captive insurance companies, and other organizations "the Kiss of Life." We keep them growing and prospering [or doing good in the case of educational, religious or medical organizations] until such time as they are merged, acquired, sold off, or liquidated after having accomplished their purpose.

A few years ago I was a one-man-show. But as we grew to an organization with nearly a billion dollars under our control, it was necessary to broaden our management base. We did this by hiring a number of experienced corporate executives from the USA and elsewhere. Today our staff is over 200 people in eleven countries. Our executive staff and board of directors include top-notch administrators with experience gained in major corporations. The Firm of Mark Harris will surely survive me although I am still in my thirties.

Corporations, Trusts, Foundations & Asset Protection

Typical providers of these offshore services are lawyers or Certified Public Accountants like myself. I am not typical because I moved abroad, acquired foreign citizenship, and became a "PT" more than ten years ago. Now I help our clients with their offshore set ups and administration. But we also run them, and file all necessary papers and tax returns. Although anyone can form a corporation without a lawyer or accountant by merely filling out the forms and paying the government fees, there is a mystique about this business. The impression is often given that one must have some sort of license to do it. That isn't true. Normally anyone can simply walk in the door of a "Registrar" or some similar name, fill out the application, and pay the money. Instantly (or within a few days) you get a corporate charter in the name of your choice. You can't use a name already taken, and there may be restrictions on use of the name "Royal," or "Bank" or obscene words. But aside from that any name or combination of letters is O.K. The corporation (foundation or trust) can then legally do business just as if it was a human being. Every corporation is a "legal person." A Corporation is immortal (it can live forever) and its owners are not personally liable for the debts or mistakes of the corporation. That is everything you need to know about corporations in order to form one.

Someone who specializes in forming corporations usually works with lawyers based in many jurisdictions to form corporations, trusts, or other legal entities. Each jurisdiction is popular for different reasons. These reasons usually have to do with the fees charged and the fact that corporations are exempted from taxation or taxed at a very low flat rate.

Panama, where I operate, became the best place to incorporate shipping companies because of its bargain basement fees and the lack of maritime regulations that smother shipping in such countries as the USA. Today Panama is the world leading offshore; dollar based banking and corporate center. Panama's currency is the USA dollar and American currency circulates freely without restrictions here.

Normally, the process of creating a corporation entails filling out a simple government form. It asks for the proposed name of the new corporation. Who are the directors and officers going to be? How much paid in capital will be involved? What will the corporation do? The form is filled out, filed with a government office, and a fee is paid. The government office or "Registrar of Corporations" then hands out a piece of paper called a corporate charter. This document merely says that "XYZ, Ltd.," has been formed under the laws of Panama, or Ireland, or Hong Kong, and is authorized to do business anywhere in the word. The government office gets anywhere from $1 to $2,000 (depending upon the jurisdiction and type of corporation involved).

Every year there is an annual renewal fee. This is normally lower than the start-up fee. All tax haven jurisdictions like Panama, Bermuda or the Cayman Islands derive substantial government revenues from these incorporation and renewal fees. The lawyers or accountants involved add on a mark-up for their services and usually provide directors a registered office and a mail-drop service for the corporation.

A non-profit foundation, charitable corporation, or a Church is typically free of state incorporation fees — though lawyers or accountants who set them up usually won't do anything for free. A family foundation costs a little more to set up and staff than a simple non-profit corporation. A Bank or Insurance Company Charter is the most expensive. In order to get a bank or insurance company charter a certain substantial amount of money must be actually on deposit in the jurisdiction that issues the charter and licenses. The lawyer who merely fills in the forms (total time as little as five minutes) gets a fee of between $250 and $25,000 for his setting up services. Sometime these attorneys are worth the fees, more often they are not. Our fees (we employ in-house lawyers) are very reasonable, normally about half of what you'd pay elsewhere. The true value of our services comes from the fact that we *implement* the client's plans and give ongoing services to achieve our client's objectives.

[Author's Note: Marc Harris, my favorite "much more than a banker" has a big but highly efficient organization down in Panama. He invites readers of this book who might be interested in giving the *KISS OF LIFE* to their own offshore corporation to make an appointment to visit with his firm. The "tour" is free. To make the most of this visit, the client should have a preliminary idea of what he wishes to accomplish and express this in the form of a letter to Marc M. Harris & Co. (Address at start of this chapter and again in Resource Section), asking for an invitation and appointment on a date of mutual convenience.]

Chapter 16

An Essential Truth Everyone Else Overlooks

JUST came back from our local business bookstore with half a dozen paperbacks on the subject of "Offshore." Wanted to find out what the competitors were writing about. Before pronouncing my book finished and ready to print I just had to check. Maybe I missed something. No such luck. It turned out (IMO) *they* were all missing something. Most were pushing the benefits of going offshore after a few chapters of gloom and doom. There seemed to be an attempt to panic the reader into taking action to buy the products and services their books were so obviously pushing. Swiss annuities for instance. A book treating annuities favorably inspired a whole chapter here where I said that Swiss annuities were worse than worthless. Another book was pushing offshore banks, trusts and asset protection schemes that were never fully explained. I suspect that after being drawn in by these books and spending up to $50,000 on corporations and asset protection plans that do not really work, few buyers will use them. No one will use them effectively. Such schemes as offshore foundations need the kiss of life to make them real. An empty shell corporation is also worse than worthless. If it were worthless, you would throw your money away once. A poor mug who is conned into an asset protection plan for domestic assets for several years will throw good money after bad. Eventually he wakes up and says "no more of this nonsense."

Missing Were Any Objective Approaches To The Subject

Maybe I have missed a good objective report, but of the half-dozen titles I found in a major bookstore, all the authors, by and large, seem to have never lived or invested abroad. Therefore, they know little or nothing about the realities in other countries. Their books are little more than sales pitches for dubious products or services. I make a few mild recommendations here and there only because I know that not all of my readers are do-it-your-selfers like me. You may want your hand held or you may want to confirm that you have not misunderstood a crucial concept in this book because of my lack of clarity. In those instances, you may want to visit with one of the precious few consultants in the field who have enough ethics to want to help their clients.

Perhaps I have missed some worthy material. If you have (or in the future, do) come across any good books or even good articles on this subject please write me c/o the publisher and let me know. Send used books (after you have finished them and marked up the interesting passages with your comments) or send copies of short articles to the attention of me, Peter Trevellian. I will try to reciprocate by sending you a swell present, maybe an unpublished chapter of an upcoming book. In trade for a good book, I will send you my latest book. If I already have, or cannot use the book you recommend, I will return it! I get some of my best ideas from intelligent readers. What do you get out of it? Before putting together the inevitable updated, expanded, revised and improved all new version of what you are reading now, I want to consider all ideas, and your comments. Please consider yourself the member of a club existing for mutual assistance and the exchange of information and ideas. Besides contributing to the betterment of humanity, you will get a dandy free new book. That is what you get out of it.

Are Things Really So Bad In The USA?

Answer: Only *some* things. The economy is fine. Investments can be very profitable. My competitors in our marketplace of ideas have missed the biggest point! In one otherwise excellent book, the author rants and raves for some twenty pages about how bad the USA is as a place to live or invest. He correctly says that parochial Americans in particular need to open their minds to the possibilities abroad. He is right about the need for all gentlemen of property to consider other options. But in my opinion he is wrong to find the USA wanting in *all* respects. The reason to go offshore is not that the USA is a bad place to invest or that opportunities are so much better in other places.

The point that these other authors forget to make is that the USA and almost every country in the world treat foreign investors and foreign visitors (i.e. tourists) different and far better than their own domestic citizens. Thus to get the best tax deals, the best grants, loans and special consideration, it is infinitely better to be a "foreigner" in the USA — or anywhere else you may choose to live and do business.

Foreign Investors Are Treated Better In Every Country Than Domestic Investors

The reason that USA citizens must move some of their assets offshore and that they must be prepared to move themselves offshore is simply this: In the years since Al Capone, the United States Government has steadily eroded our old constitutional rights to life, liberty and property. Too many ordinary activities have been made felonies. The rationale may have been to further the alcohol war during prohibition, the domestic anti-Communist war during the McCarthy era, and later drug wars and environmentalist causes. Many innocent people were caught in the grindwheels of these wars. When we see that the USA has roughly ten times the people in jail per capita than in France thinking citizens must do something to protect themselves from arbitrary arrest and prosecution.

As to the laws protecting property, only a few short years ago seizures were unknown. They were constitutionally forbidden since the days of the American Revolution. Today, government seizures of property without due process has grown to multi-billion dollar proportions. The Wall Street Journal reports many stories where the only offense of the person whose property was seized was that he had a desirable property, coveted by a government official. In more than one case, seizures involved raids and cold blooded murders of the property owners by government agents. Government agents even when found civilly liable for murder of innocent civilians go on to get rewards for their efficiency and medals for their bravery.

Normally there is some warning before anyone is hit with criminal indictments and property seizures. However, if the asset placement and second identity paperwork is not done well in advance. The warnings may come too late to move yourself and your assets to a safe place. A PT is Prepared Thoroughly.

Back to poor Al Capone. At the time of his indictment for (criminal) tax evasion, he was a big investor in Canada where it was legal to own distilleries providing alcohol for thirsty Americans. He would not have been prosecuted there for any activities having to do with violations of the Volstead Act (dealing in booze). Why? In Canada, he was not guilty of any crimes. Unfortunately, Capone had not read PT and he died in prison. He could have moved to Canada at the first sign of trouble where he was a "respected, honest businessman." Other people in the same business, Joe Kennedy (father of the President) and the Bronfman family of Seagram's fame compartmentalized their activities PT style. They made money out of prohibition, but did it through corporations, and in Canada, where it was legal. Today their money is "respectable."

The USA Is Great — Especially For Foreigners

For foreigners, the USA is one of the best places in the world to live or to invest and make a buck. [Foreigners are not treated as badly as locals. Why? Several reasons: One is because they have some protection against arbitrary injustice from their diplomatic representatives. More importantly, foreigners have their non-US passports and can leave!]

Why is the USA such a great cash cow, such a great place to make money? There is an excellent infrastructure in the USA. Laws are generally favorable to business. Well-regulated securities markets, and a very good road communication system completes the picture.

By world standards, service and quality is high. Workers are non-militant. Prices on everything (except competent workers) are quite low, making the USA in general a cheap place to live. As to climate, everyone agrees that California has no equal. Florida is good in season. San Francisco is a beautiful and livable city, while New York is still the Big Apple. The American telephone system is the most competitive and cheapest in the world. Every consumer product or service including ethnic items from all over the world is available in the larger cities. The government is stable, unemployment is low, and outside of ghetto areas, violent crime is not really a serious risk. Illicit drug use is a problem only because the government has had fifty years of political posturing instead of a common sense approach. Legalization and control – as with alcohol and cigarettes would do more in 48 hours to eliminate the whole underworld system and the corrupt law enforcement people than 48 years of drug wars.

Capital markets are mature and well organized. This means that good business ideas have no trouble finding financial backers and any successful small business can go public. Compared to everywhere else in the world, the USA is an entrepreneur's paradise. The only thing wrong is that lawyers, bureaucrats and cops in the USA are able to target any person they please for his political activities, or "suspicion" of anything. With a few scribbles, they make that person's life into hell. Salaried working people do not have too much to worry about, but local entrepreneurs with original ideas are in very dangerous waters.

Starting a new business, buying real estate, trading in any product or service is vastly simpler in the USA than in most other countries where licensing, high entry fees, state owned enterprises or monopolies keep new people out of competition with established enterprises. The USA surely does treat a small percentage of selected citizens very badly by subjecting them to unreasonable risks in criminal proceedings, lawsuits and by imposing taxes that seem excessively high. But other countries give their own citizens just as bad a time in different ways.

The Best Of All Possible Worlds: How To Turn Big Brother From Your Jailer Into An Amiable Innkeeper

The red carpet is out for PT's or foreigners, but how do you become "foreign" in your own country? Forming a corporation abroad, acquiring some foreign partners (even if in name only) and then doing business in the States (or any country) — as a foreign corporation can accomplish this. On the other hand, one can invest passively in the publicly traded stock of multi-national corporations that use these concepts to their advantage. If your personaliy owned securities are held in the name of an offshore bank or stockbroker, the owner is considered a foreigner. Big Bro will not know (or care) that an USA citizen is the real or "beneficial" owner. In case of nationalization, foreigners usually get fair compensation. Domestics get the shaft. To be an individual foreigner in the USA, a citizen can also renounce USA citizenship and come back as a citizen (perhaps even as a diplomat) from somewhere else. Unfortunately, so many people did this, encouraged by the concepts of W.G. Hill, that the USA passed a bunch of new laws that made it much harder for an American to come back as a non-resident foreigner (and escape all taxation) after 1996. There are still a few ways around this, but if we mention them in a book like this, they too will be shut down. Still, if you read between the lines, you will get many clues!

The Social Security System Will Find A Way Out

Gloom and doom writers roast the old chestnuts about a national debt that is out of control. The same thing could have been said (and was said!) twenty years ago. However, when the social security administration (for instance) really did run out of money, the withholding tax [they call it "contribution" for social security was simply doubled. The unthinkable was accepted and life went on pretty much as before. If a similar crisis hits the USA Social Security System in the year 2020, the social security tax can be doubled again. Why not?

Could The USA Impose An 85% Tax And Get Away With It?

In Germany if a typical worker gets $1,000 a week, half of that is deducted at source for tax and other "benefits." Employers have to "contribute" to the government another $1,000 a week per worker to cover such things as medical-fringe benefits and pension funding. In the USA, this would be considered a 75% withholding tax – but in socialist Europe, it is "benefits withholding" and is the norm. Europeans are conned into believing that their tax is a "low" 50%. They do not figure the employer contribution comes out of their pay. But as it costs the employer double what he pays his worker, the true gross wage is actually $2000. The true "withholding" is actually $1,500. Some of the withholding goes for union dues and Union benefits. The unions and the main political parties are often closely related. It is difficult to tell where union's end and government begins. Also in Europe, there is a 30% Value Added Tax (VAT is sort of a national sales tax) on everything. Thus if a salaried person gets paid (by our calculations) $2,000 a week, and spends $500, the government will get another $150 of the $500 the workers were left with to spend "as they pleased." This brings the total government cut on a $2,000 paycheck to around $1650. Bottom line: Taxes (often disguised with other names) are more burdensome in most other places than in the USA! In the past (World War II) the USA did have marginal income tax rates well above 90%. It could happen again.

Will USA Taxes Be Raised Dramatically In Coming Years?

Of course, USA withholding taxes will be raised. However, they will call it "Prepaid Benefits" or some euphemism — not taxes or forced withholding — which it is. Moreover, the populace will pay, just as the Germans do. After all, they say, "It is for our own good." Most people want to be protected and paid for by the government from cradle to grave. They like the idea of the government (as a substitute parent) deciding how three-quarters of their earnings should be spent as long as they can be conned into believing "It is for my own good."

Why Do Germans And European Workers Pay Up To 90% In Taxes Without A Revolt?

Simple! Because they have been convinced, they are getting a free lunch. Having a baby is "free." Getting sick is "free." Eyeglasses are "free." Dentistry is "free." Funerals are "free." University education and of course every bit of schooling prior to grad school is "free." Many perpetual students can stay in school and on the public tit well into their forties. Retirement or unemployment is at full pay or considering the post retirement benefits, even more than full pay. The elderly get free trams and transport within Germany, almost free telephone service, and meals on wheels.

In Germany, during the working life, paid vacations increase with seniority and can be up to two months a year. Plus, there are many special paid holidays and extended weekends for such essentials as beer festivals. Transportation and vacation lodgings themselves may be subsidized or free.

There is No Free Lunch!

Of course, you and I know that when anything is "free," it usually costs double. Why? Because the costs of government administration, waste and corruption must be factored in. But to give credit where credit is due, in Germany anyway, the system is just about as efficient and clean as it could be. Many people (workers especially) feel their system is more fair than in the USA and they like the cradle to grave security. Historically, many countries have splurged so much that the high taxes necessary to support their income redistribution package did in fact put the country into bankruptcy. Employers and entrepreneurs moved enterprises abroad to escape high taxes and the high fringe benefit costs associated with each employee. This happened in the Scandinavian countries, Ireland, Costa Rica, Uruguay, Argentina.

When Will The USA's Welfare State Collapse?

Based upon the experience of other countries, the USA is still a long way from the benefit levels and high tax levels that will cause the system to break down and collapse. It could happen, but is not likely, IMO. What will happen is that the deserving rich will get squeezed a bit more, and if you are lucky enough to be in that group, it is definitely time to diversify offshore and hide most of your money offshore!

What Happens When The USA Social Security System Runs Out Of Money Again?

If a conservative regime is in power when the crisis hits, it is also possible that the age for benefits will continue to be raised [from 67 to 75?]. One thing is sure; most governments will find new and costly ways to "protect" their citizens and taxpayers! However, is it possible to live anywhere, enjoy the ambiance and good things, and not pay any taxes or "benefits withholding?" Yes! Become a foreigner. The USA is a great place to have a business or live part-time if you are not a citizen or legal resident.

The USA National Debt Per Capita Is Relatively Moderate Compared To Some Places

It is probably true that every single American man, woman and child owes a substantial sum as their share of the national funded and unfunded debt. What critics of the USA forget to say is that in many other countries, notably Italy, Germany and Brazil the per capita liability is much higher and growing much faster. But they all muddle along. An USA Congressman recently said that every asset in the USA stands behind the national debt. That was news for a few diehards who still believe in private property. At least we have a clear window of government's attitude: "Private wealth within the grasp of government, is already the property of government!"

Despite all this, millions of people will find many new ways to prosper in the vast USA market! Is it possible for you to reap the benefits but also say "I refuse to contribute any more?" The answer is again yes — especially if you are a foreigner!

Crime Is Worse In Most Of The World

Many writers and politicians claim that crime is out of control in the USA. Compared to many other places in the world where you cannot leave your house or apartment empty to go out shopping or to dinner without a 100% chance of burglary, the USA is not so bad. But is it possible to live in a place where the risk of being robbed, assaulted, burglarized is nil? Of course it is! You simply choose to live in a country or an area that is crime free. In the worst (lawless) countries, there are always guarded subdivisions or condo apartment complexes where one can relax in complete safety and security. Crime is a problem facing poor little people. IMO a lot of poor people do not have sense enough to realize they and everyone has a lot of options open to them. Many individuals would rather stay where they are and complain rather than move to improve or redress their situation. If you are reading this book, the odds are that in the next year or two you *will* make a few moves to earn much more money, pay fewer taxes, and enjoy life more. Nothing will happen if you grunt and retire this book to a shelf. You have to make things happen. I can only give you options you might not have known about. Private criminals are not nearly as dangerous to you as self-righteous and all-powerful bureaucrats, police, prosecutors and tax collectors.

Privacy Doesn't Exist In Most Of The World

Privacy? In Germany, before a German can move to a different town or a different address, he must notify the police in his present town and in the town of his birth. He must get a certificate of good conduct to be able to buy, rent and make the required registration sign-up at any new residence. For every important transaction most Europeans need a government issued "family book" containing parents' names, children's names, marital history, job history, criminal record, etc. In Germany and in most European countries, the degree of control and required paperwork to do any small thing (like opening a bank account) is unimaginable to an American. Yet, it is possible for a "foreigner" in Europe or in the USA to breeze through life in complete anonymity without a thought for such things. If a foreigner runs a red light or throws litter on a street, he is let off with a warning from the local cop. A German might well have to pay a large fine or do 25 hours of community service. I cannot think of any place in the world where being seen as a foreigner does not insulate you somewhat from government interference in your personal and financial affairs.

Nightly Police Registration Required In Most Of The World

If police want to find one of their citizens in Europe, since every landlord and hotel keeper must (under penalty of heavy fines) register everyone staying on their property every single night and have an identity card for them — it is possible for the police to know where anyone is at any time. Once, in Italy, where I found a hot date one night, she insisted upon calling the police to "register me" if I stayed beyond midnight. I felt this was a ploy to get me out of her bedroom early, so I left in a huff. Then I learned that due to "anti-terrorism" laws, there really was a stiff fine and jail sentence potential if anyone gave a "new friend" a place to sleep without reporting it! That was a few years ago. The law is still on the books, but like so many laws in wonderful, anarchic Italy, it is largely ignored today.

Name Change Impossible In Most Of The World

It is virtually impossible under any circumstances, (outside of the USA, England, and Ireland) to change names. You need a personal decree signed by the President in places like Italy. Most of Europe is the same. Such decrees permitting a name change are seldom granted. In France, you cannot even name your kid whatever you want to name him. Every French kid must be named after a Christian Saint! In the States, a person can start a new life and get a new name by merely filling out a name change form and having it notarized. There is not even any requirement that it be filed as a public record. Such ease of identity changing is unthinkable to a European or anyone living in a civil law country.

All of the above leads us to the one conclusion that remained unseen to my colleagues writing about the "Offshore" world:

A PT Is A Foreigner — On Paper

For the best treatment and exemption from the burdens of ordinary mortals, we should become a foreigner, on paper at least — wherever we live or do business. If you are a perpetual tourist just passing through a country, you escape all taxes — even V.A.T. I have friends who have lived and worked as unregistered tourists in high tax countries like the USA and Germany. One has been practicing as an international legal consultant for thirty-five years. He leaves the country regularly and comes back in, with a different passport.

When investing in your home country or abroad, do it only as a foreigner or a foreign corporation. Come in with no cash — expertise only. My rule is "risk none of your own money," and get involved in a deal only if the government gives you such things as free, all risk insurance against everything, a twenty-five year tax holiday on all business profits, grants to build a new factory, grants to train your workers, grants of land, guarantees of no problems with environmentalists, trade unions, etc. You also should try for personal tax exemption, immediate citizenship, and passports for you and your family. All this is available — in Ireland or Austria, for instance.

Why should any government give you this special treatment? The answer is simple. They want to create new employment opportunities. If you will employ 25 or more workers and you "Mr. Foreigner" will get such a red carpet welcome – you will think you died and went to heaven.

With almost 240 different political entities to choose from, there is certainly no shortage of governments in the world. The *"Invisible Investor," due to his unique perspective*, is free to regard governments as something like those big hotel management groups, which rent space and provide services in their hotels. Hotels are okay for a visit, but you would not want to stay in them forever. There are just too many interesting places to visit. Why park yourself in one hotel (one country) for a lifetime?

You must be careful about long-term commitments, like buying a permanent establishment (i.e. expensive home), voting, or taking out citizenship in a place where you would like to live. Such acts could put you in a similar bind to what you just escaped. It is better to stay a tourist, just passing through. The government would have power over you and your assets again. Do not be like the long suffering husband who on the first day of his divorce goes out and re-marries, moving smoothly from the pleasant limbo of temporary freedom to another hell. I am not saying that all marriages or all permanent commitments to a country are hellish. I just say after you have gone "offshore," either financially or in person, stop, wait and think! Do not give up your PT status without very good reasons.

Keep liquid. Keep your options open and for the first few years at least, avoid permanent entanglements. This goes for all investments or alliances with governments, institutions, and individuals. Relationships with your wife's relatives, the local church, or a favored lodge or country club can all be terribly restrictive. Once you have given others dominion and authority over you, you are no longer free.

The essential truth is that Freedom is an option, but most people never realize that the option exists only because they never think about it! We do not need to give any government control over our lives or our money!

Chapter 17

Judgment Proofing: Owning Your Own Bank, Asset Protection Trusts

SOME lawyers say "pay me $50,000 or so and I'll protect your *domestic* assets with offshore trusts, foreign corporations or other asset protection plans?"

Forget it! They lie, or else they are pretty stupid.

Asset protection plans simply will not work to protect *domestic* assets from creditors or government agents unless the plaintiff's lawyers are so lazy and incompetent that they will not (or can't) pursue the matter to its logical conclusion.

Rather than give a technical explanation, I will simply tell the story of a self-styled genius at asset protection who operated out of San Francisco about fifteen years ago. He was trained as a lawyer and sold plenty of St. Vincent Trust Authority Bank Charters in his heyday. I would not mind naming him, but I forgot his name. It was something like "Howard Lauritzen III," — a classy name. Hungarian or upper class Jewish, you know the sound: "Rich. Very Uppah Crust. The ring of pure crystal and 24 Karat Gold — even better than my new name, Peter Trevellian."

If any reader can refresh my memory on this case or tell me what ultimately happened to the chap, I'd be most grateful. Like many lawyers, Howard believed so much in his own products that when I told him "You'd better never get a Federal Judge angry at you," he responded in wonderment, "Well I really don't own anything any more, what could they do to me?" Let me tell you exactly what they can do, and what they did to poor old Howard.

Lauritzen was in the business of selling bank charters. He went to little countries like Comoro, Vanuatu and the Maldives where Lauritzen convinced local politicians that they could make a lot of money (personally and for their country) by issuing these bank charters to his clients. The new bank charters were purchased at an average price of $1000 and sold to con men and people who wanted to be conned at $20,000 and up. The con-men bank buyers printed impressive certificates of deposit and other documentation, and managed to pass them off at a discount for cash. The other bank buyers were people who were conned. They wanted "asset protection" and tax freedom for their appreciating stockholdings. They got neither. Most bank buyers got *nothing' but trouble* for their $20,000 (or more).

As it turned out, the IRS was able to get a list of these banks and their American owners by raiding Lauritzen's office. With a little bit of co-operation from most of Lauritzen's legitimate clients who were all too eager to confess their sins in return for "just a fine," the IRS knew exactly what everyone was up to. While the IRS was taking their time to make a tax fraud case against him, Lauritzen got sued by one of his own clients I believe, and it was at this time (too late as usual) he (Lauritzen) called me up for a consultation. I warned him that his best course of action was to retire (i.e. disappear) to his mansion on the beautiful island of Mustique in St. Vincent, and to stay there very quietly. But no: He felt he would beat the rap, and in so doing, would get publicity that would help his business.

Cutting to the bottom line, there was a judgment in favor of his ex-client against Lauritzen for a substantial amount: The $25,000 paid for the bank charter, and another $25,000 for solving the client's problems with the IRS. The court had ordered Howard (under penalty of contempt) to pay it, or show by testimony under oath that he did not have sufficient assets to be able to pay.

Lauritzen came into court on the hearing day and asked that a public defender be appointed to represent him. "I have already exhausted my resources in defending this case." He said.

At that the judge turned red as a beet and in a very controlled rage, quietly said to Lauritzen:

[Paraphrased]

I will not have a man who lives at the most prestigious address in town, and who arrives daily for court in a chauffeur driven Mercedes limousine, who sends his two children to the most expensive school in town try the patience of this court with such a frivolous request. Denied!

The attorney for the plaintiff was then allowed to question him:

Let us get down to business:

Who owns the condo you live in?

Howard: I am not sure exactly, but I believe it is an Isle of Man Trust. I am just the caretaker.

Who is the real owner of the many mortgages against this property held in the name of several post office banks from postage stamp islands?

Howard: I have no information on that sir.

Who owns your car?

The Society for Prevention of Cruelty to Children, a non-profit group in Costa Rica.

Why do you get to use it?

I am their fund raising representative for California.

Where do you get your spending money?

I get expense allowances from various charities and foundations abroad that I work for. But they do not pay me any salary nor am I able to ask for cash advances.

The actual examination took hours, but when it was over, the judge said essentially this:

I believe your story is a load of cock 'n bull. You have tried to set things up to make yourself judgment proof. But you seem to forget that I have absolute power of disposition over any property in my jurisdiction. My preliminary finding is that all your local property, regardless of how it is held, is within the power of this court to dispose. I can deliver a master's deed to your condo (or your car). Any buyer that shows up at a public sale and cares to bid for your property will get good, incontestable title.

The judge went on:

It does not matter who holds legal title. I decide and decree who owns property in this country and I set the time and place of disposition I will set a sale date where there will be an auction of your things to satisfy the judgment against you. All your bogus mortgages on the property I will declare fraudulent unless within thirty days you have some legitimate bankers come into this courtroom and testify exactly why they made you such loans. I want to see proof and documentation of all these loans, trusts and foundations and I want all officers, directors, and signers of what I suspect are your bogus foreign benefactors in my courtroom thirty days hence. I will appoint a special mater to hear the evidence and consider it in light of my preliminary finding of fraud and perjury. I am a fair judge; I will give you the benefit of the doubt. If you can prove to my satisfaction that not all this offshore stuff involves an attempt to bamboozle this court and defraud your creditors, I might find in your favor. But if you bring a pack of liars into my courtroom, they will all find themselves in jail for perjury.

I have asked the District Attorney (who is sitting in the courtroom now and has been taking notes) to review your testimony today with an eye to bringing perjury charges against you. Until I see you again in thirty days, I order you held in County Jail without bail. **Your request for a public defender is denied.** As to your offshore assets, which have been discovered and listed by your creditor, I intend to order you to have them sold posthaste, and all proceeds delivered to the clerk of this court. If you do not comply with my orders, you will be jailed for contempt until you do comply.

I find you to be a flight risk. You will stay in our custody until this case has received its final disposition. Enjoy your stay in our county jail.

Bottom line?

The witnesses Lauritzen had lined up to support his claims wisely failed to show. Lauritzen eventually got five years in the slammer. His local assets were sold at auction, and his creditors were paid in full. I am not sure if he was able to keep his known foreign assets. However, after he served his five years, he was scheduled to stay in jail until he sold all the assets in his "offshore trusts." I suspect any visible property was taken away.

Footnote: When another chap in the same business (of selling bank charters) saw what happened to poor old Howard, he volunteered to become a USA informant if they would let him go on with his lucrative enterprise. The Buerau-rats agreed to accept a full report on all his new bank charter clients in exchange for witness protection privileges. Therefore, it happen that many people who wanted to escape taxes with an offshore bank charter found themselves and their secrets turned over to the IRS. Who can you trust these days? No one who sets up or operates any offshore services from within the USA that's for sure!

Domestic Assets

Moral of the story: Asset Protection Trusts and Offshore Bank Charters are a nice way for con-artists and lawyers to make money. Some lawyers may even believe in them. Truth is, they simply do not work to protect the house you live in, the car you drive, or the local brokerage or bank account you treat as your own. The form or structure does not matter to a judge. They were not born yesterday. They can spot B.S. when they see it.

A court can use its "equity" or powers to be "fair" to see through any corporate or trust "veil" and set it aside — if the judge chooses to. Even assets like pension plans or annuities, long perceived as being beyond the reach of creditors are vulnerable, particularly where there is a claim of fraud or a government agency (as claimant) is involved. There is no question that the IRS can seize any asset in the USA.

No Asset With Situs In The USA Is Safe From Seizure!

The most far out example of a seizure involved two alleged Colombian drug dealers. Neither had ever visited the USA. They did no business in the USA. Yet (fearful of their own banks in Colombia seizing their tainted money) they settled accounts between them in dollars at a Swiss bank in Switzerland. The USA intercepted some communications, decided that the "drug money" was in the Swiss Bank's dollar account in New York City. Without any court orders or proceedings in Switzerland, the USA Treasury seized the money. They gave the drug dealers a month to come in to testify personally to prove that the money was not involved in any illicit transactions. Nobody showed up at the hearing. Moral of the story, if you have any reason to fear the wrath of the USA, keep your assets out of the country, and never consider using dollars as your medium of exchange or savings. And of course, be ready to leave your homeland if serious problems of any sort develop.

"Asset protection plans" will work against a determined plaintiff only if the assets are well hidden abroad, *and* if the true owner cannot be forced to testify because he is either outside the jurisdiction, or in such pathetic bad health that he is incompetent. If these conditions are present, there is no need to spend the money on an asset protection trust. Why? Because if your enemy cannot grab the assets or put the strong arm on you, there is no case.

Serious Problems: Divorce

One in two marriages end in divorce. Where money is involved, there is usually a dogfight.

No assets = no fight.

People active in business and with known substantial assets face two serious lawsuits per year, on average. Judgment creditors can get everything you have domestically — but nothing abroad. You have two choices if you become a judgment creditor. Stay and lie, as Mr. Lauritzen did, or disappear until the heat is off.

No assets & no body = no lawsuit.

The IRS takes an extra hard look at people of local, regional or national reputation. It is part of their deterrence program. If you are profiled in a newspaper or magazine, it will probably bring serious tax problems. Low profile or no profile (abroad) = no IRS problems. High profile visible palatial homes, luxury cars, and conspicuous consumption guarantees heavy scrutiny and many confrontations. If you want a stress free life, stay out of the public eye and keep your investments invisible.

Chapter 18

Worthless Schemes - Worthy Schemes!

*A*RE you on as many sucker lists as I am? My Post Office Box yields a rich daily harvest of enticing schemes all promising to make me richer, preserve my assets or a combination of both. I hope that in this section I can help you recognize and avoid the worthless — yet not overlook the few gems that come your way. My suggestion is that if you have time, do read your junk mail. It is always amusing and good for a few laughs. If it "almost" sells you something, keep the letter in a special "good sales letter" file. If nothing else, a good example of convincing prose may itself be valuable. Some day, (even if you are not in the direct mail business) when you need to convince someone to use your product, maybe you can push the same buttons (with similar words and ideas).

Foundations: Do They Work? Yes — If You Give Away Your Money!

Would you send for a free brochure on this plan? "Protect your home. Have your land title held in a family trust like the one Rockefeller uses." Do not bother! The trust that Rockefeller uses is called the Rockefeller Foundation. Old Man Rocky gave away most of his money and property to fund such little things as the University of Chicago. You can still give away your money and keep control to a certain extent, but no USA-based lawyer or accountant can show you how to do it effectively. How to do it? With a non-deductible "gift" to a foreign foundation or non-profit organization, set up by yourself. Can you do it yourself? Not unless you have some technical training and have a lot of time to experiment and possibly get it wrong. Usually, you will have to be put in touch with one of the few people in that line of work that know the subject and are not crooks. See our "Resources" section for a few suggestions. Probably the firm in Panama we have mentioned a few times (The Harris Organisation) is the most reasonably priced of the competent and honest operators. We used to like a couple of lawyers in Liechtenstein, but they charge five times as much. Thus, we are no longer keen on them. A foundation can be set up with a foreign board of directors who will do exactly as you say. Although (for tax reasons) there should be no written evidence whereby you keep control, there are "99 easy ways" to ensure that your intentions are carried out.

Escaping The Goldilocks Tax On Retirement Plans

In the USA, over the past three decades, many individuals took advantage of special laws that promised them a tax break if they provided for their own retirement with a "qualified plan." It could be a self-administered pension plan, profit sharing, 401K, ESOP, or IRA. The basic advantage of the plans (said the government) was to allow individuals to set aside funds, free of income taxes, that could be invested and accumulated free of capital gains and income taxes. The funds would be paid out as income after age 59 when the (retired) taxpayer's tax rates would be presumably lower. As with any government plan there were miles of red tape to squirm around in, but to many of us, the plans looked good. We went for the bait and spent years carefully nurturing and looking after our little tax-free personal retirement trust. *With usual government perfidy or what I call "Soviet Logic", the government eventually penalized any of these plans that were "too successful."* Success was defined as meeting objectives: Building up the fund enough to provide the comfortable retirement income desired by the participant. The net result was that today, with high-net-value retirement plans, the government will take 75% of the retirement nest egg pay-out in penalties, and the taxpayer gets to live on a quarter!

A friend asked me about participating in such a plan about thirty years ago. At the time I told him, "Sure, go for it as long as it can be administered from abroad, located abroad, and can't be interfered with or seized by the IRS." In the early days, it was possible to set up a plan this way, but the rules were soon made more restrictive. My friend, now ready to retire with nearly $4,000,000 in his plan just learned that he gets to keep only $1,000,000. His reaction? "I spent half my life tending that little garden and making it grow. Before I give the government three-quarters of my money, I will give it all away to charity." That is what he did. Sort of.

The same guy, who had to do two years of community service protecting endangered snails, tadpoles and swamp vermin moved his pension money abroad. Donated it to a Foundation his offshore lawyer set up to Protect Human Rights. As a practical matter this means he gets to use the half million per year of annual income from his $4 million Foundation (and capital if he wishes) to help defend, advise educate and liberate victims of government oppression, like he was. He will use part of his money to become a kind of a PT godfather. To the extent that he personally assists in these matters, he is entitled to take expenses and reimbursement for his time. As the Foundation is based abroad and he is based abroad, Big Brother has no say in how he uses the funds. To him, Big Brother is the Problem he had to escape from, not the solution to anyone's problems. Although I say this elsewhere, I repeat: Its no use, fighting city hall. I still admire the Tadpole Man for his tenacity and discovery of a way to beat the Goldilocks Tax.

Domestic Foundations

There was a time (until a few years ago), that a wealthy individual could get a tax deduction for the current value of appreciated property (like stock in the family business). He could also provide a prestige job for his descendants in running a respected organization set up for some noble purpose. We have all heard of the various foundations that give grants to budding geniuses in music, art, and photography. Even today, there are hundreds of thousands of lesser-known foundations. These foundations fund the bulk of the good and useful work in the United States and the world. Government funding makes small problems bigger.

Long before there was an income tax, the Carnegie Foundation built wonderful public libraries in most of the small towns of America. Today, the government soaks up money like a sponge and actively discourages serious and creative charitable giving by limiting and red-taping activities to do with charity. The man on the street does not know much about giving his money to groups (or his own foundation) abroad. No wealthy people who are knowledgeable give their money domestically. A domestically based foundation makes the government your partner, with ultimate veto or seizure power over your assets. As it turns out, many Americans are now channeling their money abroad even if it is going to be spent back in the USA. That makes sense. It keeps control where it belongs: In the hands of the donor or the people, he designates! Too many politicians and regulators want a finger in your pie. They want control over your income, you savings, your pension funds, and even your charitable foundations. If they do not like what you do, they investigate and they confiscate.

[Author's Note: Skip the next paragraph if you are Already Libertarian]

As this book goes to press, the USA is currently investigating almost all worthy conservative and Libertarian organizations. Someone should tell them its time to move their assets and their egghead's (intellectual's) abroad to safer headquarters. America is the New Soviet Union where original ideas must be repressed and authors must be silenced and jailed. I have a better idea:

If 99 out of every 100 politicians and government employees were fired and sent home to do some useful work, and if welfare were phased out over the next five years, more people would again have more money. They could leave their money to good causes that would take us back to the good old days of rugged individualism and self-reliance. If taxes were cut by 99% and we returned to the golden days of free markets and prosperity experienced between 1880 and 1910, what do you think the net result would be? A society where half the people, supported without working are channeled into a useless unproductive life, living on government or welfare checks. There is why you have a drug problem! Entrepreneurs and busy productive people do not have time to hang out at home, stay stoned and tuned in to mindless MTV type entertainment on the boob tube. Support the Libertarian Party and reduce Big Brother's power.

[Commercial is over]

Phony Charitable Deductions

Other schemes in the junk mail purport to show you how to give away money or property and get such large tax deductions that you gain real cash flow (in tax savings) while it also helps your soul fast track to heaven. Every letter soliciting your consideration asks for your telephone number. First warning: Unless you enjoy endless calls from insurance salesmen or Jehovah's Witnesses, don't give out your telephone number when responding to any of these mail order solicitations. On the other hand, if any junk mail offer promises "more free informational brochure upon request," if there seems to be any credibility, I always ask for the full scoop. I should not have to tell you to have any brochures sent to a mail drop. Do not use your real name, and be sure it is impossible for the advertiser to make personal contact with you. You do not want to appear on any database — and you just do not want to be bothered!

Government Entrapment

I have not mentioned it until now, but the government itself has undercover agents who place ads offering various kinds of tax-evasion schemes. The government agent in the worst of these cases will steal your money, and then testify against you for a reward. It is a cruel world out there and these days you have to worry not only about ordinary swindlers, but a new group of crooks (usually with new identities and references provided by the Government Witness Protection Program). They are out to entrap as many innocent people as they can lure into their deals. The government-sponsored people often are provided with a cloak of legitimacy that is very convincing. How do you spot a sting operation? I do have several ways, but if I put them in this book, they would become known to the opposition and lose effectiveness. If you ever become a consulting client, remind me to tell you how to protect yourself from undercover cops and private pirates who have been given a license to steal by Big Brother.

Ignorant Believers

For the moment, the number of undercover agents out to defraud you is considerably less than garden-variety swindlers who are sometimes ignorant people who themselves do not know what they are talking about. In the lunatic fringe tax-revolt groups there are many "packages" being sold to provide "complete protection" against everything from income taxes to parking tickets. None of them will work, especially if they involve any abnormal activities that raise a red flag — like filing a blank (but signed) income tax return with a letter "taking the Fifth Amendment." The jails are full of people convicted of "Willful Failure to File" for doing exactly this. But the loonies (some of who believe in their product) continue to sell thousands of advice packages for several hundred dollars each. One secret package ["Never Again Pay A Parking Ticket"] tells you how to convince a judge that paper dollars issued by the Treasury are "illegal money". That is why you cannot pay your parking ticket. The last guy I know who tried this got a very sympathetic judge who agreed with him and said, you do not have to pay with thirty of those bad, illegal dollars. "Here's a choice: Thirty dollars or thirty days!" Next, case.

How To Identify Gems Among The Junk

One big problem is that people without legal training usually cannot tell the "real" goods from complete and utter frauds. But the first rule to remember is that any domestic or onshore asset (like your home or car) cannot be protected from potential plaintiffs or government seizure by simply putting title in an offshore trust or corporation. Even if you go through the motions of paying a monthly rent to the offshore "owner," any plaintiff's lawyer worth his salt will assume that it is yours. As it is "within the jurisdiction" & thus under a court's complete control (regardless of who owns it on paper) any judge can easily assume it is really yours and confiscate it. Remember: *All assets within the jurisdiction are subject to seizure regardless of how title is held.* Maybe I had better say that again and put it in nice big, bold, dark letters:

All Assets Located Within Any Jurisdiction Are Subject To Seizure By The Government (s) Controlling That Jurisdiction — Regardless Of How Title Is Held.

So called constitutional arguments and secret plans of the super rich available by mail order, are always worthless — if the secret plan involves putting your home, car, business, property or bank account in some other name. It does not matter if you use a church, an indigenous native trust, a mumbojumbogogogotototo, or whatever! As long as the asset is in the USA, it can be taken over by any number of local, state or federal agencies or courts for any number of reasons — or no good reason at all.

Many offshore arrangements cannot be legally promoted or sold domestically, for obvious reasons. The government does not like to lose control over its citizens or its assets. You can be informed of the opportunities offshore generally by books like this (until it is banned), but no one can solicit you. And no domestic (USA licensed and based) lawyer or accountant can inform you how to go offshore most effectively without risking his own license.

The unfortunate part of this is that if and when you are solicited, it will probably be by a crook who will take your money offshore all right — and that's the last you will see of him or your money.

Rule: How To Avoid Being Conned Or Losing Your Money

Do not send serious money offshore to just any guy with a post office box. Unless you are dealing with an old line, established bank, make a visit to the guy's office. Then before sending money (not after!) check his references. Make sure he is real. Not just a smooth talker with a fancy office that may have been rented for the day, just to con you. Make sure anyone you deal with is an established person with good references from banks and professional people, preferably someone in your own town. Call the references. If there is any doubt in your mind, take a pass. Better, yet when you go offshore, do not use a one-man show. Even if he is honest, what if your one-man accountant, lawyer, or money manager dies or gets sick. Use a firm with more than one partner or officer. I'd say you want at least half a dozen back up people. Alternatively, use an established stock-broker or bank. As we said, never use a foreign branch of an American broker or bank. You might as well stay at home because big brother controls them and big brother will still control your assets with them. A foreign branch of a USA law firm or accounting firm is not so bad. They may be cautious with a new unknown client, but if you come well introduced, you may get very good advice from them because they are more aware of your special needs. For our Cana-dian, German or other non-USA readers, the same advice applies. You usually can get decent help from expat lawyers or accountants of your own nationality based offshore. Do not be put off by the fact that many of the important members of the firm are former govern-ment, law enforcement, officials. The standard pattern is that they train with the government, and then move to the other side. On the other hand, don't you suggest anything by starting out "I know this is illegal, but can I get away with it?" They might suspect you are an undercover cop. Rather say, "This is what I want to accomplish, how can I do it"? "Are there other ways?" "Do you have any other sug-gestions?" "Is that the only way?"

If It Is Too Easy And Too Simple, It Probably Won't Work

Another example of fraud? There are zillions of variations, but often a salesman will try to tell you that if you put your money into a foreign corporation or trust, your foreign "entity" can accumulate money for you tax free. Further, they will have ways for you to control the assets and to withdraw your money secretly at any time. Unfortunately, the tax collectors in the USA have made rules so that if you have any kind of control over foreign corporations, trusts, or otherwise, you have to pay taxes just as if the "entity" didn't exist. Besides this, other rules make it a major crime if you do not file annual reports listing exactly what securities and cash you have abroad and where it is kept. The only things that do not require such filings are assets like gold bars, diamonds, paintings, stamps, and coins. The trouble with so called collectibles is that they are sold to you at retail prices. They earn no interest while you hold them, and unless you are very lucky indeed, you will lose a lot of purchasing power when you seek to cash them in.

We hear stories of people who buy a painting for $30,000 store it in a French villa and sell it ten years later for $10 Million. But the odds are in real life, when you buy a $30,000 painting (or piece of jewelry, collector coin set, etc.) you'll sell it ten years later for a lot less. The only exception is when you have expertise in such matters and are essentially a dealer yourself. Dealers set and control the big spread between bid and asked prices for their own benefit — not for their clients.

The Only Simple Thing That Works Is Secrecy

Further (and back to conventional asset holding like cash or securities), in terms of either lawsuits or tax matters, to get any tax or asset protection benefits from most (but not all!) offshore structures, you have to keep them secret. If questioned under oath, to be judgment proof, my experience is that you have to deny the fact of their existence and your connection to them. Obviously, if a local lawyer or accountant can contradict you and show papers, you could be in serious hot water for perjury. Judges are on to the fact that almost all these offshore asset protection schemes are in fact scams where the settlor (person who sets up a trust or something similar) does keep control. If there is any control suspected, the judge can say "Mr. Smart-Guy, here's what you will do: You will pay your judgment to Mrs. Ex-wife by making your trustees in the Isle of Man pay her $50,000 out of your trust. Until you do, you will sit in jail for civil contempt (willful failure to obey a court order). I know you have told me you cannot control what your trustees do, but you will just have to try harder to meet your obligations. This court will not let you live the high life with a generous income from an asset protection trust while your poor ex-wife is forced to go on welfare. Come back to see me after sixty days of bread and water in a concrete box with a bunch of degenerates and homosexual rapists."

Boy Scout Mentality

Most Americans, being of the Boy Scout Mentality (at least at first), are not capable of lying convincingly under oath. Acting ability often improves after a bout in court where the defendant perceives that he is the *only* person telling the truth. But avoidance of confrontation is easy and that is a far better option. After some personal experience in Court where I did tell the truth and was awarded some time in the country jail for my honesty, I resolved to never place myself within the power of "authority," ever again.

The Two Step Secret That Does Work

This author has long felt that the only surefire way of protecting assets is to first *move the assets abroad.* Then either move or *be ready to move your body completely out of the jurisdiction* so that there is no possibility of being placed in the position where lying in a court of law is necessary. With all your property and your persona in parts unknown, there simply is no case to prosecute. In the USA, there are no convictions in absentia as there are under civil law. A tribunal or government agency can only act when your hot little body is there — or if they can grab local assets. There are limited circumstances when they will kidnap or extradite people from foreign countries. (Needless to say for any outreaching activities outside the jurisdiction you must be a pretty big fish; they must know exactly where you are and they'll need plenty of time to make the necessary arrangements with their counterparts abroad.) There are also a few ways to seize foreign assets of USA citizens. But both of these situations, asset grabs or ass-grabs, require you to act like a stupid sitting duck: The plaintiff, be it private or government, has to know exactly where you are. They must know exactly where the money is.

Only in the movies is the U.S. Marshall or the Mafia Hit Squad able to track down the marked man "every time." In reality, the world is so big that by simply breaking ties (temporarily) with past contacts and choosing a place where there are not too many fellow Americans who would recognize you, anyone can disappear until things cool off. The same rule applies obviously, not only to Americans, but also to all people who want to lay low. Hard as it may be to believe, there are many nice places in the world where someone can be totally unknown even if they have made the cover of Time, Fortune, Business Week, Life and have been "done" on CNN. Where? Anywhere along the Black Sea, Mauritius, Goa, the former French or Spanish colonies, or just about anywhere they do not speak English. For normal fade-away, just about anywhere that your hometown gang does not frequent is a good hideout.

Objectivity Is Always Affected By Secret Commissions [To Your Accountant Or Lawyer]

Any well-informed lawyer or accountant (or even any businessman) who has been involved with these things over the years can steer you away from lousy deals if he isn't trying hard to sell you one himself. Just in case you did not know it, lawyers, and accountants normally get commissions of up to 20% of the money you invest in deals, tax saving schemes or asset protection arrangements. They will always recommend arrangements where they get payments known in the trade as "front end load." So their recommendations are not always objective. If you ask your own trusted advisor directly if they are making any commission on the deal they are pitching you, they will usually answer honestly. A "yes" answer is your first hint about their objectivity:

Magic Question: How Much Do *You* Make If I Go Into This Deal?

Ask anyone trying to sell you anything "What is your commission on this deal, if I go into it?" Then, get the answer in writing! Very few licensed professionals in your own country will risk lying to you (in writing) about any secret commission deal. Of course a con-man salesman will sign anything or do anything to get hold of your money. The deal may be good or bad, and it is no sin to get an undisclosed commission. But once again, if a salesman, consultant, an accountant or your own lawyer is getting a big portion of the cash he wants you to put into a deal, stop. Consider this:

A)   His motivation is likely to be more towards filling his own pockets than in furthering your best interests.

B)   If the up-front commissions [front-end load] are substantial, then you obviously have significantly less of your money working for you on the deal! Why? Money that had been taken out for a front-end commission obviously is not earning interest or dividends for you.

Finally, do not assume that accountants, lawyers, or most financial advisors know anything about making money grow. They make their serious money on commissions and probably earn less than you do on their own investments. If they were so smart, they would be as rich as you are! *Look for and create your own deals at home or abroad!*

The Vast Majority Of *Advertised* Business Opportunities Or Tax Shelters Are Strictly 'Suckers Only'.

A lot of the schemes advertised under "business opportunities" will put money into the pockets of the sellers of kits and forms, seminar organizers or mail order book promoters, but won't do you much good. As business deals virtually all tax motivated, arrangements are lousy. You are much better off grazing in familiar fields of endeavor and paying the taxes. Let us consider a few categories:

Tax Loopholes Or Tax Avoidance Schemes

There are really are loopholes! Some of these legal loopholes are actually intentional — to encourage a certain type of economic behavior. For instance, years ago, investments in low-income housing could throw off tax benefits considerably greater than the amount of money actually invested. Lawyers discover them and for a commission, put their clients into these situations. Once in a great while, a character like Nevada White (see chapter about him) comes along and publicizes these deals in a way the common man can understand. They advise a "do it yourself approach." These opportunities do not last long. Either the loophole is closed, or the chap exploiting the loophole is accused of some crime and is himself shut down. See our chapter on Nevada white.

Do It Yourself Deals That Did Work

Norbert Dacey, the man who wrote the book about doing your own arrangements to avoid probate was hounded for *practicing law without a license* until he had to leave the country. The same thing happened with Ted Nicholas who put out an excellent mail order book about forming your own domestic corporation (without a lawyer) to reduce taxes. These gambits always worked and they still work, but the establishment put such pressure on Ted and Norbert that they had to fold their tents. Yet, con-artists and fraudsters seem to go on peddling the same worthless ideas for years and years.

The Kiss Of Death

Really good tax loophole deals get the kiss of death just as soon as direct mail promoters start pushing them. Another sign is once they are advertised in professional journals or trade papers and sold to medical doctors, airline pilots, or CPA's. When the Wall Street Journal does a page one column one feature article or profile on someone or some scheme — then you know the jig is up.

Swiss Annuities

Here is something that has recently been getting a heavy push at offshore investment seminars aimed at Americans. As with all such deals, it makes no investment sense, and once it started to become a big thing, it made no tax sense either. Recently received a brochure from a Swiss Insurance Broker. He makes his money on commissions yet calls himself an INVESTMENT COUNSELOR. It had quite a few impressive charts and graphs. The general impression conveyed was that anyone who bought a Swiss Annuity thirty years ago enjoyed a consistent 30% per year compounded return ever since. There was a warning that past performance is no guaranty of similar results in the future — but it was in fine print. Nobody pays attention to such warnings anyway. Did "investors" really make 30% annually? No! The impression about past performance is false.

What Is An Annuity?

What is an annuity? In its simplest form, an annuity is purchased with a lump sum you pay to an insurance company. They figure your life expectancy, and pay you back your own money in periodic payments over your life span, less ten or twenty per cent of the initial contribution as a commission. When you are dead, the payments stop. Your heirs get nothing. The insurance company then invests your money in bonds and other conservative deals and adds to the payoff figures a certain amount for interest. Typically, this is about half of what you could earn if you made a similar investment yourself. Such a deal!

Real Investment Return On A Swiss Annuity

The real return on a Swiss annuity in Swiss francs has been closer to 3% per year. The Swiss Franc has gained considerably against the dollar during that period, but the German Mark and Japanese Yen have done even better. A simple savings account in any of those three currencies would have given any saver a better return than what was gained on Swiss Annuities. In other words, it was not the Swiss Annuity that gave a good return, but rather the choice of currency. During the Nixon era, high inflation caused the dollar to drop considerably versus the Swiss Franc, but in more recent years, the gains resulting from currency appreciation have been flat. Or to put it another way, the big currency gains are a thing of the past, not the present. Almost any offshore (non-USA) stock or bond fund has done considerably better than any annuities.

To repeat, the seemingly high (prior year) return indicated in the mail-shot charts is really a non-recurring gain on the currency exchange. Further, the chart in all such promotions chooses the years carefully, starting at a historic low point in order to make the product being promoted seem to be a "sure thing."

Funny Thing About Swiss Annuities Everybody In Offshore Industry Now Sells Them. Why?

Although any good investment advisor does not believe in Swiss Annuities, their sales and public relations people have done such a great marketing job that the stupid public wants to buy them. When I asked Harris, my Panamanian money manager friend why he (reluctantly) sold them as one of his offshore products, he said "Everybody else carries them and if I couldn't offer Swiss annuities, some clients who have been pre-sold would just go to someone else. Some clients have decided that they want Swiss annuities, and there is nothing I can do to change their mind."

Diamonds Are A Girl's Best Friend?

There is another myth! DeBeers cartel operating out of South Africa for a century has cleverly advertised and promoted an intrinsically worthless product. In nature, diamonds are not nearly as rare and valuable as they are cracked up to be. If the truth were known, so many diamonds are mined that without all the hype, the value of any stone would be worth little more than baubles at the bottom of your fish tank. What's more, perfect stones (i.e. diamonds) can now be produced synthetically. How did the public get conned? The DeBeer's syndicate signed up all the diamond producers. The deal is they buy 100% of all production at several times the price that a free market would support. The cartel assigns production quotas and sets wholesale prices. By keeping excess diamonds off the market and by setting the wholesale prices to go up slightly each year, they have created an illusion of value (as the Swiss annuity people have done). DeBeers won't sell to jewelry stores who don't play the game and keep the retail prices well above the levels set at the DeBeers "sightings" a sales to the retailers.

Everybody Wants To Get In On The Act!

The Diamond Cartel got very upset about twenty years ago when a bunch of outsiders decided to horn in on the carefully honed marketing strategy of DeBeers. A couple of decades ago, diamonds were (for the first time) promoted by a group of con-artists within DeBeers greater con. Diamonds were promoted as "investments," rather than pretty status symbols women would wear at parties. Promoter's charts correctly showed a consistent increase of nearly "10% per year over inflation" for seventy-five years in wholesale diamond prices. Although that sounded like 10% or more in uninterrupted appreciation, it really meant that if inflation in a given year was 2%, diamond prices were raised 2.2% in that year. Ten per cent over inflation! Get it? The swindlers were able to operate in an unregulated area of commerce that had long been the exclusive preserve of the DeBeers people.

Investment Diamonds Become The Rage

The 1970's saw an immensely successful promotion of "unset professionally graded diamonds" sold at "wholesale prices" in transparent plastic sealed envelopes with a guaranteed buy-back at a minimum profit greater than the prevailing interest rates. The contract was imprinted right on the packet. As a result of enthusiasm generated by this promotion, "investment graded diamonds" imbedded in plastic took a roller-coaster ride going up 50% in a year or two before falling to way below where they started. The marketing company was able to bid up prices on their own products and support those prices as long as they were selling far more diamonds than those coming in for redemption. It was a Ponzi scheme of course. The company giving the guarantees disappeared (as might have been expected) and did not pay up when the prices of their diamonds headed South as the result of negative publicity. Nevertheless, they had bilked the public out of a billion dollars. Although the scandal was generally known and received big publicity, the fact that diamond jewelry is always "keystoned" or marked up nearly seven times its wholesale cost never got out to the public. As a result, some people still believe that diamonds are a good investment, or as the song says, "A girl's best friend." The truth is that if you buy a nice diamond ring for $7,000, the wholesale or buy-back value is likely to be around $1,000. Not exactly, good ways to make money, unless you are the jeweler-dealer who sells at retail and buys at wholesale.

Oriental carpets, rare coins, paintings, ceramics — all "collectibles" are sold to the public at whatever the traffic will bear and most dealers will buy only at 10% on the dollar. If you have a collection to be sold, before you accept a dealer's offer be aware of this in advance.

Back To Annuities

We do not say that most of the issuers of annuities will go under like the investment diamond people did. Large Swiss institutions are very solid and IMO, they will not default. Why? Because any insurance company that issues annuities is getting too good a deal: They are using your money without having to pay full market rates of interest. Why can buyers be conned? Inflation in the post World War II era was usually lower in Switzerland than in the USA. As a result, the Swiss franc used to go up against the USA dollar by a few percentage points each year. But in some more recent periods like 1984-85 and again in 1997 the Swiss Franc lost a substantial amount of its value against a strengthening dollar. Now that inflation in the USA and Switzerland are equalizing, expectations should not be the same as they were in the Nixon era. These days, the dollar regularly goes into periods of great appreciation or depression versus the Swiss Franc. The volatility range is about 50%.

Rotten Performance

Example? During the period from 1980 to 1986, if you had invested in a Swiss Annuity at exactly the wrong times, you would have lost over 50% of your capital in dollars. Depending on timing, other currencies like the Deutschmark or Yen have also done much better over the long term than dollars. But that was in the past. Nothing is such a sure thing any more. Many investments denominated in a huge variety of currencies have vastly outperformed the Swiss franc over the short or long term.

Where Do The Swiss Invest?

The Swiss themselves invest most of their assets abroad. The biggest pool of Swiss capital is invested in the USA! Where? New York Stock Exchange common stocks. Swiss sophisticated investors would not touch local annuities with a ten-foot pole. Why? The person pushing Swiss Annuities is an insurance salesman. He or she gets a fat commission [up front load] on every dollar or franc put into an annuity deal. To recoup this up-front load, the customer cannot cash out at any time. He, under the terms of the contract, must wait several years to break even. Under the best contracts, to pull out, you lose at least one-year interest. This penalty is needed to pay your salesman's commission.

Lucky You?

You could be lucky, cash out of an annuity early and make up the commissions you have paid and break even on a favorable currency fluctuation. You are infinitely more likely to discover that a Swiss annuity contract won't turn out nearly as well as simply buying any Swiss stock or any bond and keeping it in a box. Without the big front-end load commission, you would be ahead from Day 1 by not going into an annuity. A Swiss annuity is like a Swiss mutual fund or investment trust with a big deduction on day one. There is no such thing as a "No-load" annuity, as far as I know. There are plenty of no load or low load investment vehicles around.

Sucker Deals

Why do some (foolish) people buy annuities? Why diamonds? Why the paintings of some no-talent artist? The main reason is usually good advertising and P.R. In addition, because dealers and commission salesmen are paid very well to unload these sucker deals on a gullible public. Annuities are certainly not an "investment" any more than diamonds are.

I Haven't Finished Beating A Dead Horse!
[More On Annuities]

Let's look at the life span figures the insurance companies use on annuitants: For most insurance purposes, standard mortality tables are used. But for annuities, the insurance companies assume you'll live an extra few years. If you do not survive till an extra-ordinary age, they will make a very substantial windfall on all the money left in the actuarial portion your account. But they will even make a profit if you live forever because the annuity pay out is normally less than they earn with your capital.

Let us look at a 50-year-old American male with US $100,000. If he wanted to make an intelligent and conservative investment of this money, he'd go to a Swiss or other offshore bank. If he wanted a conservative investment in a strong currency, he'd say, "Buy me US $100,000 worth of German Grade A 20 year corporate bonds yielding 9%." This is exactly what I did a few years ago. At the same time I did this, a Swiss Insurance Broker was trying to sell me an annuity. Let us compare what actually did happen with my German bonds to what would have happened with my annuity.

I held my German bonds for four years receiving around US $40,000 in interest during that period. At the end of four years, I sold my bonds for $175,000 because interest rates had gone down. This meant the bonds went up. I made a capital gain on the bonds; in addition, I made another gain on the currency. During the four year holding period I was always liquid, and I could do what I wanted with my money or leave it to my heirs by simply seeing to it that an envelope containing my bearer bonds was handed to them upon my death. My $100,000 became $215,000 in three years.

If I had bought a Swiss annuity, I would have had a contract to receive CHF4,000 per year for the rest of my life. In the year I sold my bonds for double what I paid, I could cash in my annuity for $90,000. When I died, if I did not cash out before that, the annuity contract would terminate. My money would be lost. My heirs would get nothing! The typical annuity contract allows certain variations like an ability to borrow against your own remaining money in case of certain specified emergencies. You then pay the insurance company an interest rate on the borrowed money. What they charge you for borrowing your own money is considerably higher than what they are willing to pay you! But the fact remains you are essentially illiquid. Most importantly, and to repeat, with a standard annuity, when you die, your capital vanishes without a trace. Of course, there are many variations on the annuity contract, but they are all written so that the actuarial odds favor the insurance company, and not the customer. No matter what the plan, the salesmen make a nice commission, and the insurance company makes a nice spread on what they pay out vs. what they retain.

Besides stupidity, why would anyone buy an annuity when they could buy a bearer bond (possibly even from the same insurance company) yielding near double what they get on the annuity? And especially when the bond could be sold anytime for a nominal commission while the annuity could only be liquidated by incurring costs much much higher. With stocks or bonds, there is a chance of capital gain aside from currency appreciation. With an annuity, currency appreciation is the only chance for a capital gain. And the currency appreciation of Swiss Francs during the past 10 years has been anything but steady and dependable.

I could not think of a single intelligent reason to buy an annuity under any circumstances. But a broker who sells the stuff once told me why Americans could be sold on them.

The Boy Scout Mentality

The broker explained "Once I tell any American that Swiss Annuities are a *legal* way to protect wealth and hide money, their eyes light up. I know I have made the sale. You and I know that Europeans are not such Boy Scouts and would always rather buy a Swiss (unregistered) bearer bond that yields nearly double what an annuity does and is easily sold for a commission of around 1/4 or 1%. They would keep the bond in a safety deposit box and I venture to say that of the billions of dollars earned on bearer securities, virtually none is ever reported to tax authorities. But some Americans believe that there is an "eye in the sky" that knows they have unreported interest. They would feel guilty about having a secret bank account, or bearer securities. They fear they will be discovered and go to jail. Of course they won't unless they open their own big mouth to brag. But many Americans can't resist telling everything about themselves to anyone who asks. Annuities were the thing for them — at least until the laws were changed in 1996 and the annuities lost much of their protected status. What happened was, the IRS became aware of the magnitude of American holdings of Swiss annuities, and they changed the rules, as they always do. But until the rules were changed, many Americans, being less sophisticated about such things than the wealthy residents of other countries, would rather put their money in a loser deal where, for the moment at least, there was no reporting requirement. Annuities did not have to be reported on income tax returns in the USA.

Now, although the implications are not all that clear, it appears that the "Boy Scouts" get the worst of all possible worlds — a lousy investment, no secrecy, and they are tied up long term with an illiquid investment. Once again, that always happens with the so called "legal" schemes once they get popular. There are many better ways to invest money, but most Americans starting on the offshore path like the idea of getting away with something and doing it legally. Therefore, that legality is the clincher when it comes to selling Americans annuities. Creditors cannot get at the contents of a safety deposit box or secret deposit abroad, but technically it is a crime to go bankrupt and hide your assets in such a way. Americans are Boy Scouts, and at least many of the ones who go to investment seminars abroad are eager customers for annuities which still can't easily be seized by creditors or even the tax collectors, for the moment anyway."

The key word dear readers, is "for the moment" or "for the time being." For long-time, and still today, promoters of asset protection trusts and Liechtenstein Anstalts (Foundations) were touted as secure places for assets to be hidden. The far away Cook Islands (near New Zealand) were often touted as the place to have an asset protection trust. Then in 1995 a judge in the Cook Islands hearing a fraud case announced that "This jurisdiction and its laws will no longer be used to protect criminals who launder money or defraud creditors in other places."

The quasi-boy scouts who wanted to defraud the IRS or their creditors legally lost again!

As to Liechtenstein Foundations or secret accounts, they are "protected" only as long as they are secret, and if the person who controls such accounts is silly enough to allow documentary evidence (like bank statements) to fall into the wrong hands, then government agents or creditors can always attack known assets.

In the opinion of this writer, it will just take the right case to crack open all *known* offshore annuity accounts for creditors. An American judge will ask a known or suspected "bad guy" if he has the power to borrow against his Swiss annuity. If the answer is yes, the judge will order him to turn over whatever cash he can get to his creditors or the government as a forfeiture. The alternative will be to rot in jail forever under a contempt of court order. There is no question that a judge could make this order even now with no changes in the laws as they stand. It is further likely that an American court order concerning a Swiss annuity could be enforced against a Swiss Insurance Company. There is not one single Swiss bank or insurance company that doesn't have US Dollar assets, stocks, bonds, or pending contracts — even if they don't have any offices or "do business" in the USA. The mere fact that they have USA assets of any kind makes a company vulnerable to rulings of an American court. They will cave in to the slightest pressure and no doubt make a deal where as in the Nevada White case; they get to keep a third of the assets in return for giving up the customer.

Secrecy Offers The Only Safety

In my opinion, the ONLY safety for assets is secrecy. If no one but the owner knows it exists, and if there is no public registry where the true owner's name can be found, the asset is secure. Anyone who thinks they will securely protect their assets by openly purchasing an annuity is deluding themselves.

Is there anything good to be said for annuities? If you are absolutely sure you will beat the odds and live to be 299 years old, you will possibly make out almost as well with an annuity as with a bank account or bond. Aside from that, my advice is "Don't be a sucker!"

Gold!

Some writers attribute magic to gold. Gold is no more or less valuable on any given day, than any other commodity. Over the last twenty years it has been relatively constant in price which only means that if you bought some ingots at US $400 per troy ounce twenty years ago, and it is $400 per ounce today, you have lost the 6% per year or whatever interest you might have earned on an alternate investment. You are not just 60% down (6% times 10 years) you are down (roughly) another 20% because of the compounding effect, and certainly even more for inflation. Then if you factor in what you would have made in the average common stock mutual fund or income fund over the same period, your relative loss goes to 95%. If gold performs as it has in the past, you will lose 95% of your purchasing power over the next twenty years. But even if the price of gold moves up smartly, because it doesn't earn any interest or pay dividends, it must move up at nearly double the inflation rate just to keep up with other common investments. *In other words, IMO gold coins or bars (like annuities) are one of the worst things anyone can hold for investment.*

Gold bullion coins buried in the yard or a safe deposit box abroad are safe (sort of) but then so would be stocks, bonds or for that matter an apartment building you own secretly abroad. Real estate you could get a tenant for would bring in rental income. If well located, and bought at a time when real estate prices are depressed, probably some appreciation too.

Gold Company shares (mining stocks) in general have performed much better than physical gold. That is because they are a business, producing a product. The product (Gold) must sell for more than the cost of mining & refining.

Medallions & Collector Coins

Collector coins and medallions are typically sold by dealers or outfits like the Franklin Mint at high markups. A private person who buys retail may never be able to sell them at more than a small fraction of prices paid. If you go into coin (or coin and stamp) dealing buying at a wholesale ($1 for instance) and selling at retail ($7.95 for example), you may make some money after paying overhead, rent, insurance, advertising and all the usual expenses. Then you are a dealer. Used car dealers make money too — but few people would suggest that used cars are a swell investment.

Gold Futures

Gold Futures? The vast majority of all Commodity traders are like slot machine players. They start with a can of money. They play until they lose it all. It is just a matter of time. Commodity brokers on the other hand make commissions if the customer gains or loses.

Investments Held In The Name Of Swiss Bankers

Vaunted Swiss Bank Secrecy has been so eroded in the past twenty years that keeping known assets there is no safer for Americans than keeping it in any country without bank secrecy. The Swiss Department of Justice has caved in to the Americans and will do just about, whatever they want. If the American IRS gives a name to the Swiss and merely accuses (without proof) that named person of some crime under Swiss law (like money laundering) the Swiss will send out a notice to all their banks freezing or "arresting" the assets of the named person. Any American who opens a Swiss bank account using an American passport and his own name might just as well count on having his assets seized if he ever gets into any sort of conflict. Surprisingly, the Swiss are said to protect Italians, French, and Germans much more.

Chapter 19

How To Create Your Own Deals

*T*HE average bloke has as much idea of how to make a deal as how to prepare Creme Bruleé. Yet becoming gourmets cook, or an entrepreneur is easy. In this chapter I will teach you how to become both! You will see how the same thinking process will make you a dealmaker and a first class chef as well.

An entrepreneur looks at a main street full of dirty cars and visualizes his profitable spanking new automatic car wash. The same guy looks at his first portion of Creme Bruleé in a French restaurant and doesn't see a desert, but rather a deal — a new product he can put in a can to sell as an upscale "energy booster."

How about a great chef, visiting the corner super market. He looks at many potential ingredients and thinks about how to combine these elements into a mouth watering delight – a taste treat his guests will never forget. He sees a jar of fresh clotted cream, a stick of butter plus some honey or brown sugar. A delicious dessert that does not yet exist turns him on. The end product is visualized, smelled and tasted.

A cook, a dealmaker, a creative expert in any field looks at diverse elements or raw materials. They are constantly putting together finished products — in their minds. If you try to develop this mind set, it will be only a matter of time before you too become a creative genius.

Before we move on, I had better tell you how to prepare Bruleé a la Trevellian (simple version). This skill comes in handy if you want to make a desert and just happen to have these ingredients lying around. The main thing is French "Fresh Cream" which has certain tartness. In France it can purchased any place they sell food. Abroad? Only in gourmet delicatessens. The name alone, *Creme Bruleé a la Trevellian* will impress your next date or guests. [When you say you got it out of a book on "Offshore Finance", they will *really* think you are something else.]

OK. You start with a very shallow casserole pan of the sort you can heat from the bottom and broil with. Copper bottom is best for even heat, but make do with whatever material you have around. Ceramic is O.K. Heat some very good quality butter, not margarine in your pan and sprinkle brown sugar over the melting butter in the bottom of the pan. How much? Not a lot. Maybe two tablespoons of butter & two tablespoons of very dark brown sugar. The very best tasting brown sugar comes from the Philippines.

The brown & delicious flavor there comes from the rust in the pipes of the Filipino processing plants (only joking). But it sure does taste better than any other brown sugar. Caribbean brown is second best. You can get away with Demarara Sugar if you must. Any sugar will turn a nice caramel color if heated with butter. Heat gently and swish around with a fork. Turn up heat enough so the mixture begins to turn a lovely brown. This is the Bruleé (or a dark coppertone) color — the trademark of this desert. Pour out half the hot golden syrup into a waiting warm bowl. Then (to the broiling pan, not the bowl) add the "Fresh Cream." This is NOT just ordinary fresh cream you get in the USA. It's that special French stuff I told you about. In England it is called "Clotted Cream" but the American's – well, outside of big towns like New York City, San Francisco and New Orleans, they just don't know what's good. That's when you get creative.

You may have to play around with substitutes like ricotta cream cheese until you get something that tastes good. If in America, you may have to whip up your *Creme Bruleé* with what they call "sour cream." Tone down the sour cream if you want with a bit of "whipping cream" and maybe add one or two beaten egg whites (or whole eggs) to stiffen the mixture. [If you put the whole eggs in with a little flour, you end up with *Crepes Suzette*.] There is no "one right way" to cook a dinner or to make a deal. The expert always ads a personal touch. A secret pinch of this or that to give it his trademark touches. Cinnamon and powdered ginger are both good little ingredients for desserts. Try adding a pinch or three.

Putting all this stuff together in a very smooth blend (a blender is OK to use only if you don't have a fork). Put the white goop in the hot pan, and very fast put the pan under a broiler already very very hot so the sugar mixture gets a little scorched. Fast. Like 30 seconds. Max. You do not want the cream to liquefy. Then before things cool off. Pour the extra sauce and a shot glass or two of liquor over your Bruleé. Use something very high proof that burns like Grand Marnier (Cherry, Lemon or Orange Triple Sec). Then shove it back in the oven until the heat from the broiling element (or gas) causes your casserole pan to explode in a rainbow of flames. These fireworks will really impress your guests. They might burn the house down too. But it's all part of the excitement.

If you like Japanese Blandness, just use some tasteless vodka. Anyway, set the almost finished desert on fire one way or another. Use a match if you are afraid to put it back under the broiler. Then enjoy watching the wicked flames of this sinful snack. When the fire goes out after a few seconds, be sure the candles are still burning (so you can see). Then try eating the stuff. It is hard to go wrong unless you burn it. But don't worry about the flambé sauce burning your dessert. Those flames are strictly decoration and the heat is all dissipated on top.

If your first attempt to make Creme Bruleé doesn't smell good, look good and taste good, play with the ingredients till it does. You might also check out another recipe.

Another suggestion. If Bruleé is not your thing, go for the pancakes (*Crepes Suzette*). Alternatively, leave out the cream and try it (butter & brown sugar) with bananas instead of cream. Do not mash the bananas. Just split them once, lengthwise. It will be flaming fried bananas all right with brown sugar and butter sauce. But that is only worth four bucks. *Banana Flambé a la Trevellian* with the story of where you got the recipe is worth $39 (in perceived value) as a romantic serving for two. Serve with violin music and candlelight. It is all in the packaging and presentation.

How Do You Make A Deal?

Putting together a deal is not so different from cooking something successfully. That's why I told you all about experimenting & ending up with Crepes or bananas if your first product didn't' come out right.

Let me spell it out. You will see certain ingredients. There are always ingredients around for putting together a successful deal or a successful meal. Anyone who bothers to open his eyes will always find a few hungry people. They may be hungry for love, power, food, money, health, prestige, beauty, and amusement. This is your *market*. None of the other jerks standing around with their hands in their pockets can see what you see. Why? They did not buy this book or have a mommy or daddy who was a role model. They were not asking the right questions, like:

How can you sell 25¢ worth of bananas for $39 — and have your customers praise you for one of the great culinary experiences of a lifetime? I just showed you. This is what an entrepreneur does 99 times a day. He has ideas. More ideas than time to try them all out. Some work, some don't. But if you don't try, if you don't experiment and fail many times, you can never make it big.

Find a need and fill it. Or *create a need and fill it.* Create a new product out of whatever you have plenty of, and figure out a way to make it appealing.

The Ultimate Entrepreneur

Years ago, a master marketer, Joe Cossman made millions selling rubber shrunken heads that were (for a time) hung from every rear view car mirror in the USA. He also invented the ant farm (two pieces of glass with sand plus a few ants sandwiched in the middle). However, my all time favorite was the "Spud Gun." Cossman tells it this way: "There was a massive over-supply of potatoes one year in America. Nobody wanted to see another potato at any price. The government came up with more and more recipes for potatoes.

I said, to myself "They are going about this all wrong. There are only so many potatoes one can eat. What other uses are there for potatoes?" So I picked up a popgun (toy) pulled off the cork, stuck it in a potato. I cut off the potato so that when you shot the popgun, a chunk of the potato went flying. Eureka! That was my prototype. The later improved model had a child safe potato chunker so there was no danger of the kids taking out a chunk of themselves with my new toy.

My sales campaign went 'Buy your kid a spud gun. Do your patriotic duty. Help the farmers.' We got a lot of free publicity out of that, especially when I had a load of spud guns and surplus potatoes dropped off at the Chicago Commodities Exchange. We sold a lot of spud guns to the brokers and gave away a lot more to the media people."

Cossman made a million or more on Spud Guns in an era when a million was real money, not just the price of an average waterfront home.

Now you know how to make a deal. If you didn't get it, at least you know how to make Creme Bruleé, Pancakes *(Crepes Suzette)* and fried bananas.

What Does This Have To Do With "Offshore?"

That's a good question. In the last chapter, I said, "Create your own deals." My current squeeze read it and said "I just hate it when some smart ass know-it-all author in a 'how to book' tells me something vague like 'Create your own deals' without a detailed follow up." So to keep her happy and so you will not hate me this is the baby talk explanation of how to create your own deals — onshore or offshore...

How To Create An "Offshore Deal?"

What do they have offshore that we do not have onshore? Find it, bottle it, and sell it. People are already selling anonymous bearer savings accounts from Austria called Sparbuchs and a similar product from Italy. These accounts cost nothing to open (except for the money you deposit), but the going price in the USA was to be $500 each. I know that the folks at Expat World and Scope have moved about 10,000 of these Sparbuchs out by mail order. The only thing unique about them was that they could not be advertised and sold legally in America. I guess that is why they sold so many, so fast. Lately people are selling "bank introductions" by mail at $1,000 a crack. Then they get a commission from the bankers for bringing in clients. I can introduce you (for nothing) to plenty of bankers who will take your money.

Maybe in Europe I could sell introductions to Sears & Roebuck or J.C. Penny. On second thought, that is not as ridiculous as it sounds. Why couldn't you sell catalogs you got for free? *Computer Shopper,* which is only about $4 in the USA goes for $25 in Switzerland. The Japanese especially are very hungry for imported mail order items. Maybe you could sell *translations of catalogs.*

Get me started and I have a million and one ideas.

What do you have in your home country that they *do not* have "Offshore?" Same instructions. Get foreign licensing and sales rights on some local American product. It may have appeal somewhere just because it is exotically American.

For The Passive Investor

If you have already made more money than you can spend, then why do deals? Just find a few money managers, apportion your assets in securities or other passive investments, and let your managers break their *cohones* for all those good deals and hot investments.

My personal technique is to divide my assets up into equal tranches (that's financial jargon for portions — like bundles or packages). I give tranches of about the same amount to three or four different money managers. Then, after a year has gone by, I compare performance.

Next, step? Weed out the poorest manager, and replace him. This process goes on continuously. With any luck I make a pretty good return — tax free of course. I even play around — having a few bucks with Harris my Panama financial guru. So far its been very profitable, but no matter how much he makes me I will always stay diversified with investments in several countries and in many markets. That was true even before I read Nevada White's chapter, "Don't Make My Mistakes." As you recall, he was doing so well with one particular money manager that he transferred all his assets to one place. Next thing, Big Brother grabbed the entire mother lode and poor Nevada was broke.

See back pages (Resource Section) for specific suggestions, names of banks and money managers.

Chapter 20

Best Places To Hide Money Offshore

*T*HERE are quite a few offshore banking centers where the USA is much less likely to look and where there is far more secrecy than in Switzerland. All the usual tax haven — bank secrecy places are no secret. They are certainly well known to tax authorities. Certain countries like Germany even publish a "Black List" of tax havens and offshore money centers. When any local citizen has reported dealings with places on the *black list,* those dealings are always flagged for further investigation and a detailed audit.

The USA doesn't follow the same path. Offshore dealings do not trigger an audit, *per se.* But politicians (of all countries) watch ads and read best selling books. Then to get personal publicity, they publicly *point with concern* at popular practices. Bureaucrats pander to politicians, and the next thing you know, they are going after the exposed situation. What should this teach you?

1) If everybody is doing it, don't do it.

2) Hide things in unlikely spots. For instance, English speakers will usually patronize banks and brokers where English is the prime language. No government people will be looking for you or your assets in an unlikely place. Like Panama, Uruguay or Singapore. There are many wonderful vacation spots and bank havens where I'd venture to say there are very few Americans. I have mentioned a few here, but have not mentioned all of them in this book because once I do, they may become favorites. But you can go to the Internet and look up facts about every country

in the world. Check on Fiji. No extradition treaties last time I looked. Good infrastructure and communications. Great beaches. Speak English. I could say the same things about Mauritius and the Seychelles. Israel too.

As long as a particular "offshore" country is not perceived as conniving in creating a major drain on USA tax revenues, they are not going to be pressured. The department of state is far too busy buying UN votes and pressuring national governments on a myriad of other causes. To avoid some eager beaver bureaucrat applying the usual big brother tactics and undermining these last few bastions of banking secrecy and efficiency, I will not mention any more of them here but will offer a few more places and secret techniques as suggestions to individual consulting clients depending upon their objectives and needs. [Note: I am not trying to get you to purchase my consulting services by holding out secrets, nor am I trying to conceal anything. Just making contact, much less hiring me as a consultant is such a formidable task, it will be beyond the capabilities of most. You don't need me, the answers are here. If you read this book carefully, and look for the names of these places in other contexts in my various books. You will find them. You must learn to read between the lines. The constraints of writing partly for the USA market make it essential for me to be discreet. I fear I am not discreet enough!

The Best Place To Hide Yourself Or Your Assets Is The Least Commonly Used Hiding Place

The basic rule is "Hide a diamond in a pile of sand." Or if you still don't get it, try to think independently of the crowd. Again! If everyone is doing it, it's the wrong thing to do. Realize that if a certain tax avoidance (or evasion) scheme or banking location is being touted in books or at widely advertised seminars, that particular game (if it ever was any good) is already over. Publicity and big advertised seminars is the kiss of death. Nobody is advertising and holding seminars telling you to go to the Sultanate of Brunei (near the Philippines) and invest there. Have you heard anyone touting Gambia (in Africa)? I am not saying those are the best places, or even good places. But at least if you have a creditor problem or if the tax collectors are after you, they probably won't bother to look for you or your money in such off-the-beaten-track places. Not unless you have left them a road map by telling potential informants of your intentions.

For Americans, a place that uses American money and has no exchange restrictions can be interesting. Panama runs on New York City time and, having no currency of its own uses greenbacks as legal tender. Liberia used to be in the same category, but that changed recently when the local two-bit dictator made it mandatory to exchange greenbacks for worthless local paper money. Anyway, Liberia is too inconvenient. Panama is not a bad choice as it is far less popular with Americans than Cayman and the Bahamas. But what's good is you don't have to get there via a direct flight. You can go via San Jose Costa Rica, Tegucigalpa, Honduras, Guatemala City, or Mexico. If you would like a real adventure, you can even drive there on the Pan American Highway from the USA. Another possibility is Argentina where the local currency is pegged to the dollar and changes hands at one to one. Uruguay is the banking center for South Americans. You will not find many gringos with accounts there. Finally, there are some of the Asian Tiger economies. Everyone in the orient deals in cash. They have no conception of "money laundering" and the costs of forex transactions (changing money) in any amounts is nominal.

Back To (Yeech!) Switzerland

Even perfidious Switzerland can be a safe depository if you have your assets registered in another (new) name. Needless to say, it is essential that your alternate (new) identity is not known to anyone BACK HOME who might want to sue you or sic Big Brother onto you. Giving the devil credit, most of the smaller Swiss banks give very good service. They answer the phone on one ring, don't screw up your orders, and unless you are an American they don't care much about how much cash you move in or out.

Who *Shouldn't* Know Where You Keep Your Money?

1) First and foremost, keep it a secret from any lawyer, accountant, financial advisor or anyone holding a license currently living or practicing in your home country. Whew, that was a long sentence. Read it over again. Due to conspiracy laws and reporting requirements, all USSR (whoops, excuse the typo, USA) professionals including doctors, lawyers and accountants have been co-opted. They are now essentially government agents. Attorney-Client privilege does not apply if you tell your lawyer about any *future* questionable activities you plan on engaging in. If your attorney does not report your plans to authorities, he is automatically guilty as a co-conspirator. With legal niceties like this lurking in the woodwork, I would not trust a USA based attorney (or CPA) whit any sensitive information.

2) Potential ex-employees, potential ex-wives, ex-lovers, and potential ex-business partners.

3) Add to that list all friends, relatives, casual and intimate acquaintances plus anyone who might sue you or dislike you for any reason plus anyone who knows your (old) name.

There you have **a list of those *who must not know anything* about your offshore finances.**

Chapter 21

How Your Enemies Get Leads On Your Whereabouts And Assets

ALMOST every government has tax collection staff assigned the job of ferreting out high net worth individuals who don't pay "their fair share" of taxes or those who do not file at all. In recent times, merely having substantial assets is enough to make someone a target in the USA. There have been many instances reported to us where people who pay vast amounts of taxes (like the infamous Leona Helmsley) are investigated and then either criminally indicted or subjected to seizures for actions that were previously considered "normal." People outside of bureaucracy sometimes wonder how the lottery works. Who will be the next person to be targeted? "Will it be me?" In a recent discussion, a former officer of the Inland Revenue Service of Great Britain explained their system to us. His words can prepare us well:

Real Estate Purchases And Sales

The biggest single source of leads for a heavy tax office investigation is the record of taxes paid that flows into their office when an expensive residential property (real estate) changes hands. An offshore company owner or any new name in the property owner's register guarantees a discerning follow up. What is involved? Normally there is a personal visit to the property by a tax officer to ask the occupant, neighbors, seller, and lawyer who handled the transaction "Who is the real owner? Who are the people using the property? How much time do they spend here?" If the person they decide is the power behind the scenes (i.e. the real owner) does not have an iron clad fiscal address somewhere else (where he actually pays income taxes), he will be deemed resident for tax purposes a target to be personally interviewed.

Property ownership records are the most lucrative source of leads. Why? Because real property, being illiquid, can be seized. It provides tax authorities with a valuable asset that can be frozen or seized. A person who owns expensive property can be presumed by local authorities to be a resident, subject to taxes. The starting point of bureaucratic logic is "If a person owns an expensive home or rental property, he either lives there (and as a resident, owes substantial income taxes) or, the property is rented out and substantial income taxes are due on the rental income.

Never Own An Expensive Home!

Thus, the Most Important Rule for PT's? Never, ever own property unless you are willing to either:

1) Pay income taxes in the locality where you own a home — based upon your visible assets and lifestyle or

2) You own your property in a tax haven where no taxes would be due or

3) You regard your local property as disposable (and you don't mind .abandoning it). Property mortgaged for more than it is worth would be in this category.

Media Exposure — Avoid It!

A special unit in every tax office develops leads by monitoring the media. Agents are constantly clipping newspaper articles and especially the magazine section feature profiles. Any person written up in an article emitting the scent of wealth (or tax avoidance) will trigger a check of the subject's recent tax returns. If that person is a foreigner, it will also likely cause the immigration department to review his or her status. Has the person been in the country for more than the allowed six months? Other agencies also get leads on potential targets from the press. The same is true of radio and television: Talk show guests. People who are the subject of news spot about their business activities, lifestyle, luxurious home, or expensive sporting activities are all likely to be subjected to further investigation. If there is no record of the taxpayer or if the amount of taxes paid are inconsistent with the information noted from the media, then a personal follow up is made. Surprisingly enough, when there is news of a big burglary or kidnap for ransom, if you don't already have enough trouble, the tax people will be over to investigate you.

What's the lesson? **Publicity can be the kiss of death.** Unless you want bureau-rats investigating your personal life and finances, **stay out of the newspapers, off television and off the radio.** The mere fact that you are mentioned on the news as the owner of an art collection, race horse, or that you love helicopter-skiing [or any other very expensive sport], will eventually cause you to come to the attention of authorities. They haven't been cruising the Internet for suspects except for kiddie-porn peddlers. But the cops will surely be putting detectives on the net-surfing circuits.

If You Don't Like Heat, Stay Out Of The Kitchen

It goes without saying that once you are involved with any criminal associations, arrests or criminal investigations it will open a bag of worms. Probing questions and investigations take place. Government agents will explore all possibilities asking themselves and each other, "How do we get rid of this bum?" Obviously, brawls, traffic violations, lawsuits, all activities leading to possible confrontations are best sidestepped. Avoid attracting heat if you don't want to get burned!

Another source of leads is readily available lists of expensive "thing" owners — and to a much lesser extent, long term renters. Thus, public records may be used to zero in on all registered owners of Rolls Royce's, Land Rovers, Ferraris, BMWs, Cadillacs, cellular phones, speed boats, yachts, renters of large boat or plane mooring spaces, long term tenants of expensive houses or apartments. Lesson? Don't own or (at least in your permanent hangout area) even rent very expensive things that would indicate you have a substantial income or high net worth. Merely having things registered in a trust, company or offshore name will not deflect scrutiny unless the expensive boat, and plane or car is really used mainly in a tax haven.

In places like Monte Carlo, the only cars that look out of place are the ones costing *under* $250,000. [Only joking. There are plenty of low profile people in Monte Carlo with cheap cars.] In your own country however, investigators for an ambulance chaser or collection lawyer know enough to zero in on the real owner/user by simply observing the situation and asking questions. Merely pretending you are a caretaker or renter won't wash if the private eye hasn't had a lobotomy.

Information Exchange Treaties

Income flows such as interest or dividends sent abroad to a foreigner are now regularly reported between governments of some countries. Thus, a British person who gets interest or dividends from USA banks or companies will have these dividends reported to the British tax office and vice versa. Beware of governments having an exchange of tax information treaty. There will be a crosscheck to see if your foreign receipts are being reported on a local tax return. If there is no tax return or if they are not reported "there comes trouble." How to avoid this problem? Simply have your assets held in their own name by an offshore institution in a tax haven or place with bank secrecy. Offshore banks and brokers always hold client investments in straw names. That is why if you ever got to look at the corporate shareholder registers of IBM or General Motors, you'd see less than 3% "real names." Most registered stockholders are interesting entities like Vaduz A Nominees, Vaduz B Nominees, etc.

Note for the umpety umph time that I've told you Switzerland's bank secrecy has been eroded over the last few years. For Americans a Swiss account is almost as vulnerable as an account at the corner bank back home. Swiss bank accounts held in the name of American citizens are no longer protected by bank secrecy! A foreign trust or company you have set up in a jurisdiction like Switzerland or even Canada can help protect your privacy — but only if no one knows or can find out the name and the location of the assets. How do investigators find out where you've moved your money? Phone taps. Paper trails. Loose lips.

Informants

Tips from informants are a big source of leads: Jealous neighbors, disgruntled employees, unhappy relatives, jilted lovers or spouses. Business associates who make a deal to get out of trouble themselves by putting you into the soup. Housekeepers or snoopers who simply want to collect the rewards that most governments now offer. How to minimize the Risks? Avoid confrontations and conflicts. Avoid telling friends your financial secrets. Never tell anyone personal information that could be used against you. If your immigration papers are not in order or if you fear that an enemy will find out your whereabouts or status — these are the last things you should discuss with anyone.

Use Of Large Amounts Of Cash In Countries With Money Laundering Laws

Cash payments or deposits. In many countries, new money laundering laws supposedly enacted to catch drug dealers are being used by bureau-rats to cast an ever-widening net around all lovers of privacy. Merely purchasing travel tickets or a car for all cash gets reported to the local police or tax agency. Likewise making a substantial cash deposit, wire transfer, or withdrawal in any bank, currency exchange, gambling casino, etc. The net result of any "suspicious transfer" could be a request for a "little interview" where your entire lifestyle and finances are probed in detail.

Commercial Mailing Lists

Magazine subscriptions, club memberships, mailing lists. The late Gay Edgar Hoover, unlamented head of America's FBI found himself personally on the mailing list of the Mattatachine Society, a gay organization. He made great efforts to have himself taken off even though he was said to be a fan of nude-boy art and was quite pleased to have a free look at this sort of magazine. Yet Hoover was aware that the contents of mailing lists or customer lists are often used by snoops, government agents and reporters to make conclusions about peoples habits, inclinations, finances, hobbies or lifestyles. Marijuana users were often entrapped because their subscriptions to *High Times* lead local police to them or more often because ads placed by Federal Agencies for paraphernalia, seeds, or grow lights were used to identify and entrap home growers. If you must, get publications, mail or faxes that are sensitive sent to a buffer address or person. Buy newspapers or magazines at a newsstand. For unavoidable, sensitive stuff like PT or Libertarian oriented publications, have such mail and books go to an anonymous name at a rented private mailbox. Be sure the box-renter intermediary does not know your address or true identity. Don't pick up any very sensitive stuff (like ID cards or passports) personally. Have these documents forwarded to you via a mail drop in another country!

Once You Are Investigated

Although the following sources are not usually used to get leads that bring about investigations, once a person is targeted, you can count on this sequence of events with any investigator for any bureaucracy in any country:

Telephone records: These are easily obtained and will always yield a rich harvest of information for further follow up. Investigators will get a record of every telephone call (or fax) made to or from the phone in your home. In all jurisdictions he will know of all things charged to your phone (including collect calls). The investigator thinks he will know the identity and whereabouts of all your friends, bankers, brokers, and business contacts. But will he? Not if you placed all-important calls from a public phone using an anonymously purchased phone calling card or coins. Important! The only calls made from your telephone should be to the local Pizza Joint.

Credit card records: If the same name or address known to the investigator is on your credit card, even if it is an internationally issued card (from another country) any investigator can learn almost everything there is to know about you. What trips did you take? What hotels did you stay in? With whom? If you charged toll-roads, and gas, your hourly movements can be plotted. By following up and contacting hotel(s), agents will get the numbers on identification cards or passports used by yourself and your companions. If a charge card is used every few days, he can precisely establish your whereabouts and movements. For tax purposes, charge account records can prove you were inside a given country long enough to be subject to its income taxes. To keep your affairs private, get a credit card in a different name or in a company name and use it carefully and sparingly. The worst mistake you could make is to have a credit card that leads to your mother lode of bank deposits or other assets. Always have your credit card (if you must have one at all) from where you have a small bank account fed by deposits not providing an information highway (a paper trail) to your serious money.

Mail cover and communications taps: Once you are the target of an investigation, your incoming mail can be monitored and photocopied to determine the location and identity of your correspondents. If bank and broker statements regularly appear in your mail, the nature of your assets is revealed and your goose is cooked. In most countries, even if local mail is theoretically protected against opening, *foreign mail is never subject to privacy* protections. The theory is that even a small letter could contain some illegal narcotic substances. Thus, the "incidental discovery" of other information that can be used against you is justified, these days, by the international drug war again. We all know this drug war is an excuse used to invade the privacy of all persons.

E-mail: Copies of all your correspondence as well as all Web Sites you have visited are easily available to investigators. # PGP encryption: good privacy is good protection.

Anonymous remailers: Can offer some protection, but these outfits are regularly pressured to roll over. Non co-operative service providers are sabotaged and shut down by Big Brother. If your anonymous remailer or mail drop is located abroad, your home government can't normally pressure them!

Lawsuit records: Your own testimony or the testimony of others concerning you is a rich source of information for bureau-rats. Many agencies regularly alert each other to interesting tidbits that might be developed into further investigations and prosecutions. Government prosecutors or investigators have a policy of turning over leads to their fellow operatives in other jurisdictions or countries. They know such co-operation leads to juicy prosecutions with evidence already given under oath. If a statement can't be retracted without subjecting the speaker to prosecution for perjury, it is much stronger than many other types of evidence. Rule? Stay out of court and if possible, never have your name mentioned in anyone else's disputes.

Keep your house and office clean and clear of evidence: Imagine a search of your home or office. Right now! Every record, every scrap of paper, and every computer disc is seized. Imagine that the whole truth as thus revealed was known about you. Consider what if every letter, every computer file, and every item in your premises was subjected to in depth scrutiny? Suppose the person going through your things was a determined bureau-rat whose promotion depended upon putting you in jail. Don't kid yourself. Not only every PT, but almost everyone could be charged with some offense. But you say, "An in-depth search of my home, my office and confiscation of all my possessions? It couldn't happen to me?"

It cannot happen to me: Famous last words! It does happen many times — even to low profile people. In one instance, reported recently on television, the whole world saw a photo of a missing child who had been abducted by her own father in violation of a local court order giving custody to the mother. In a far away country, a viewer of the program via satellite reported a single father, a neighbor she didn't like, was the kidnapper. His kid didn't look anything like the missing one. He didn't look anything like the father as shown on TV. But while they were out, because of this false report, his premises were searched. What happened? It turned out the cops found old letters and photos indicating the kid was indeed separated from its mother. The father and daughter were using different identity papers than another set found in the house. This meant major problems for the dad and child who had been living quietly for many years. The mother involved in this unrelated case didn't care about them any more, but the house search none-the-less uncovered compromising evidence of victimless crime. Dad went to jail; his daughter to an orphanage.

In other cases, a search for drugs or becoming a criminal suspect based upon a tip has resulted in many an unexpected search of premises having absolutely no connection with the original case. But evidence and clues picked up were then used against the householder who had been erroneously targeted. *Moral of the story: Never store files or anything that is even slightly incriminating in your home. Obviously, this goes double as to items on your person or in your car, boat, or plane* — especially when crossing borders. A search at an international crossing is much more likely than at any other time. Where should you leave your most sensitive things? Perhaps in a safe deposit box or rental small storage facility in another country with no trail to your real living address or the name you commonly use. Better yet, destroy or get rid of papers, photos, and anything else you don't really need. Another possibility, mail incriminating, but needed documents ahead before you cross a border.

Doing it legally: Every PT who is not already victimized by government starts out with the idea of doing it legally. But after a few years, no one [except perhaps a few lawyers or very high profile individuals] feels that it is worth the trouble to have every move checked and approved by an expensive army of accountants and lawyers. For instance: Many rich Swedes and newly rich Russians have discovered that if they stay at home and do the business that made them wealthy, the tax laws are so confused and contradictory that they would need to pay five or ten times their gross income to comply. So they move to a tax haven and only "visit" their homeland when absolutely necessary to do business. They want to do things legally, but after a while they find that there is no Eye-In-The-Sky watching them. As a PT they are free to do as they want, not as a myriad of governmental laws and regulations say they should act.

The bad news about Monaco: Many wealthy individuals move to Monaco to make it their tax haven home. I know I did in 1979. It seems like a good idea at first, but after a while, we learn that Monaco is over-crowded, very noisy, full of dog-poop on the streets, and that nosy Monaco authorities expect you to actually live in their overpriced apartments more than six months (continuously) per year.

Further, these same Monegasque authorities act like parents. They want to know everything about you. They require forms, forms, and more forms. Telephone conversations are probably all recorded automatically. Your mail may be intercepted. This is easily solved by having a mail drop across the road in France, or down the street in Italy. Information is exchanged with France and other countries. The Monegasque Gestapo may not be after you for income taxes, but the local authorities and those of many other tax havens want to keep resident foreigners on a short leash.

Typically, the person who went to Monaco as a tax-exile makes other arrangements within a few years. That is one reason why the turn over in Monaco property is one of the greatest in the world. In Bermuda or Cayman, other tax havens, people get what is locally known as "Rock Fever." Tiring of island life and petty gossip, they opt to become more internationally oriented PT's. But go back home to high taxes and lawsuits? Never!

In a song of the 1920's called MAKING WHOOPEE, the poor guy singing the ballad relates that he tells the judge his income is ten bucks a day, and then the judge awards his ex-wife twelve. Maybe it was a joke, but in the case of many personal consulting clients of your author, tax authorities levied fines and penalties on individuals that would bankrupt many an honest man. These fines were well beyond the capacity of my clients to pay and no solution was in sight except becoming a P.T. But back to "doing it legally."

Only USA Citizens *Must* Give Up Citizenship Everyone Else Can Just Move

Under the laws of all countries except the USA, local and national taxes can be entirely avoided (legally!) by simply moving out of the jurisdiction. For USA citizens, an additional step required is to shed the USA passport and citizenship. The next step (for everyone) is to establish a legal residence in a tax haven or a country that will treat you as if you were in a tax haven.

Take the case of the United Kingdom. People who are non-British, who move there from another country, can get legal residence papers without being considered domiciled for tax purposes. But to keep a tax free status, foreigners who live in say London, must jump through a lot of hoops:

Tax returns must be filed although no taxes will necessarily be due. Income earned abroad (outside of UK) is tax-free. Capital gains earned abroad are tax-free. All money spent in England must come from "Capital" not income.

In other words, a rich Swede living in England must put say £1,000,000 in a Swiss bank account and instruct the bank that all interest income from this account must go to still another account. Then the bank must provide statements and proof that all funds remitted to London came from a capital account, untainted by any income having been deposited to it.

Any property that is lived in and owned by the foreigner should be owned by an offshore company or trust. There is a minefield of little details one must be aware of in order to be legally tax free and unfortunately having the most expensive consultants you can find does not always guaranty you will be passed and approved by the authorities. In fact, once in an audit situation, the government itself is likely to make mistakes and assess taxes and penalties — no matter how many experts you had on your side to avoid confrontations.

There are many complex requirements to be resident yet non-domiciled for tax purposes. Thus, many people feel that it is simply easier (if they want to spend time in England) to come as a tourist for six months, and file no tax returns. As a practical matter, anyone can come and go as they please. The key matter is to depart before six months have gone by. In the UK, if one can prove with rent receipts that six months are spent in Ireland, there would not necessarily be any passport exit stamps, and one would be tax-free. With far less time, trouble and professional advisory fees, life can be equally tax fee and considerably simplified by being a Perpetual Tourist and on paper at least, never spending more than six months in any one country. The net result of being such a PT however is that there is some danger that one would be targeted as a tax evader. What does this mean? You get notified, usually by mail, to come into the tax office for an interview. Once interviewed, it is the beginning of the end. Even if ultimately exonerated, getting your personal parts in the wringer of an investigation is always expensive and uncomfortable. Thus the PT way is to:

DEMATERIALIZE "Beam me up Scotty!" Take steps needed to avoid official scrutiny. Obviously, avoid any interviews! If unwanted attention ever comes, simply get out of town in a hurry. Abandon use of your mail drops and exit the area (or even the country) at the first whiff of trouble. Do not return until things cool off. A year or two later, consider resettling but always in a different home — probably with a new identity. Learn from your mistakes and don't repeat whatever it was that brought the sniffers to your doorstep.

A PT wife who couldn't really comprehend what her husband was up to once asked me: "Why can't we be like everyone else?" "What exactly do you mean, I questioned. "Why don't we and live in a nice pretentious house with servants, join a country club, and forget all this business about tax-havens, offshore deposits, moving about and being low profile?"

The answer is that modern governments won't let you be a free person. Nor will they let you hold on to your assets. They insist that you waste your money on lawyers, accountants, and so much paperwork that you have little time to pursue your own interests. If you are lucky enough to have substantial wealth or income, you can choose to be like everyone else. But then you will surrender to government much more than half of your income and wealth. You'll spend time and energy plus you'll hire a staff to comply with reporting laws regarding income taxes, gift taxes, capital gain taxes, social security taxes, wealth taxes, estate and inheritance taxes. Unfortunately, even paying a huge amount in taxes does not guaranty that you will be free from unjust prosecutions or criminal charges. Ask Leona Helmsley. She and her husband were real estate millionaires who paid huge dollar amounts of taxes and did nothing more than what every other real estate operator was doing. Her particular scam was taking some unused carpeting from a hotel she owned, and installing it in her personal home without declaring it as additional "imputed" income. Her income would not have been increased by more than 1% if she reported her little game properly on her income tax forms.

Every accountant keeping records for owners in the rental property business assumed that criminal fraud would never be charged unless the chiseling involved sums amounting to over 33% of reported income. This "one-third" was the announced, long accepted rule of thumb, the ground rules of engagement. Sort of like (in some places) you can always exceed the speed limit by 5 miles per hour and no cop will bother you. The IRS might sue in a civil case over an improper deduction or suspected failure to report some income. They might even go after civil penalties and extra interest. However, as long as the taxpayer didn't get too out of line they didn't have to worry about a criminal prosecution. The government prosecutor, a piece of scum who wanted to get some politically useful publicity (and ultimately became Mayor of New York) chose to arbitrarily ignore the long acknowledged 33% "rule of thumb" and make an example of Leona. So much for wanting to be like everyone else. You are not secure even if you try to be like everyone else. "Everyone else" has their ass and their assets at risk! Only prosecutorial discretion stands between you and the jailhouse door. The choice, as Hamlet once said, is to PT (hold on to your freedom and assets), or not to PT and thus to lose them. Hamlet says: "One must take arms against a sea of troubles." The net amount of time spent by many wealthy non-PT's on thinking about taxes and dealing with the government is probably close to fifty percent of their total waking hours. The cost is at least fifty per cent of their wealth. The net amount of time and money spent on similar concerns by the PT [once initial paperwork is in place and life-plan is established] is probably closer to .01%.

When Residence In A Tax Haven Is Necessary

If a PT is immature enough to want an attention-getting car, a splashy home, and all the attention from con-men, thieves and kidnappers that go with a lifestyle of conspicuous consumption, then the best place to indulge is in a tax haven. There at least, excessive government harassment will not be part of the package of troubles. But for those willing to take up a more simple and solid upper-middle-class lifestyle, PT plus low profile is, we think, the only way to go. A PT can live anywhere and come and go as he pleases. Applying for an "official" permit simply gives a government power over you that IMO it doesn't need and shouldn't have. If you want to live in a tax haven rent an apartment there and stay as long as you want. Don't register. If you consider yourself "Passing Through" you will never be bothered. This author lived for two years in Monaco without registering. No one ever questioned my right to live there.

Reader comments on these thoughts are most welcome. Your constructive criticism or corrections will help us all get it right. Please contact the author from time to time. We PT's have to hang together — or else we'll get hung, alone!

Chapter 22

Three Tax Exiles Speak Out: Could You Be Happy After Leaving Your Home Country?

*R*ECENTLY, a group of four middle aged, expat American friends, who now base themselves in Paraguay, Amsterdam, Monte Carlo and Thailand, got together to enjoy each others company over a few beers in a bar in the Thai coastal resort of Pattaya. All had become practicing PT's before they'd even heard of the concept. Your author Peter Trevellian hosting the group, was one of them. For the benefit of those who do not fully appreciate the pros & cons of being a tax exile, I (Peter) decided to take notes on what the other three had to say about their past and present lives. Names & identifying facts have been changed.

How Albert, Barry And Carl Became Exiles

The cast of characters starts with the tale of:

Albert, a fifty year old Dealer in Arts, antiques and "anything else I can make a buck on".

How did you, Albert, happen to relocate "offshore?"

Albert: I was real estate developer. I made plenty of money in the USA, but from around 1980 found it harder and harder to do business, make profits and still comply with a steadily increasing number of silly or crazy environmental laws. One empty city lot where I was building a house (with all the necessary permits having been granted) was soggy, boggy and low.

Nothing lived there aside from *Culiseta Annulata* (common mosquitoes and their larvae). To get rid of the bog and its many bugs (as I had done on dozens of prior building-lot preparations), I filled it in with several truckloads of earth, dredged out of the swamps for the foundations. The net result would have been dry land, and many pretty little recreational lakes. This, in the eyes of the local greenies, turned me something worse than an axe murderer. To make a long story short, I was criminally indicted for violation of the *Wetland Protection Act.* This bit of nonsense makes it a Federal crime. to drain swamps or make any swampy wasteland productive.

After many hassles, I emerged from the experience with a felony conviction and a several year community service sentence in lieu of jail. If I did not do the community service "with enthusiasm and a proper attitude" my bureau-rat supervisor could have my probation revoked. Half of my net worth had gone for attorney's fees (which by the way were *not* tax deductible as a business expense — even if I had won).

Maybe I had a bad attitude, but I felt screwed by the system and unwilling to remain a part of it any longer. Also, I couldn't stomach working on a community service projects to rescue endangered mosquitoes and gnats. Of course, I am kidding about gnats. It was snails, toads, and leeches!

What Happened Then?

Albert: I decided to check out Mexico as a place to lay low. Before finishing my community service I went abroad on a tourist card (sort of visa). You didn't need a passport and this card, issued by Mexico was good for six months. It could be renewed indefinitely by crossing out for a few seconds, and then going back in again at any border of Mexico. My passport had been confiscated. But I was able to move my money out of the USA.

In my first six months as a fugitive, I met many men like myself in Mexico. Most told me to keep going South for prettier and more agreeable women. Costa Rica, the Dominican Republic, and Paraguay were particularly recommended. So after acquiring a set of identity documents, I kept moving in a general Southerly direction — staying for periods in Belize, Guatemala, Costa Rica, Panama,

Colombia, Peru, Argentina, Brazil and finally, Paraguay. I found that in the third world, in general, attractive young women are still attracted to wealthy older men. Companionship was a concern for me, but it was not a problem after a short stay in Antiqua, Guatemala where I learned Spanish very well and got it on with my dollar an hour "Maestra" or Spanish teacher. Once I could speak the local lingo, my relationships with the opposite sex blossomed.

I am now based in Paraguay. Have been there about ten happy years. It is easy to make money and stay out of trouble. The police settle everything with a wink and an appropriate *mordida* or tip. The main industry of the country is smuggling. Everything comes into Paraguay tax-free. Because of the neighboring countries' protectionist taxes and other levies on liquor, tobacco and luxury goods, there are good profits to be made.

Prior to my experience in the USA, I wouldn't have considered going into an illegal business, but if you can be jailed for making mosquitoes homeless, I figured I might as well go whole hog and do something really bad — like importing Kahlua, cars and other contraband. [I don't believe in illicit drugs!] There is no income tax in Paraguay, no matter how rich you are. Thus, I am happy to live where I do not have to keep any records or worry about audits. It was easy to get a Paraguayan passport via a local lawyer. My total cost to become a naturalized legal and registered citizen was under $10,000. It took about a year. I have renounced USA citizenship because if I didn't I would be committing another felony every year by not filing any USA income tax forms. Besides, I still had five years of community service in lieu of doing time at Club Fed. If I go back, for breaking parole, I would get five years-hard times! With things as they are, there is no point in trying to make a deal or ever going back. In the meantime, I can travel anywhere I want to go on my Paraguayan passport — usually without the need for a visa. Best of all, Paraguay is quite unfriendly to the Big Brother up North, and would never co-operate on an extradition — especially of one of their own citizens. Frankly, I do not think any country would extradite me for the crime of cleaning up a swamp! But I shall be careful and low profile anyway.

I left the States because I had no choice. A couple of decades on, I'm glad the choice was made for me. I would never go back to a country where I was so over-regulated and over-taxed that I never experienced real freedom. Yet the funny thing is, when I lived in the USA I had no inkling that there was any other possibility. I was like a bird in a cage. I thought I was free because I could flap my wings and make a little squawk now and then. But it wasn't until I got down to Mexico that I realized in the rest of the world you could actually fly! That is a metaphor.

Advantages And Disadvantages Of Being A PT?

I've got a stress free-life now. I have had no trouble making money South of the border, even though I left the USA with not quite enough capital to make it strictly on investment income alone.

The disadvantages of leaving — especially when you are forced to leave suddenly, are that you leave behind old friends, contacts. It can be a wrenching and lonely experience at first. If extroverted, you soon make new pals. You lose the "social standing" you built up back home.

In my case, as a convicted felon, my social status was nil: I could not even vote any more! And believe me, it was no great loss to leave my ex-wife's alimony claims behind. My few remaining friends visit me in Asuncion, and express envy over my lifestyle down in Paraguay. My grown kids love to visit me in exotic places like the Moravian Chaco Desert or tropical Phuket. As long as I pay for their trip, I can have them around during all their vacations. But I don't. A once a year visit is sufficient.

Without Big Brother defining everything that's any fun a crime in the USA, and requiring me to fill out forms every time I get in the car or go to lunch, it's a new world. I love my newfound freedom and those local experiences I have everyday. In addition, I live far better now (on much less money) than I could ever have done in the States. I have several maids, a governess for my new baby, a driver, cook, and a gardener. The price of all these servants is dirt-cheap. What I pay for the whole bunch is about what I'd pay for one domestic in New York City.

Helpful Hints For New PT's?

Do not constantly compare things with the way they were "back home". You will annoy the people in your new country, and frustrate yourself. It is third world. That means bodies are cheap, and infrastructure could be a lot better. Some things in Paraguay are forty years behind the times. So what if they don't have four lane highways and Sarah Lee Cheesecake? You don't get lovely Paraguayan Harp concerts at lunch in London's Savoy Grill but you do here. Any electronic gadgets or other big boy toys you can't find in Asuncion, you can buy in the bigger cities of South America. Or you can send for things by mail order or have a friend bring in stuff for you. You might even make some money by importing (for the local expat market) some of the things you miss.

Don't Complain. Accept And Learn New Customs

Eat local foods. Above all, learn the local language. Read the local newspapers, and become a minor patron of the arts or otherwise be a good citizen and part of the new scene. Join clubs like Rotary or Lions. You will make new friends! As an "exotic" guy of independent means, you will probably be accepted at the highest level of society. Fit in as well as you can. Be flexible. Don't always seek to hang out with expats or other PT's. Do not flaunt your wealth with any status symbols — cars, clothes, watches, etc. It can only bring trouble. Being well off enough to hire a few servants at $50 per month apiece that is one thing, but appearing to be seriously wealthy will only attract burglars and kidnappers in South America. On balance, I think the quality of life for me now is better in South America than it was in the USA.

The Wealthy Man Who Left Forever

Barry, age 62, despite his modest appearance and comments, was (and may still be) the major stockholder of a New York Stock Exchange Listed Company he founded to sell organic health products.

Same Question: How Did You Happen To Leave The Land Of The Free And The Home Of The Brave?

Barry: I made quite a bit of money in mail order, most recently in vitamins and other honest organic "not tested on animals" products. My first company went public. I walked away with three million bucks, which was big money at the time (1970's). After that, I started another non-competing business. In one mail shot a few years back, I offered a bonus can of vitamins for the first fifty people to respond to my order for another product, I got a few thousand responses as I expected. To keep them all happy, we sent them all the "free" vitamins. Would you believe this turned out to be a crime, according to the Federal Trade Commission? They also had plenty of other complaints about my business such as the fact that "vitamin" isn't a politically correct word now "vitamin" is illegal to use in ads. (You have to say "food supplement".) After illegally opening my mail, and raiding my office and apartment for records, they wanted me to plead guilty to a dozen felony counts and do five years of easy time in a country club jail. Unlike Albert, I decided not to fight and go through all that nonsense, but rather to take a powder. I had another worry too. I had been a very minor marijuana dealer when I was a kid in the 1960's and although the statute had run out on that, I figured it might come up at my trial, and give the judge an excuse to grab my entire net worth as "the fruits of crime." He might have sentenced me for six lifetimes and thrown the key away. The justice system is so crazy, you can't begin to predict what will happen to you. That's why I left early, at the first whiff of trouble.

What Happened Then?

I moved my ass and my assets abroad and established a new business in Amsterdam where, among other advantages, I can continue with my vitamin mail order business into the States or anywhere else without worrying that I am going to be sent to prison as a felon just because I give out a free bonus can of vitamins, or because I call my vitamins what they have always been called, namely vitamins — not "food supplements."

Advantages And Disadvantages Of Living Abroad?

Besides smoking pot, I didn't pay taxes in my youthful grass dealing days nor did I file any government papers before I got involved with going public. After twenty years as a Boy Scout, paying hundreds of thousands in income taxes, and in and out of lawyers and accountant's offices — I am finally back in the underground economy where I feel most comfortable and free. I will always be underground. No licenses. No paperwork.

My main hangout is Amsterdam, but I like to get away from Europe for the winters. Usually I go to Bali, but I get stopovers in Thailand and Singapore included with my cattle-class round-trip-ticket for $900. Sometimes I stay in Goa or Sikkim. I am not a legal resident, but have the right passports to live anywhere for as long as I please. Identity documents are easy to come by if you make the effort.

I certainly do not pay any taxes anywhere, nor have I become a legal resident anywhere. No government knows where I sleep. I have not renounced my USA citizenship, but if they won't renew my passport I don't really give a hoot. I have picked up at least one other "Paper Trip" passport on my travels. I suppose I probably should file USA income tax returns because with the $70,000 earned income deduction and a little creativity, I wouldn't have to pay any USA tax — but I just don't like the idea of being tied into an annual record keeping obligation and the possibility that they will call me in for questioning or an audit. My idea of freedom is to be free of having to justify my existence annually to Big Brother. Therefore, I will not buy into the system by accepting any "obligations" to file any papers with any government unless I absolutely have to.

The Eden Press "underground books" published out of California has been useful, as have the Hill, PT books. I don't go along with everything said in those books, but they certainly have been a major source of ideas for me.

Any More Helpful Hints?

Keep on truckin! For those not familiar with cartoons of the Great Crumb, this means just go on one day at a time. Be ready to move like Bambi when Big Brother comes a gunning. I never learned Dutch because they all speak English in Amsterdam. After all, I was one of the original guys into natural products after the USA government began spraying poison (paraquat) on marijuana. Everything I dealt in had to be organically grown on mom and pop dope farms in Mendocino County, California. I kept my customers healthy when the US government was infecting millions of smokers with canker sores and ultimately cancers inside their mouths. The decline of pot use and growth of cocaine addiction in the USA was a direct result of this government sponsored poison spray activity. I had to retire from my mellow business when the vicious Colombians took over the USA markets.

I was pleased to find the old California Haight /Ashbury ambiance in Amsterdam today — where marijuana is legal, tolerated, and doesn't cause the physical damage of cocaine. My attractive hippie casual workers (in my own vitamin business) are very caring and accommodating. Good people. It comes with the territory. I don't have any servants, and don't want any. Cars are polluting and I wouldn't drive one. I get around on a bike. I guess I am an arch-greeny, myself. In fact the only thing I can agree with Albert on is that the USA is a dangerous place for anyone with an original idea, a streak of individuality or his own creative business. How they can put people in jail for marijuana related offense beats me.

When the Wall Street Journal reporters came round to do a front page profile on me a couple years back, I just said: "You must have the wrong guy, I don't have 3c jingling in my jeans." I sure don't need the kiss of death that a profile in their rag would bring me. I am only going along with this "interview" now because Peter Trevellian says my advice to others might be a help to people in the same boat, as I was — like-kindred souls. Anyway, I know that my name and identifying "facts" in his story will be changed enough to make me unrecognizable even to my own mother.

Tale Of A Tycoon

Carl, 57 years old, Trader, Tycoon and Investor

How did you become an expatriate?

Carl: Before I moved abroad to become a PT, I was an entrepreneur with a dozen different businesses. I seemed to thrive in an atmosphere of deal making and stress. I spent a hundred grand a year on Chartered Accountants just to keep my books and make sure I did not have to pay any taxes. We did this with offshore trusts and Marc Harris types of legal "structures" as we used to call them. Mostly. I didn't feel unfree, because I regarded every single new tax or regulating law, no matter how stupid, as an opportunity to make another million. All I had to do was figure a way to get around it, one way or another. That's what I had lawyers for. Mark Rich and I had a lot in common though he had a higher profile. For instance, when the US government during the Nixon era, set two prices on oil, one very low, lets say $5 a barrel on domestically produced oil used domestically, and $9.99 on imported oil, I just bought all the USA oil I could get for "domestic use". Then I exported the "domestic" to where it was needed. I sold at full world price or I traded for imported oil to be delivered Stateside. This had to be done before everyone else figured out how to do the same thing. And I must admit a few government bureaucrats on the inside, also in my employ helped me with advice and proper timing. When everyone and their brother got into these deals in a few months, the law was repealed as unworkable. So for a short while, I made $5- each on ten million barrels. For readers who have never been in such deals, your gross sounds very good — $50 Million in my case, but after commissions, bribes, shipping, insurance, transport and taxes, I was able to clear maybe $20 Million.

This exact same activity (arbitraging domestic vs. foreign oil) is exactly what got Marc Rich into trouble. I was one of several hundred others who did the same thing. Most of us simply were not targeted. Marc Rich had a high profile. Nobody ever heard of me outside of my professional contacts. There were similar deals made by me every year of my life — and similar profits. Usually I made out like a bandit. I cannot think of a single year that I didn't clear over a couple of million bucks. The secret is good government contacts — and they have to be paid off. Whenever there is a lot of government interference in the free markets, there are opportunities for people like me to make serious money. What "libertarian types" see as something nearly sinful, I see as opportunity calling. With ever changing subsidy deals and parities, tariff tinkering and price supports, there are a lot of sure things for insiders.

Another example of how I made all this serious money? For Instance: Whenever there was a major devaluation of any currency, for a few days before local prices adjusted, I bought commodities at the old, pre-devaluation prices (in the local currency). Obviously, they will rise in price to world market levels.

Peter Trevellian: "I don't understand, please explain."

O.K. Coffee is 1,000 Cruzeros a pound in Brazil and sells for $1 a pound in the USA. 1,000 Cruzeros equals $1. [To keep the example simple we are omitting obviously needed calculations for shipping, insurance, and processing.]

All of a sudden the Brazilian Government says "Cruzeros will stay the same value for internal transactions, but they are only worth 500 to the dollar for international deals. The reason for this devaluation is to help our exports says the Trade Commissar. Full of noble impulses and tipped off a few days before the devaluation, I decide to help the government of Brazil's exports. I buy ten million pounds of coffee at 1000 Cruzeros (or 50c per pound) and then sell the coffee at $1 a pound. I make $5 million on the devaluation. Get it? It's a legal commodity trade.

If it's so easy then why doesn't everybody do it?

Carl: That is the most stupid question you have ever asked Peter. I suspect you are pulling my chain and really know the answer. *Everybody doesn't do obvious things to make a buck because not everybody is smart like us.*

Did Something Go Wrong?

"Something" always goes wrong in every deal — but you do your best to wiggle your way out of your mistakes. If you are talking about the oil deal, in my case, sure there were minor glitches, but I came out smelling like a rose. The statute of limitations has run out long ago, so I could not be prosecuted as Marc Rich was.

Although what I do is usually legal, various government agencies in the USA were always on my case for evading the spirit of the law, or one thing or another. If you are in my business, you have to expect problems with the regulators and tax collectors. The trick is to quit while you are ahead. Of course the funny thing is, even if you are in the most legal of businesses or professions, some government agency is always breathing down your neck. My doctor nearly went to prison for prescribing pills that worked, but were not approved for the particular illness that she prescribed them for. My butcher actually did go to jail because his smoked hams that had somewhat higher water content than was legally allowed. And this was in spite of his hams being selected as the best gourmet hams in the USA. It was probably the technical violations of federal standards that made them so outstandingly juicy and delicious. The truth seems to be that the only thing keeping anyone in or out of the criminal justice system is blind luck — good or bad.

Eventually, I decided to pick up my chips, move to a tax haven, retire and play for smaller stakes. I chose to rent a waterfront apartment in the Monte Carlo Star, which I regard as the best apartment building in the world. Although I didn't ever become an official resident, my office is in my third and spare bedroom. No more big staff, no more big deals like I used to do. I am quite happy in Monaco, living mainly on my investment income. But I do enough deals to keep myself in bread and jam. I notice the Prince recently called his little Principality a "Sunny place for shady people." I suppose that fits.

Your Passport?

Because I wangled an EU passport by marrying an Irish girl for a while, I am able to come and go as I please in Europe. Being a PT living in a no-tax country, I no longer have to worry about an accountant, lawyer, or filling in any tax returns.

Don't You File USA Income Tax Returns?

Carl: You must be kidding? You are really in a leg-pulling mode this afternoon!

How Can A Reader Make Money Like You Do Now?

I still buy and sell things like rare stamps, coins, paintings and such, but always privately — never through dealers who would add a 300% mark up. If I cannot buy something for half of what I know I can sell it for immediately, I don't buy. How can you do this? The answer is read, study, and develop some expertise. Keep your eyes and ears open. Read the classified ads. Go to auctions. Do not be taken in and buy an Elvis guitar or an Abraham Lincoln autograph from some huckster at a seminar. Know values and pick up such things at auction and estate sales. And by auction I don't mean Christies or Sotheby's where they get top dollar. Try Druet Galleries or other government auctions in Paris. Distress sales are always a bargain hunter's paradise. Classified ads are also good. Making money by buying and selling things, anywhere in the world is easy, if you put your mind to it.

Any Hints For Staying Out Of Trouble?

Stay invisible. Do not get on any computer database, at least not in your real name or at your real address. Nobody except your one nightstand should know where you sleep. Maybe its best to keep a separate studio just for that — governments have been known to send in hookers to steal or copy businessmen's files. Also strangers in your house can cause all sorts of potential problems. Once a hooker in a friend's apartment found two passports with the same guy pictured — different names and birthdays. She went to the cops to make a deal and got herself an informant's fee. Have at least one alternate identity. But never leave conflicting papers in close proximity. I feel they should not even be kept in the same safety deposit box! Use cash not credit cards. Or maybe use a corporate card not linked to yourself. Don't ever get any financial statements mailed. If your bank or broker will not hold your statements, change banks. Do not tell anyone any information that could be used against you. Stay clean. No traffic tickets. If you get a traffic or other fine, pay it immediately. Stay clean on the small stuff, and they will never come across you to sniff around and get you for the big stuff.

Do not associate with people likely to get themselves into trouble. This includes nuts, kinks, Nutty Party Members, dope users like Barry, drunks or smugglers like Albert — or high profile authors like you, Peter!

Advantages And Disadvantages Of Your Expat Life?

At certain times in your life, maybe you want to be a major player. Then you have to be visible. Publicity and a high profile may help your career. But it always invites trouble, in the form of lawyers, con men, tax collectors, accountants, and insurance salesmen. You sue and get sued. But that goes with the territory.

When you decide to quit, becoming a PT is a little like building a wall around yourself to protect your privacy, your ass, and your assets!

Carl's Final Thoughts?

Our lifestyle is not for insecure people who can only thrive in a staid and familiar environment. It's for entrepreneurial types who love to make deals, enjoy adventure, challenges and changes; it's the most freedom you can get in an unfree world.

~~~~~~~~~~~~~~~~~~~~~~~~~~~~~~~~~~~~

Peter Trevellian: Thank you Albert, Barry & Carl. You are three completely different guys, yet you all call yourself PT's. You identify with a certain mobile, independent lifestyle that you all seem to enjoy and thrive upon. Most informative.

Chapter 23

Where To Get Good Ideas,
Reliable Advice And Sound Counsel

J UST as in business, the best deals and the best ideas won't come gift-wrapped and all tied neatly in red ribbons. If you just write a check and don't have to do any thinking or work, it may well be "garbage in and garbage out." To go offshore successfully, you might want to study a lot of technical material yourself. Or, you have to find someone reliable and intelligent who has already done it successfully and is willing to share knowledge with you. Maybe you'll have to pay for this knowledge. But good information is worth paying for.

Look around for PT oriented accountants, lawyers, or offshore advisors in your hometown, and it's like looking for true love in a brothel. You are looking in the wrong place. Even good reading material in your own country will be hard to find. The best books (forbidden or underground) are never found on bookstore shelves. Palladin Press and Eden Press mail order catalogs carry some good books on the subject, but these firms are often harassed because of it.

This book, Invisible Investor cannot tell you the whole story (as much as we'd like to) because of the "chill effect." Big Brother has spent a lot of time and millions upon millions of dollars to shut down anyone writing or saying anything too useful. They are today trying to come up with new ways to silence the flashes of truth that appear on the Internet. See back pages for interesting Web Sites where you'll get information channeled to you via sites beyond the control of Big Brother.

Technically proficient PT's visiting your home country to give seminars or private consultations are usually not so rash as to reveal their secrets to new clients who might be undercover agents out to nail them. Abroad, it's another story. If you have a trustworthy and financially successful old PT friend who is living abroad as an expat, he (or she) might be able to point you in the right direction. If you go and visit bankers and stockbrokers in offshore jurisdictions like Panama, The Dutch Antilles, Andorra, Singapore, Monaco and Luxembourg you will surely get some ideas. Bankers or consultants in one place will tell you what is good about them and wrong with their competitors. But amidst all the puffery and conflicting stories, the truth will emerge. Sure, it would be nice to have the original W. G. Hill hold your hand through all of this, but at $10,000 for a year's retainer, he is too expensive for most of us. Besides, he has to be convinced you are bona-fide.

The proper approach on an initial visit with any banker or consultant is to explain (whether true or not) that you have over a million dollars and want to protect it in an upcoming divorce. Don't talk about laundering money, avoiding taxes or frauds upon creditors. Bankers and financial service providers (always wary of a sting) do not want to hear anything of that nature — especially on a first encounter. An upcoming divorce is a good line however. Years later, after you know them well, you can discuss anything.

As you get advice and education from a variety of sources, you will begin to develop a picture of the offshore world as it really is.

Offshore Newsletters & Offshore Seminars

Writer/Consultants who are based abroad, like Harry Schultz in Monaco, Larry Abraham in Santiago, Marc Harris in Panama and others, are usually abroad for a reason. The reason is that they were oppressed or threatened by government in the place they came from — almost always the USA. They tend to express their sentiments and give many good hints about living and investing abroad within their publications. Because they are so busy, they usually have no time to engage in a lot of personal correspondence, but sometimes they sponsor smaller group conventions or tours abroad for their subscribers. Most attendees at these sessions feel they learn a lot and get their money's worth. *Also, it is a good place to make interesting friends and contacts.* If you ignore the hype to sell you obviously unsuitable investment deals these meetings can be extremely valuable. Speakers can express ideas abroad that would not be tolerated in your own home country. These newsletters and a few others are listed in the back of this book under resources, along with trial subscription prices and a summary of the information you are likely to find in them.

Consultants

High priced consultants, who may charge up to $10,000 for a single visit, are ONLY for those who have a very substantial net worth. They might be good for individuals who don't want to waste time with bankers and stockbroker types who are inevitably trying to push some specific investment deal on them in order to make a commission. Some consultants are better than others are naturally. Just as with restaurants, the most expensive is not always the best. If they have written a book or pamphlet, you can get a feeling for whether their ideas are compatible with your own.

Some advisors, particularly lawyers who, not being real PT's, still visit or maintain offices in their old countries, are so "straight" that they are unable to offer truly helpful suggestions as to what offshore schemes will work and what will sink. I give clients who are thinking of using me on a $10,000 two year retainer basis an opportunity to consult with me one-time for $1,000 (deductible from the 10K) to find out if I have anything to offer them besides a lot of hot air.

Expensive Bad Advice

One very good lawyer of my acquaintance advised some clients (at a fee of $250,000) to spend a few years on a god-forsaken island in the middle of nowhere as part of a scheme to inherit a sizable fortune tax-free. As it turned out, after the Rich Grandpa died, they got their money. Returning to the USA, as their lawyer said they could safely do under existing law, the tax collector changed the rules *retroactively.* The government found that the action in their changing residence was *tax motivated and thus fraud.* Then the government made the clients pay not only the 60% estate and inheritance taxes they would have paid, but also fines and penalties that left them with nearly nothing. So in our example here, the clients paid big attorney's fees, and lost 3 years on the Mariana Islands — all for less than nothing in the way of gain.

Peter Trevellian, Consultant

My own reputation is that I tell my clients what they can do to push the envelope to the edge without getting into trouble even if the enemy knew all the facts. I have a good feel for what will work and what will trigger an investigation or audit. Beyond that, I can give clients a good idea of what they can get away with risk free. Of course, I always keep in mind that "trouble" is like a virus. It can infect you regardless of fault, and the proper medicine or antidote for trouble with government is the flexibility to move out of danger and to already have your assets strategically placed well in advance. My fee, by the way is $10,000 for two years of unlimited (but reasonable), retainer consultancy. Needless to say, as a Libertarian, I can't work with any person who defrauds others or uses violence to further his ends. But if you have divorce problems or are being pushed around by the bureaucrats, I'd love to try and help you.

"Does It Work?" Or "Is It Legal?"

My own experience has been that it makes far more sense to go for a plan that works — not something that might not work, but like the Mariana Island scheme referred to above, is "technically legal." Why? Because the government is always changing the rules. If your partner in a business deal did what the government always does, you would call him a crook. I rely on good common sense.

At least in Great Britain it is different. There is a certain amount of stability. Certain kinds of offshore trust arrangements will work, even if they *are* tax motivated. In the USA, any government agency that wants your money (or your body in jail) can custom fit you with a large choice of violations, and if they can't do that, they can and will get your fanny with perjured testimony. If none of that works, they will pass a new law or create a new rule to make something you did in the past an offense. Heads I win, tails you lose. Ever since the fall of the Soviet Union and South Africa, the United States has become by far, the most dangerous country for an honest man.

Ass & Assets Abroad! Still The Best Preventative! Still The Best Cure All!

Once you are physically abroad, and once your assets are also abroad in a secret location known only to you only then you are safe from predators — governmental or private. You do not have to stay away forever — just so long as the heat is on. It may be a couple of years at most. But generally, the whole world is an open oyster to anyone with a million dollars or more in assets. You can make it with a lot less — perhaps with nothing if you have chutzpah and earning skills. But these days, a million in offshore assets should earn you close to $2,000 net spendable a week. That is enough to live middle class style anywhere, or like a maharajah in the Third World.

More than that, and you can live very well anywhere on the tax-free income from a million bucks — even in expensive Monaco!

The Client Who Wouldn't Be Deterred, Detoured Or Derailed

My old friend and mentor, W.G. Hill announced that he was retired from the lecture circuit and unlimited consulting for all comers.. And that is true. Outside of an occasional book or newsletter piece, he doesn't want to be an active player any more. But if a potential client is very determined and persistent, I know he can be coaxed to give aid counsel and assistance. Can you convince Hill you are a decent person he'd like to know as a friend? Do you have legitimate needs? Are you a non-violent person who feels endangered or has already been raped by the system? Hill doesn't need or want the money any more. On the other hand, he says he can't be bothered by a lot of poor slobs. All his present friends or clients have to be wealthy male chauvinists like him. His retainer-fee is $12,000 per year, payable in advance. This is the story Hill sent in during 1997 — about his last consulting client.

I present this piece as a little end-of-book treat for readers who will get here (as a free bonus) what amounts to a $10,000 session with the old master himself:

My Last Consulting Client: Gentleman Jimmy Wants The Best
By Dr. W. G. Hill

Once upon a time not so long ago, this chap whom we'll call "Jimmy," was criminally indicted for some very technical crimes. They came under the general category of "insider trading."

Jimmy, who had no reason to lie to me, explained that he was totally innocent of the criminal charges made against him. Like so many, he had been accused by a man who was in deep trouble himself. This villain then implicated and falsely testified against over a dozen people. Why? To get himself immunity. In other words, a real criminal turned in (and testified against) a dozen innocent people (most of whom were later convicted) in order to make a deal where he, the accuser, the real crook got off Scot-free. It happens all the time.

Jimmy went to trial twice and was twice acquitted on appeal. But perhaps I shouldn't say acquitted. His case was dismissed for improper conduct on the part of the prosecution. This improper conduct by the Department of Justice was in bringing charges they knew to be false, supported by (bought and paid for) witness testimony the government knew to be perjured. The people who did the bad deeds were commended instead of fired. Incredibly, the government came back with the same charges a third time. Jimmy was now considered a whistle blower and troublemaker. Why? Because he hadn't bent over and let the government kick him in the pants. Because he beat them in court two times. And nothing is worse than a trouble making whistle blower that is found innocent by a jury. The bureau-rats were out to get him good. As Jimmy had already spent over $2 million on his legal defense and was again facing (another million in legal fees plus) twenty years in jail if he lost, he jumped at the chance to plea bargain to a felony. The deal reached was that upon pleading guilty, he was to be immune from any further prosecution forever. He then spent 90 days in a so-called country club Federal Prison

Camp for white-collar criminals. While in prison he came across my books and the Hill PT book in the prison library. He decided that after his release he would seek me out to help him along with his life plan.

Making Contact

Jimmy wrote to my previous publisher and was then placed in touch with consultants who claimed to be me (more or less). He quickly discerned (through questioning) that his incompetent advisers were not the genuine articles. Finally, one of his letters pleading for an audience found its way to me. After a good deal of thought, I investigated his past and his story.

I had made the irrevocable decision to take no more clients at all or ever again. It turned out that my irrevocable decision could be changed with the right motivation.

This guy was my ideal client. After our first session together, I gave him the OK to join my inner circle of less than six advisees that keep me on permanent retainer. What made me take him on? He had been wronged by the system, he was intelligent, and he was determined to get on with his life and to get even by living well. He wanted to get out of Big Brother's orbit in an effective way with no negative side effects. Also important to me was that he had no hesitation about offering me $12,000 cash up front. This was and is my usual one-year unlimited consulting fee.

What Advice Did You Give Him That Was Worth $12,000?

My first counsel was that he should formulate his own plan based on the premise that "If he had not had his problem, and if he had no criminal convictions in his past, what would he most like to do with the thirty or forty years he had remaining in his life." Thinking in this way, and maybe factoring in a hypothetical life expectancy of six months always leads my clients to formulate a worthwhile plan.

Once we established that he would like to have a large waterfront estate in a tropical paradise with a bevy of disponibile (Italian word meaning agreeable) beautiful young women at his disposal, I showed him how to make this happen. He could have done it himself by trial and error, but because I had already been that route, I was able to make it happen in a few months instead of a few years. There was no big secret. I spent the last 20 years writing a book called *Sex Havens*. While exploring abroad every day (joke!) I was also looking at real estate. So I knew where Jimmy could find the illusion of love and some nice waterfront property. Both cheap. It was in Southeast Asia.

Then he wanted to jettison his USA passport and get another one legally and quickly. Because of a criminal conviction, most respectable countries would not accept him as a citizen or even a resident. But I quickly found a first class country that had a passport infinitely better (than the American) for travel. I knew from long trial and error with other clients, that this English speaking country would disregard any "crime" that was not a crime under its own laws. As they had no law against insider trading, he was quickly accepted for residence. After two years, he was eligible for his passport. As I write this, we are trying to decide if it's a better idea for him to renounce USA citizenship, or simply to fade away quietly.

Interestingly enough, this particular country (where he settled in) had many islands where his dreams of a tropical paradise with running, hot women and cold beer came with the territory. There were very few costs or taxes involved in his new life, and no onerous regulations or record keeping requirements. He was amazed at the relative freedom. He couldn't even conceive of it before. One of his concerns — proper medical treatment was allayed when he went locally to the herb doctor for treatment of a painful old chronic condition that American doctors could not cure. He'd spent some $48,000 on treatment over the years. A local guy took care of him in a series of visits that cured him completely. The bill? US$32.

Americans always have the wrong idea that the only good doctors and dentists are in their home country. Because of the many restrictions on American medical practitioners with regard to innovative treatments or drugs, the opposite is more often true! Competent (and incompetent) practitioners exist all over the world. In many places, certain procedures are more reliably executed than in the USA. For instance, cosmetic surgery is better and cheaper in places like Brazil. Perio-dentistry work is arguably done better in Switzerland, Germany, or Israel. Far more effective drugs and medications are available abroad. Why? Without the many prohibitions and restrictions of the USA Food and Drug Administration good medicine is tested and goes to the shelves in two or three years instead of ten to fifteen. Any cures for anything appear in Europe five or ten years before they are released in the USA. The FDA is so busy protecting the terminally ill against medicines with unknown side effects that the patients die.

A Consultant Is Not Necessary, But Just Like Going First Class; It Is A Luxury To Make Your "PT" Trip More Comfortable

I could go on more, but in summary, for $12,000 I made Jimmy's dreams come true almost immediately. After a year, like most of my clients, we were good pals. He forgot that "his best ideas" came from me. He began to slack off and do a few things I felt were out of keeping with his best interests. As we had become social friends and he knew a lot about my personal life by that time, his answer was "You do it, why shouldn't I?"

All I could say was the preacher's line "Do as I say, not as I do!" The truth is that I personally am sometimes guilty of not taking my own good advice. It has gotten me into trouble and cost me money more than once. My personal problem is trusting too many people and being too open. But of course I err on the side of caution with regard to my clients.

In any event, Jimmy, like every other PT I ever knew, is currently happy as a bug in a rug. He settled in a luxury oceanfront estate with one of the members of his original harem. Trying to stay active in business, he started several international businesses to recoup his losses back in Big Brother-land. He is able to travel back and forth to his old homeland — but he paid a high price for this dubious privilege: Two million dollars in legal fees, a lot of emotional stress, a divorce, a criminal conviction and finally 90 days in the slammer. Had I known him before his indictment and first trial, I'd have told him to leave immediately before any indictment was laid. My standard advice "Lay low till the heat's off!" There is always plenty of warning that trouble is afoot. If you disappear for a while, the prosecutors have other fish to fry, and you are forgotten. The statute of limitations run's. You are free.

Even if you win in litigation with the government, you always lose. With their infinite resources and their vindictive need to skewer every target one way or another, even if you are acquitted it is likely you will be brought in again with the usual suspects and harassed — until they have their way with you. If they finally get you and you lose a court case (as he did) you lose even bigger: A criminal conviction (even if you feel you were innocent) is like a bankruptcy or flunking out of school. It is a personal defeat and badge of shame that haunts you forever. You cannot vote, you cannot own a gun, you cannot deal in securities or real estate as a broker, and you may not even be able to get a license as a barber! In these modern days of forfeitures, even before a conviction, most people lose their freedom and all their money too.

Unfortunately, every person unjustly accused thinks they will beat the rap — just like the innocent heroes who usually get acquitted in the movies! They are almost always wrong. Persons indicted for federal crimes are convicted in 98% of all cases. The prosecutor who handled Jimmy had a motto on his wall: "The Guilty are easy to convict; the Innocent are a greater challenge." Thus, innocent defendants should not be very surprised when they wake up in jail — denuded of their assets.

In virtually all cases, as a convicted felon old friends will shun you. Within a year your spouse will stop visiting and will get a divorce. The pressures of getting along all alone (with a husband in the slammer) are too great for most women. There are few wives like Winnie Mandela who stuck by her husband faithfully for almost three decades of incarceration. Unfortunately, she was not so faithful after he was released. But the average wife decides to get a divorce on the day of the conviction.

Child custody or visitation is seldom granted to convicted felons (if the matter is in dispute). In business, your name is "Mud" after doing time. Innocence does not matter. Once a jury has convicted someone, the general perception is that the person convicted is a "bad" person. This is not to say that every person incarcerated in a USA prison has been unjustly convicted, but based upon an informal survey of my clients, it appears that the figure is close to a third. This could mean that there are literally a million or more people like you and I who were simply unlucky —their lives shattered by unwarranted criminal charges.

Jimmy's Special Needs

Lately, Jimmy has eased up trying to get back to (what is for him) normal and away from the PT mode. He lives only in one place. I feel Jimmy is mentally unprepared to make a sudden move again from his new country if any circumstances warrant it. He is not as prepared as he should be. He has bought property and fixed assets instead of renting, as he should have done. He owns a capital-intensive business that is anything but mobile. He trusts the woman he lives with far too much. She has been a nice obedient girl so far. But any ex-hooker living with a guy old enough to be her grandpa may well have a hidden agenda. In my opinion, his little bit of fluff should not be trusted with the keys to the kingdom. She knows everything and could bring him down with a quivering of lips. I have mentioned all of this to him, but like all my ex-clients, once their immediate crisis has been solved, they fall back into old patterns of somewhat sloppy behavior. The possibility of another cycle of disappointments thus becomes more likely. I tell him this, and he says, "Look at you!" I do, and then resolve to clean up my own act. But he doesn't stay PT (Prepared Thoroughly) and sometimes I don't either.

[End of submission by Hill]

Bottom Line?
By Peter Trevellian (back again)

Let me know if you enjoyed the above piece by Hill. With a few good fan letters to send him I may be able to get him to submit a few more tales for future books. Now we go back to my advice.

Become a PT Prepared Thoroughly! Move enough assets offshore to survive any crisis, and get your second identity or passport when you are not under pressure. These two moves will go a long way to insuring your future happiness.

If you foul up on anything else, as long as you have at least one alternate identity and one secret mother lode of assets to draw upon, you will be better off than most people will.

If you want your hand held through a crisis and can afford me, but not Hill, fax Peter Trevellian c/o Shamrock at 331 5301 3118 or e-mail me at shamrock@netcomuk.co.uk. Remember to ask for and insist on the original PT. That is Peter Trevellian with two "L's"

There are a few less expensive consultants I would also recommend, and they are listed in the back pages of this book.

Chapter 24

Prospects For Individual Freedom In Our LifeTimes — Taking A Long Perspective

*S*TUDY history. You will find human society is much like a river: At first it flows quickly and simply in one direction: A torrent of water breaks through a highland lake seeking the shortest route to the sea. It goes in a straight line downhill. Then, every river or creek gradually bends like a snake. The great Albert Einstein once wrote a paper explaining the mathematical reasons why flowing water can't help meandering; turning in upon itself with curves of ever greater complexity. Depending upon the river flow and terrain, there may be shallows, rapids, eddies, branches, even dead-end ponds or lakes. Life forms grow and adapt to the changing river. Usually, changes are almost imperceptible, but every once in a while there is a big flood. Then, for a time, the river flows relatively straight again — for a little while. Until it begins a new cycle of convolution. In human society, it seems that groups of human beings start off with simple rules and gradually develop ever more oppressive and complex systems to benefit some members of the group at the expense of others.

Sooner or later, all the bends or kinks are eliminated by a major change in form of government. This fall of bureaucracy can be the result of war, epidemic, or simply exhaustion. But surely as a river develops bends, a new bureaucracy will eventually grow up to replace the old. At the same time this is happening, crime rates, prices, human fertility rates, social organization and a billion other things go through cycles. Humans try to make sense out of these changes (and some are naive enough to think they can predict the future). Carl Marx and Lenin thought they had done it and said so in many books. Main prediction? The inevitability of Communist Quasi-Religious Dictators of the Proletariat leading humanity into a perfect state of Utopia.

For a time Communists numbered about half the population of the world and they all believed that the State (i.e. all governments) would eventually wither away and everything would self-regulate. Now even professing communists take Marx like most non-fundamentalist Christians take the bible. What's that? As symbolic inspirational stories, not to be believed in a literal way. No one believes that someday all governments will whither away. There are many however who believe that the heavy hand of government and bureaucracy is always getting heavier, and rugged individualism and personal freedom is eroding at an ever increasing rate. True or False? How about you? Are things worse now than they were twenty years ago?

Let's take an objective look. What is perceived as an onerous burden to one person (a tax?) is perceived as a career opportunity to a student studying for a career as a tax collector. A goodly number of people at any time believe they are living in the best of all possible worlds at the best of all possible times. Simultaneously, others feel oppressed. Can both be right? Yes! Someone who has a good job working for a bureaucracy can, and usually does think everything is hunky-dory. Someone in jail for a crime that they perceive as normal conduct (like calling a public official a jackass) might disagree. Most wars have been fought because those on different sides see the same things from a different point of view. Someone with the PT mentality who isn't living the PT life will perceive his situation as intolerable. "Everything is going to hell. Nothing is as good as it used to be." Is that what you think?

It's All Relative

What is the reality? Simply that some people in any society (or fish in any river) will have it good (or bad) some of the time, most of the people will have it good (or bad) most of the time, and a very few people will have it very good all of the time. Some of those whom we think have it good will think that things are terrible. Moreover, some whom we perceive, as being in terrible straits will think their life is full of rewards and satisfactions. Happiness or satisfaction is a state of mind, a perception. Your reality is not necessarily my reality. Should I put it in baby talk? In Joseph Stalin's time, nobody can deny that from a personal freedom & material point of view Joe himself (materially at least) had it pretty good. No one else in the Soviet Union lived as well as he did. However, I venture to say that if we asked Joe if he was happy, he'd disregard the material aspect to focus on the fact that his life and the political system he set up was in constant danger. He survived only by deporting, jailing and murdering a few million of his (perceived) enemies every year. I could have made the same observation about Mao, Mussolini, or Hitler. Today in Russia, there is a new system emerging offering vastly more individual economic opportunity & personal freedom. There are many newly rich Russians. Where before everyone had a job, now many are free to be homeless and jobless.

In Russia, for the first time in 75 years everyone (theoretically) has the legal right to engage in commerce, travel abroad or communicate with foreigners. At the same time, in modern Russia, there is also more personal danger to the non-political guy on the street — from violent criminals, and from economic circumstance. Would you be happier there? Most locals are not happy. The majority is voting to return to the security of Communism! Achieving stability, security and prosperity (or whatever social goal people in general agree upon) plus encouraging individual freedom always involves a balancing act. Sometimes the main goal of a large group of people is enforcing certain religious rituals and beliefs. You can never please all the people and so, there is constant tinkering.

The Price Of A Pleasant Landscape To Look Upon

In England under Labour and in Russia under the Communists, there was no visible and certainly no widespread homelessness. Think about why? The price of not seeing drunks and urban living in cardboard hovels involved forced labor camps; the liquidation of social

parasites in the Communist World and the institutionalization of mis-
fits in the "Free" World. Few people complain about the incarceration of categories of bad people that they themselves do not feel they
fit into. One way to read current events in trend setting countries
like the USA, where more and more people are being jailed for less
and less (in the way of offenses), is a decline in personal freedom.
Nevertheless, a decline in freedom for those in jail can also be inter-
preted as an increase in freedom for those outside. Those not incarcerated are free from disturbance by those offenders sent away. Such
theoretical discussions alone do not answer the important questions:
A P.T. almost by definition is a non-conformist in a highly
regulated, highly taxed, first world society. Thus, a P.T. must adapt
in a special way. "How do I cope?" you ask. "How do I get for
myself and my family a material lifestyle better than everyone else
— or at least better than average?" Merely asking this question would
be offensive to a socialist who wants all people to be 'equal.' A
good Communist or Patriot should never ask: "How do I avoid con-
scription, confrontation, imprisonment and perhaps even death at the
hands of my own government?" He should say, "I wish I had more
than one life to give for my country, right or wrong. Take my money
too, while you're at it." Of course, we don't buy into that way of
thinking.

The answer to the question of how and where to live for a PT is not
difficult:

1) WHAT IS IT YOU WANT MORE OF?

2) MONEY? POWER? FORBIDDEN SEX? GAMBLING?
   DRUGS?

3) MAYBE YOU JUST WANT A MORE MORAL ENVIRON-
   MENT WITH

4) NO SEX, NO DRUGS, NO GAMBLING, WHERE EVERYONE
   EATS GRUEL.

Figure out what kind of behavior is being rewarded in the town (or
country) where you live, and what kind of behavior is being pun-
ished. Then, take the obvious path to make more money; to get more

sex, power, immortality, glory or whatever it is that you think you need. Obviously you must avoid activities or behavior that get you into trouble locally. **If you can't exist comfortably where you are, or can't get what you want where you live; then look for opportunities (and restrictions) elsewhere in the world.** Consider a physical move to where greater opportunity for your particular diversions or perversions exist. You want to go where what you like is perceived as the ordinary, legal way of life. Your particular river (the place you live now) may have too many bends for your taste, but for the foreseeable future there will always be plenty of other rivers. Most fish are stuck in a particular river, but you can choose to move to the environment that suits you best!

Want To Get Rich?

In some countries, entrepreneurs are richly rewarded. In the USA, Japan or Europe this is still generally true. It is truer in unregulated, new fields of endeavor like computer software. It is hard (but not impossible) to go to jail for coming up with a best selling original innovation in software or hardware. But try to be innovative in American or Swiss banking or pharmaceutical marketing and you will be breaking a million and one rules.

Soldier Or Cleric

In countries like the Philippines and Thailand, it pays better to be a politician or army officer than a businessman. In Iran or anyplace where religious know-nothing -else people are in sway, being a traditional community religious leader is less dangerous and leads generally to respectability, power, and a good standard of living.

Where In The World Should I Be Heading To Get What I Want?"

You should match your personality and talents to a community that appreciates (or at least tolerates) you. Thus, the question to be concerned with is not "Where is the world heading?" but rather, "Where in the world should I be heading to get what I want?" The world's communities, as we know, are heading in a myriad of different directions — all at the same time. Moreover, this is where the P.T. concept comes into play. By identifying several countries or communities where the work and recreation you like is socially acceptable, you will avoid going to jail.

Where To Smoke Pot Legally

If you like to smoke grass, you do it in Holland where it is legal. In the Netherlands, you can get stoned at most any coffee shop for the same price as a beer in your hometown. Obviously, if you enjoy beer, do not move to the Muslim world. If you hanker for unconventional sex, no matter how kinky your taste, there are places (described in Hill's fine book, *Sex Havens*) where you can legally and openly do what you love most. If you want to earn a lot of money, or have power over other people, there are places in the world where you are far more likely to succeed than in other places. Having more than one passport (for Americans) and an open mind is all you need.

It doesn't really matter that ecologists are making life difficult for real estate developers in your particular suburb. There are plenty of nice places in the world to develop (or depending on one's point of view, despoil). Ecology isn't fashionable in most of Africa. Even if you are a homicidal maniac, you can always find some place in the world to be hired as a mercenary and hack away at innocent victims. And if you don't want to be an innocent victim, as a PT you can always go and live somewhere that is relatively safe from violent crime (like Monaco, New Zealand, Japan, or Liechtenstein).

Is Individual Freedom Being Eroded All Over The World?

It is silly (in my opinion) to say things like "Individual Freedom is being eroded all over the world." It simply isn't true. There are different sorts of freedom and different sorts of slavery going on in hundreds of different places. You and your family can have a Swiss Family Robinson sort of freedom by becoming hermits on an uninhabited island. Living with or near other people always involves some compromises and some advantages. My idea of an ideal place to live is one where I pay little or no taxes, don't have to risk getting my ding-dong shot off in any street-gang war, and have a first class

Chinese take-away nearby. My family and I can get what I want by living in any one of a dozen prosperous tax havens.

Would You Rather Retire & Smell The Flowers?

Once I had enough money to live well on, I quickly found more satisfying things to do than running a business. My business career was a stepping stone; not something I wanted to do until I croaked in my office swivel chair. It was no thrill or satisfaction to spend most of my time defending inevitable private lawsuits and fighting public regulatory agencies. I found that being a recognized local celebrity was a royal pain in the arse. Obviously, there are different strokes for different folks. It is also a function of age. At 20-35, maybe you need to make your mark on the world, be lauded and be recognized. At 55, maybe you will want to make love and read more. A personal confession. As a young mover and shaker I didn't have enough time to be a proper father to my first family. Now I have a second family with a wife younger than my daughter and a new set of kids the same age as my friend's grandchildren. I spend four or five hours every day with the kids, and I look after my new wife much better than I did with the other one twenty-five years ago. I missed having a good family life the first time around, but got it as a PT.

Why Low Profile Suits Me Just Fine

One is that people in the public eye are envied. There are and always have been non-entities around who want to harm those they envy. Little punks with lethal weapons stalk the rich and famous. Other threats are litigants, bureaucrats or journalists who can and will cut you down with lethal legal processes and paperwork. Notoriety, display, or anything that attracts envy (or the other side of the coin, admiration) is to be avoided, at least by myself. Look at what happened to John Lennon. Gianni Versachi too. He never hurt anyone! The guy who shot him had no connection with him at all.

As a PT, you can expand your place of living options to virtually any locality. You do not even need two passports. Australian PT's live "invisibly" in New Zealand and Kiwis live in Oz. Any European can live indefinitely and invisibly in any other European country. Why? Because no passports are needed to move between countries and you can fall through the cracks. The PT, being perceived by local cops and bureaucrats (if he is perceived at all), is seen as a passing through tourist who minds his own business, keeps a low profile, and avoids trouble.

One Whiff Of Trouble And I'm Off Like Bambi

It is inconceivable that any member of my family or I could ever be conscripted into any military service, jailed for any offense, or sent a bill for income tax. In any of the places I have lived as a PT over the dozen years, if there was the merest whiff of any of the above, I was off like Bambi. The only time I had to move was when I made the mistake of confiding my PT status to my mail drop operator. To be a successful PT, your status and PT life-plan should be your most closely held secret! But that's my point of view. General Colin Powell would no doubt say that he found freedom and a satisfying career in the military when other doors of opportunity were shut to him because of his race or background. General Powell is not a PT and surely would not want to join our ranks any more than we would want to join the US Army. Fact to remember: Most people in the world are not PT material. Over half are directly or indirectly employed or supported by government! They would not go for a PT style existence even if they could. If they thought about us which we hope they will not, it would be to classify PT's as Penitentiary Targets.

Not Even All Millionaires Are Potential PT's

An individual (one of my consulting clients) became a PT & bitterly regrets it. He cashed out of a multi-million dollar business, obtained another passport, picked up all his chips and moved to a very agreeable foreign country where he took up residence with one of the most beautiful and agreeable women in the world. Yet these days he complains that his kick in life was having the prestige (and problems) that came with a lot of employees, a huge income, and a big, visible lifestyle. His old life included recognition he misses: Stuff like giving parties for the local lights, photos and mention in his town's society pages. "Now" he says, "I am a rich nobody!" He finds the PT life boring. How about you?

Even A Flash Car Is A Dangerous Possession!

My personal experience is that when I drove a ten-year-old sturdy and reliable rust bucket, I never once had a problem. But when I traded it for a shiny red Mazda sports car (costing no more than a middle class sedan), the perceived glamour of this car regularly attracted vandals (even in Monaco!). As a result of many personal experiences my PT rule is to no longer do any conspicuous (i.e. visible) consumption. No flaunting of wealth or possessions. Period. That does not mean I don't dine at Joel Robushon's (the world's best restaurant in Paris) or get a high priced massage. I do rent a luxury apartment in a high rise well-secured building. Going out for a walk with my ladylove, my rule is she doesn't drip diamonds (not even fake ones) or gold chains. Neither of us wears an expensive watch. Nor does she wear form fitting sexy clothes. I like to look at her when she's all tarted up, but we both agree that it's better to dress and act in a way that is less likely to attract unwanted attention. We make a big effort to look like poverty personified Mr. & Mrs. Dumpy, stumbling out for their evening shuffle.

How Much Dough Do You Need To Quit Working?

One clear requirement for PT freedom and mobility is either a net worth that allows you to live off assets, or a portable occupation that allows you to earn money without licenses, permits or a permanent place of business. In my travels I've met street musicians, computer programmers and English teachers who are PT's though they may not know it. My new PTO (*Portable Trades & Occupations*) book describes a lot of portable jobs or things anyone can do in a foreign country. I concentrate on ways to make money without any permits, licenses, or regular nine to five jobs.

In My Opinion, The Exits Won't Slam Shut In Our Lifetimes For USA Or European Citizens Who Want To Relocate

The outlook for PT's is good. Even if places like the USA attempt to impose an exit tax on assets, there will always be ways for people who make the effort to moving themselves and most of their assets to another country. In the old South Africa, rich people who wanted to expatriate assets and themselves often built yachts. They bought art works, jewelry, stamp collections and other portable wealth. Then they simply sailed off into the stars. A small percentage but large number of Germans and Italians (Jewish and otherwise) were able to exit Europe for the USA and South America when they saw (as almost anyone could see) that war was in the air and things were going to get worse before they got better. People killed or imprisoned by governments usually have years of warnings and plenty of signals that it is time to leave. Don't be A Prisoner of Your Possessions! A good friend of mine who was in the midst of a crisis didn't leave. Why? Because his wife insisted upon staying with her old friends furniture and familiar crockery. He will lose his freedom if he follows this foolishness. Another friend said he'd rather go to jail for twenty years than be separated forever from his old gang. There is an Old French saying "Chacon a son gout." Each to his own taste. Indeed. I prefer to be Prepared Thoroughly. The Only Certainty is Change

The Biggest Barrier To Overcome Is Inertia

Some people (probably the vast majority) think that the center of the universe is their hometown. They actually believe they could not make it or be happy anywhere else. Generations of people stay in hellholes or refugee camps where life itself is a terrible struggle. It is clear to them (from others who do escape), that a little effort and initiative would make a new life possible. But the majority doesn't make the move. They do not seek to better themselves. Why? The vast majority prefers the certainty of misery to uncertain change.

Perceptions

For people living in relatively prosperous countries like today's USA or Scandinavia, some of the most wealthy and privileged will perceive that they are slaves living in gulags, birds in gilded cages. It is clearly a question of perception. But by becoming a PT and taking advantage of the opportunities available, any person can physically live wherever they want, and escape most of the perceived negatives in their life. Finding freedom in an unfree world is possible if you simply decide what it is you want to avoid, and what is important to you. Then, you take the steps to go where you want to go and do the things you want to do.

You Can Go Back Where You Started From!

A very wealthy American guy named Dart who made his billion on foam plastic coffee cups must have read PT. However, for all his billions he did not bother to get any intelligent advice on his PT transition. He moved to Belize (a country I visited and psyched out as a potential PT Playground). Had he spoken to me, I would have told him that Belize was a dump. It would be one of the last places on Earth a wealthy PT would choose as a place to invest or deal with any government official. Dart apparently wanted to emulate one of the characters in the Passport Report who ultimately returned (as a tax free diplomatic) to his original place of residence (Sarasota). So Dart got his Consul General appointment from Belize. Then the USA wouldn't recognize him in his new role. His main problem? He did not do his entire program in a quiet and low profile way. While I never met Mr. Dart, I imagine he used high priced big name lawyers and accountants. This modus operandi almost guarantees litigation and problems.

A future PT shouldn't disclose his PT intentions to anyone in his home country — especially lawyers, accountants, politicians, journalists, or potentially hostile ex-wives. We won't go over the motivations of all of these categories but a lawyer's interest is in making continuing fees and getting publicity to generate new future clients. This is exactly what a PT needs to avoid. Someone like me, who co-invented the concept of PT, understands that the big move, when it comes, is essentially a divorce from the system. Its an annulment from your old country's minions of bureaucrats (government employees), lawyers (officers of the court) and accountants (who are essentially IRS collection Agents). It should cut you off physically from any potential litigants like alimony seeking women.

Dart could have quietly moved his money to safe havens so that Big Brother couldn't ever figure out what was where. His expatriation would have been handled with name changes in such a way as to make him invisible. He apparently has no back up passports besides Belize and no respectable countries where he could live. Although he can still do it, as part of the process, he should have made deals with desirable first-rate countries for passports. His new home country, Belize, is the corrupt African sort of Third World place that will milk a beached billionaire dry. The easily purchased Belize passport might have been OK as one of several PT flags, but its not a country where you'd actually live or have any assets. Dart needs better advice. He should have contacted the guy who wrote the PT book. It is relatively easy to get a passport (by investment, ancestry or marriage) in several countries of the European Union. The same is true in Canada, Singapore, Australia, or New Zealand. If a chap like Dart knew this, why would he choose a bunghole like Belize, and why would he handle his affairs in such a way those muckraking journalists could expose him and point fingers to louse up his PT plans?

Its Hard To Dig Yourself Out Of A Hole

Yet it is probable that Dart could still change course and accomplish his objectives. Reminds me of the comparison between Marc Rich and Mike Milken in the Hill Passport Report. One did things right, the other mucked up. Fortunately, you can usually start over.

A Pragmatist Decides What He Wants And Goes After It
A Philosopher Doesn't Know What He Wants, But Thinks A Lot

To summarize! Do not waste time on meaningless speculation by trying to figure out what will happen in the world over the next 2,000 years. Fine if you want to write a book of worthless predictions — for which there is always a market. But for your own personal use there is no point in trying to figure out where the whole world is going to go politically, socially or economically. There is not even the hope of getting any useful answers. Why? Because the world is going in many different directions — all at the same time.

A PT is pragmatic. The PT mentality merely asks "Am I happy with what I am? Am I happy where I am? Do I enjoy who I'm with and doing what I do?" If the answer is "No," to any question the next step is to re-read PT and try and figure out where in the world you'd be happier. Then pay the place(s) a visit. If the PT way of life would help achieve your goals, make a few moves to cut the umbilical cord.

If you are certain you can make major moves without an objective counseling session with a PT who has actually made it for a dozen years or more, prepare for your PT life slowly and deliberately. As all the disclaimers say, "Seek competent advice." Run your plans by someone who can advice as to your options, either in person or by mail. It probably is best (if you can afford it) to get second or third opinions as well. Be sure to ask yourself and your advisors the right questions. Like the ones Dart and Milken didn't ask:

Making predictions for the long-term future is not necessary. It isn't even helpful. The very essence of the PT is being prepared for unexpected and unpredictable changes. It is only necessary to choose a selection of people, places and passports to serve an uncertain future. If your investments are also spread out in half a dozen countries, you have far more security than anyone else does. Your predictions about the future do not have to be right. After all, the only thing you can predict with absolute certainly is that unexpected, unpredictable change will come.

If you never move your bottom, if you never travel — even then you will be better off if you move some assets abroad just in case. There are many eventualities you can't insure yourself against with a commercial insurance company. Having a secret nest egg stashed away for a rainy day can solve some of the little problems of life. These days, with the United States no longer being property friendly, it is a good idea to:

"Get your money out of the country before your country gets the money out of you."

Chapter 25

Consider The Source & Bon Voyage

*N*OW that you have learned everything there is to know about off-shore investing, let me tell you why I wrote this book.

First, I wanted to educate you. A good doctor or dentist will explain the procedures or treatment he thinks you need. Then he will let you make ALL the final decisions. I hope that you will explore your options, make up your own game plan. When it is all done, I hope you will review it with an experienced expert in the field of offshore investments and asset protection strategies. Your plan should also be also integrated with your goals in life and your aspirations for your family. Explore the possibilities with an expert because if you do not you may be missing something. You may have read this book twice and you may think you understand everything. However, from much experience with clients I know that even a highly intelligent, well-informed person can always do better with a few experts on their team. You should know that behind almost everything you read there is a hidden agenda. Someone is trying to influence you for his or her own reasons.

What Is My Hidden Agenda?

At least we are going to be painfully honest: I was royally skewered by Big Brother, By U.B.S., S.B.C., By Credit Suisse Bank and others panned in this volume. This writing kick is my way of paying them back — my method of getting a little revenge. And we'll help you give it to 'em too. If you have a story to tell (like Dr. DeBunk in this

book) send it. I will try to use it in a revision of this book or in a later
book on some related topic. You do not have to write your own
book. One chapter will do!

Could be I am a bit less charitable to my enemies than I should be.
When I wrote my first book with Hill years ago, I thought we were
alone in our experiences and world-view. After all, I figured many
people (probably the majority) get through life without being criminally accused and without suffering in an unjust lawsuit or divorce.
But with my old friend Hill having sold over a million copies of his
PT oriented books (all edited and partly written by me), it seems we
have struck a chord. And now that I know the real statistics, it's
quite clear there are a lot of productive people with serious assets
who are getting leaned on.

I usually get to see clients who have had similar experiences to our
own. Its a great pleasure to help them cope and to beat the system in
ways we didn't know about when it would have helped us.

The most important reason for writing is to have a sense of purpose
in life, and a sense that we are in some small way, influencing the
course of history. Ideas do have consequences in the real world. We
were very happy to see a proliferation of PT oriented newsletters
growing out of the seeds we planted.

My next book might be on the general subject "Divorce: Picking Up
All Your Chips before the game starts." Let me know if this is a
topic of interest.

Then too, it is a real pleasure to provide guidance for people facing
or involved in a crisis. I really know from fan letters that many
people feel helped and glad to know they are not alone in having to
deal with bureau-rats, and idiot Robin Hood judges.

Product And Service Recommendations

Of course when lucky, I get paid by my publishers. Therefore, they
get to put a few plugs in the book, especially in the Resource Section. However, my integrity is such that I will not allow my "highly
recommend" tag on anything I do not believe in. Keep that in mind
when you read the chapter at the end of the book.

My Own Consulting Business

I have mixed feelings about drumming up new consulting business for myself. On one hand, I am stimulated by new contacts and by helping people achieve their goals. I also like earning the money for talking to people about what I know best. If you ever contact me for a consultation, do it right, by submitting your ideas and questions in advance. We will be able to expand your options, point you in the right directions, and predict with a high degree of accuracy, how things will work out in your case. It could be that your plan is perfect. More likely, we will confirm that most of what you have decided upon is good — but that other areas could be improved upon. We can certainly be of assistance in certain practical things like arranging for legal residences, legal second passports, good places for your financial, social and money making headquarters — i.e. your five flags.

Most Of My Clients Come To See Me After Disaster Has Hit

Funny thing is, more earthquake insurance is sold immediately after an earthquake than in the three decades preceding it. As a geological fact, once two tectonic plates have overcome the forces holding them back and have moved (this move being experienced as an earthquake) it is unlikely they will have another major move for fifty years more. But disaster insurance sales representatives have receptive customers when people see debris around them. Reality? Insurance should be taken out when there have been no quakes for a long time (in an earthquake prone area). What am I talking about? Move your nest egg out to safety NOW. Not after it is too late. Get your alternate identity now — for the same reason.

More Investment Opportunities
Come To International Investors

Likewise, with investments, most people commit their assets most heavily and with great confidence, when a market has been rising for years. They forget that every market has a top, and after every top there's a flop. The best time to buy domestically or offshore is when things are historically very cheap. This is at the beginning of a cycle.

When you can buy a company or piece of property and get your money back out of earnings in a year or three it is relatively safe. You don't have to care about what the market does. Earnings may justify the price. But most people would rather buy into a ten-year record of uninterrupted higher stock prices. This is what the newly fashionable index funds are all about. Forget about value or earnings. You are buying something that has gone up in the past. How much would you bet on a racecar where the driver looks only out of the rear window — at the past?

A market is obviously headed for disaster when a utility company with relatively slow growth sells for a price where it would take three hundred years to recoup the investment. Yet this was the actual price level of stocks in Japan before their market collapsed. Once you become an invisible investor and an international investor, you can look for property deals like in Cuba, where you can buy property where the rent pays off the cost of property in two years. That's a 50% return. You can find stocks so depressed that they are selling at one times earnings. You might not double your money in a week, but you will probably double it every year or two as I have done with my "Panama Portfolio." I don't even think it is so risky to diversify into very high return deals. If you have several, they won't all go sour. The best returns around are in fast growth third world countries.

Do you fully understand my ideas and final suggestions? Do you realize the value of planning — making your own financial and life-goal plans? I want you to be *aware* of the need to protect your financial health by moving at least *some* of your assets to a safer haven. More importantly, I want you to widen your horizons.

Become More International In Outlook

The sun doesn't really rise and set in your hometown. Your present country is not the only place on earth where you can breathe fresh air, have the best medical care at reasonable cost, and walk the streets in safety anytime.

You Should Be Happy!

Where you live now is probably the only place on earth where life is fair and the benefits you get from government outweigh the costs. [That is BS, and MS- more of the same, just in case you didn't recognize it!] Your country is the only place where bureaucracy does not interfere with your life. [And that's Ph.D.: Piled higher and deeper!]

The odds are that wherever you currently live, play, work, and invest. The situation is far from ideal. My purpose in this book is to show you that you can easily — by a mere change of attitude and a little bit of paper shuffling — protect your assets, make more money and enjoy life more. The question is not "can I afford it?" The real question is "Can I afford not to?"

International Investments

One of the good things about being a PT is that you can look for the grossly undervalued properties on the WORLD market just after a war, revolution, or economic collapse. This is one way I have kept my money growing at double digit rates for the past thirty years. I will share my methods with clients and also refer you to some good money managers.

My Usual Clients

Churned & burned

Their stockbrokers have churned them and burned them. This means that their accounts were traded in and out so they lost their shirt — but their stockbroker has a new yacht. [Our practice is to make medium to long term investments, forget day-to-day fluctuations, and let the situations work themselves out for our benefit].

Sued & screwed

Other clients are being sued for divorce or are in the midst of serious legal problems. [If their assets had been offshore, these problems would probably not have happened. Why? Because the plaintiff's lawyers always look first for juicy assets to grab. If there are none, the case seldom gets filed].

Audited or being investigated

Many people who come down to see me have or had government problems. Just as in the other examples, a tax collector or regulatory agency looks for big fish to fry. Big fish have big bank accounts and stock portfolios. A low profile person with invisible assets is judgment proof. He is not a good target.

Cornered Cat

Finally, the last and most usual category of client is the cornered cat. He is in a situation and has no where else to run. He needs to move his assets and his ass NOW. He needs a second passport and a new legal residence. Unfortunately, when you are insolvent, out on bail or have been jailed for contempt, no respectable country wants to hear about you. Even opening a foreign bank account becomes a major enterprise. The time to get your paperwork together is before, not after you have been wrongfully accused of something. Even a "smart" lawyer like F. Lee Bailey was sent to prison on a contempt charge. To get out of jail he had to turn over his entire fortune — some deca-millions — to the clerk of the court. If he was thinking like a PT, he would have never allowed himself to get into that predicament.

Lock The Barn Door Before The Horse Gets Out

I would like by means of this book to gain a few clients who see my message early and lock the barn doors before the horses have escaped. Doesn't it make more sense to buy insurance before the earthquake?

There is usually plenty of warning. The warnings are loud and clear for wealthy citizens of almost every country. In Germany, the father of a famous tennis player (Stefi Graf) went to jail for tax evasion. He will also lose his daughter's millions, and much more in fines and penalties. How simple (and legal!) it would have been for him to relocate his legal residence to a tax haven like Monaco and to have kept his investments offshore where they would grow at twice the speed. It does not take a genius to see that. But he didn't. Probably was a "patriotic" German who wanted to pay his fair share. He did, but the government did not think the millions he did pay were enough — just like Leona Helmsley's case in New York City. She too paid huge amounts of taxes for decades when she could have sold her hotels and real estate for a billion dollars or more, packed up, and moved to tax-free Bermuda. Instead, she served over a year in jail at the age of 71!

Get Your Money Out Of The Country Before Your Country Gets The Money Out Of You!

More than ever before, wealthier, more productive people are being targeted by their tax and justice system for plucking. Many middle class people who built up a sizable nest egg are rightly worried about losing it to a "Robin Hood" legal system. Tax collectors are not the only danger. Get into court and the only sure result is that your retirement nest egg will be taken from your so-called deep pockets to be transferred to the pockets of non-productive people. The facts of any case don't matter much any more. Enshrined in legal theory is that when two people come into the legal process as adversaries, the poorest one will go out richer, and the richer one will be poorer. Of course the lawyers take their generous cut off the top. But who thinks about the fate of these poor lawyers? They in turn are shorn by the tax system taking half of whatever they earn. They are over regulated and like accountants who practice in their home country — they are practically forced to become government agents.

You Can Do It Yourself!

Next big question. You know a lot about going offshore with your investments now, and you can probably do it as an individual on your own. But getting back to my analogy of the doctor and dentist, you could also buy a book on home remedies. Would you self-prescribe treatments for everything that ails you? Some things, yes. But a regular check up is sensible. If you can afford it, it is better to buy and pay for regular expert (hopefully objective) opinions. If you are not satisfied with your first expert, it doesn't hurt to get a second and third opinion. When going off to fish in uncharted waters, it is best to hire a guide. Eventually, you can do it yourself and even guide others. But to find the best fishing holes and to avoid sudden dangerous currents, start out with a guru. You save time and can avoid making the wrong moves. Weather changes all the time, and in the offshore world, the near perfect headquarters or "flag" of today may not be so good tomorrow. Think back to the story in this book of Nevada White whose hard earned $20 Million was confiscated from a Liechtenstein Foundation — generally thought of as the most invulnerable bastion of asset protection. Had Mr. White hired someone like me to review his situation, I would have, in the course of preparing his financial plan, provided him with a checklist. My checklist would have asked him: Do any real or potential enemies know the exact location of your mother lode?

Would I have stressed the absolute need for never carrying across borders un-encoded financial statements showing secret account numbers and offshore balances? You bet! It is better to never even take them out of the institution that is managing your money. The chink in Nevada's elaborate plan was that he let two potential enemies — his cheating wife, and his disloyal secretary — in on his secret stash of cash. If somebody knows your secrets, all the numbered accounts and other standard asset protection schemes will not help you keep your money.

Hire Trustworthy Money Managers & Then 'Mum's The Word.'

You already know from reading this book that often your own big, bragging mouth is your worst enemy. Carelessness is another. Perhaps you need an outside consultant to remind you of this and to do a regular check on your security.

Some investors lose their money through inattention to their portfolio. Others lose it through too much trading. If you are a tape watcher, and if you want to trade in and out every day, we can suggest a good offshore broker. If you want quiet excellent long-term results, we have others in mind for you.

Is all this leading to still another plug for myself? Nahh! I've already made enough of them. Just go to the Resource Section, the best part of the book, and try to do it yourself.

Your Move Offshore. Don't Throw Caution To The Winds!

Can you afford to make a very silly mistake on your first offshore deal? One that will lose serious money or even worse, get you into a "situation" with your own government? In our experience, far too many individuals respond to a sucker advertisement, a telephone call from a bucket shop, or they put their money into an obvious fraud or swindle. Not only do they lose their money, but also more often than not, they are conned into throwing even more good money after a bad first investment. If you don't have sound business sense, get some reliable experts, people who have made serious money on their own. They can go over the books on any proposed deal and give you an opinion of the possible risks and rewards. That expert, if he is also a talented money manager will tell you about all the alternative investments or deals that he knows of. Unquestionably, you should get a qualified outside opinion if you are going to be investing more than $150,000.

You might get a cheap or "free" financial plan from someone (all the big American brokers offer them), but the recommendations (consider the source) will inevitably recommend that you purchase their deals. The big stockbrokers don't have your interests at heart. They just want to sell product and earn the highest possible commissions. My recommendations on the other hand, will be entirely neutral and will make a set of suggestions having nothing to do with any secret commissions. For passive investors who don't want to take the time and trouble to do a little research, I think your best bet is to go with half a dozen solid, no-load offshore mutual funds. Magazines like the ones in my resource list will help you make a selection.

How About The Big Stockbrokers?

If you were to go through the training program at Merrill Lynch or any of the major stockbrokers, you would learn that they all are in the business of offering "products" to satisfy demand. They don't always give the best advice — they sell what is "hot" or fashionable. The result is that their investors are always heavy into the tail end of a toppy market — just before the crash. Thus, major stockbrokers are always pushing (for instance) the mutual fund that had the best performance last year. The investor doesn't realize that historically, the best performer of last year is likely to have a very bad next year.

The worst performing fund or investment sector is likely to be next year's star. But it is harder work for a stockbroker to sell a stock or a country that currently smells bad. For my own personal investments and for my clients, one of my favorite money managers (who makes me a lot of money), is Marc M. Harris. Marc is always sniffing around for deals that smell bad or are yet to be discovered by the thundering herds of Wall Street. For instance, I currently have small investments — taking positions in Cuba and Russia. A couple of years ago, Harris turned me on to Vietnam. Most of my Vietnam deals have shown better than a 100% annualized return. But as they were risky, I didn't commit more than 2% of my assets to them.

Take The Plunge

Before you bought my book you were fearful of plunging into those uncharted waters "offshore." Hopefully, by now I have shown you that the best beaches to swim in may well be outside your home country that's a metaphor of course. Naturally, we mean that some foreign country may offer excellent places for investing or holding title to your money. But don't lose all your fear. A little bit of fear is a good thing. We call it *caution.*

Why Not Change The System Instead Of Going Offshore?

Mr. "X", a gentleman of our intimate acquaintance, and very unpopular with his own government, once described North American democracy as a system where politicians in power think up ways to steal the money of those not in power. Several decades ago, he helped start a new "Libertarian" political party. Believing that America allowed freedom of speech and expression, he preached some radical thoughts. One early "X" idea was to fire ninety percent of all government employees. Another was to put "None of the above" as a choice in all elections, and if "None" was elected, to eliminate the political office. This he felt would cut the number of paid elected officials by a similar number. Then he wanted to amend the constitution to abolish the income tax (among other things), and run every city and government with a competent paid manager — just as any efficient business is run. At first, politicians held him up to scorn and ridicule: "He's just another lunatic fringe guy."

Then, in the 1970's when his "Prop 13 Anti-tax Group" achieved a landmark citizen's ballot box initiative victory by practically abolishing real estate taxes in California, the Federal Bureaucrats took notice. Local politicians predicted the collapse of state government and the collapse of the economy in California. But the only result of abolishing real estate taxes was that the government was forced to deflate (a little). The local economy got a lot better.

The media took notice of Jarvis, Gann & Mr. "X" who ran for vice-president under the Libertarian banner. A so-called "Tax Revolt" movement got underway. The thing that started the ball rolling was the success of Proposition 13 in California. Of the three people on the Proposition 13 Tax Reform Steering Committee, who began to campaign for similar measures in other states, two died shortly thereafter — under questionable circumstances. The third, Mr. "X", was criminally indicted under a directive that stated: "Others must be deterred from following his example."

A law was found to make him guilty of lying on a tax return (tax fraud). He was found guilty of *not having* a foreign account that he had properly reported and listed. When the case was over he was sentenced to jail for contempt of court for *not turning over the funds in this same account* to the court. The judge who had just found this account to be a non-existent figment of the defendant's imagination now sent him to jail because he wouldn't turn over money in the "non-existent" account. Mr. "X" actually went to jail. Then for a time, until he left the country, was forced by administrative order, to cease and desist from any more "rabble rousing or attempts at tax reforming." So much for freedom of speech. As a convicted felon he was barred from further political activity like running for (federal) public office. He was not the only person who met a similar fate for similar activities. Congressman Hansen from Idaho and Irwin Schiff was another of a cast of thousands of American tax reform authors in the same boat. Many of these people were memorialized in the PT book's HALL OF FRAME.

Don't Save The World, Look Out For Number One.

Your conclusion and mine from all this should be: You cannot fight city hall without getting severely damaged yourself. The existing power structure resists all change. So, why play their game? Do not save the world, just look out for Number One. If you are lucky enough to have had a winning streak, quit while you are ahead. Do not get into endless confrontations by trying to change the rules. The rule of government always is "Heads we win, Tails you lose." It is better to walk away from the table with as many of your chips as you can carry. Move your posterior and your possessions to climates that are more favorable. That is our message. We hope you take it to heart. We wish you a Bon Voyage!

REMEMBER THE FAMOUS LAST WORDS OF W.G. HILL:

"GET YOUR MONEY OUT OF THE COUNTRY BEFORE YOUR COUNTRY GETS THE MONEY OUT OF YOU!"

BONUS CHAPTER

THE ASSET PROTECTION OFFSHORE TRUST

"Put your money in A.P.O.T.™ and watch it grow!"
A Special Report by
W. G. HILL & ASSOCIATES
Financial Consultants
PTT Publishing c/o La Firma de Marc M. Harris
Apartado 6-1097, Estafeta El Dorado
Panama City, Republic of Panama
Fax: (507) 263-6964

"For the price of a good dinner ($99) you can now have your own asset protection trust "offshore." This Special Report by W. G. Hill & Associates objectively and simply explains the benefits and possible drawbacks of such an arrangement. It will help you make your own decision.

Your questions answered in this report:

1) Is an A.P.O.T.™ something that I could use effectively?

2) Is it legal?

3) What are the A.P.O.T.™ 's main purposes, advantages and disadvantages?

4) Why do some people pay $50,000 for the same trust that we provide for $99?

What Is A Trust?

A trust agreement is simply a document drawn up (usually) by a lawyer. An asset protection trust is a way of insulating assets from claims of creditors, governments, or lawsuit plaintiffs. In the widely publicized 1996 case of O. J. Simpson, although he was a losing defendant in a lawsuit, he still got to keep $25,000 a month in spending money. Although he lost all assets held in his own name, he kept all income from money placed in trust years before the lawsuits were filed.

How A Trust Is Created?

A lawyer usually goes to a "form book" or these days a computer service. His secretary types in the name of his client and indicates the type of trust document desired. The resulting "hard copy" is printed out. This trust agreement form costs the lawyer little or nothing — maybe $10. But his charges are based upon the wealth of the client and the assets involved. In other words, a lawyer always charges his clients for whatever the traffic will bear.

During the period 1980 to 1995, thousands of wealthy people spent on average, US $50,000 — [each!] on lawyer's fees to accomplish the same results that you can now have with a $99 — A.P.O.T.™. Why the vast price difference? Why do some people pay $50,000 and others $99 for a similar document? Because some people, especially wealthy people, unlike you, don't really know how to save money on such matters. If their lawyer bills them for $50,000 they have no way of finding out about the $99 A.P.O.T.™. The simple answer is lack of information. Some people pay $10 for a certain brand of aspirin when the exact same product, turned out by the same factory can be had for $1.

The Spendthrift Trust

A trust involves at least one person and at least some property or assets. Let us say that you have a fourteen-year old, irresponsible kid who cannot even manage his lunch money. You decide that since your kid would blow any money in his control, you will make a million-dollar gift in trust to that kid. You open a bank account styled "Papa in trust for Irresponsible Kid." You hand the kid a piece of paper saying that you (Papa) will invest and manage the trust assets, collect the interest and gains, pay kid's school fees and also give him a weekly allowance for the next 21 years.

When the kid reaches maturity at a certain age (35?), Papa, the trustee will turn everything in the trust over to the kid. Until the kid reaches 35, the kid is powerless to touch the principal; the money (for the next 21 years) is also protected against creditors of the kid or the creditors of Papa. Any trust agreement can make provisions for all kinds of eventualities. For instance: "If Papa dies before kid reaches 35, a successor trustee (a lawyer, a bank or the kid's mom) is appointed to take Papa's place as trustee."

Asset Protection Trusts- Very Popular In The United States

Due to the proliferation of lawsuits, government confiscation's, and new laws enacted to "protect us" from ourselves, many if not all wealthy people have already set up asset protection trusts. By having title to assets like stock or real property held by foreign corporations or trustees, these assets can be hidden and protected from creditors. At the same time ownership benefits (like income) can still be enjoyed as before.

Possible personal objectives satisfied by an A.P.O.T.™

The Right To Choose Your Investments

American Citizens are forbidden by law from investing their money in at least 99% of the opportunities of the world. Put simply, before most securities can be purchased by a USA citizen, they must be "approved" by the Securities and Exchange Commission. Gaining such approval is an expensive bureaucratic procedure — much like winning the OK of the Food and Drug Administration for a life saving new drug. Most companies never bother. As a result, most of the world's best performing mutual funds can't be legally sold in the USA or to USA citizens. By establishing an offshore trust to hold these forbidden investments, one can often do considerably better than with the very limited, legally approved deals for USA citizens. With an A.P.O.T.™ you have the right to choose!

Low Profile And Financial Privacy

These days, if one is in a dispute with a Federal Regulatory Agency, it is very easy for a low-grade bureaucrat to press a button on his PC. He enters your social security number, and thus, quickly identifies your bank accounts, securities, and real estate. Another few buttons are pressed, and just like that your property is "frozen." Bank and brokerage accounts are transferred to the government.

With assets held abroad and in an A.P.O.T.™, it is not possible for a creditor to locate them with any precision. It is virtually impossible to confiscate trust assets. Why? Bureaucrats and plaintiff's lawyers don't like difficult investigations and long, drawn out court procedures — especially if lawsuits must be filed and pursued abroad. As a result, in most foreign jurisdictions (unless the local governments are collaborating), not even Big Brother can get at your assets. Americans can't expect any protection in Canada or vice-versa, but cooperation in seizing the assets of Americans in most countries is only done when serious crimes are involved. Examples: Drug dealers, child-porno rings, or bank robbers.

Instant, Secure And Private Access To Your Funds

With A.P.O.T.™, it is possible to instantly access your funds, in cash, anywhere in the world, any time, 24 hours per day. Rather than going into detail about this option here, you will receive full details with the papers setting up your A.P.O.T.™.

Borrowing Power

It is likely that if your A.P.O.T.™ assets are earning excellent returns, you won't simply pull funds out for consumer spending. It is more likely that when you need cash you will borrow against these offshore assets. A credit line can be arranged in advance, and your funds can be accessed anywhere in the world, instantly upon demand.

Lawsuit & Creditor Protection

It is well known that ambulance-chasing lawyers are constantly sniffing out potential defendants by identifying high net worth individuals. Keeping some of your assets in an A.P.O.T.™ can substantially lower your visible level of wealth. This makes you a far less attractive victim. Before a contingent fee lawyer will file suit, he always gets a full report on his target's assets. Since funds and properties held in an A.P.O.T.™ are invisible (or at least, less discoverable) much litigation can be avoided or favorably settled. The same reasoning (reducing your visible net worth) goes for repelling other blood-sucking pests seeking an unwarranted share of your wealth. The list includes burglars, kidnappers, extortionists, ex-spouses, tax collectors, disgruntled business associates, crooked cops, insurance sales people, and bent bureaucrats seeking bribes. The poorer you seem, the less of a target you are.

Avoiding Probate

Particularly where your heirs are likely to squabble over their inheritance, it is likely that most of your estate could be eaten up in legal fees. Also, in some jurisdictions, the "forced heirship" law provides that you must leave all or a certain percentage of your property to a forgotten separated spouse, or to a child who detests you (and vice versa). Assets in an A.P.O.T.™ can, upon your demise, be given to any person or used for any purpose you designate. Thus, once again, you have the right to choose who gets the benefit of your estate. You don't have to let the State make those choices for you.

Exchange Controls And Taxes

Many countries have controls on foreign remittances that make it impossible to move money to where it is needed. Many Chinese-Americans were criminally charged years ago for simply sending subsistence money to aged parents on the mainland. Expat Cubans face similar risks today. Wealth taxes and other taxes eat away at your savings and profits. An A.P.O.T.™ can help you save on taxes, spend or invest your own money as you please. Certain "roll-up" investment funds convert taxable income into non-taxable, unrealized capital gains. Our staff will advise you of any special arrangements that could benefit you.

What's My Recourse If A Trustee Doesn't Do His Job Right?

The most important asset of any money manager or trust administrator is his reputation. This is why it is important to deal with an established firm that has a good reputation in depth management, client references, real offices, real employees, and good communications with customers. In our opinion, The Firm of Marc M. Harris meets these tests. [The writer of this report has a substantial and very satisfactory personal A.P.O.T.™ discretionary account with this firm!]. Besides all the usual court remedies (which take too long and are too expensive), your biggest element of control is that you can complain. Letters to the local regulatory bureaucrats will cause a legitimate operator a great deal of trouble. You can also make public your griev-ances by writing to journalists and editors. Such complaints made (to people like myself), in financial publications and on the Internet will cost a trustee dearly. Bad publicity about not providing the services you bargained for will cost much more than he could gain from mismanaging or stealing your account.

In the final analysis, dealings with a trustee or even any bank depend mainly upon trust. If you start modestly and build up assets, trust, and confidence over the years, you should do very well. A fly-by-night confidence man doesn't have the ten plus year track record of the Marc M. Harris Organization.

Technical Stuff — Questions And Answers About An A.P.O.T. - By Marc M. Harris

Q: Do I have to give up control over my assets with an A.P.O.T.™?

A: Look at it this way: do you give up control when you let a pilot or good cab driver take you where you want to go in a strange country? Not really! The professional will probably get you to your destination faster and safer than you could do it yourself. If you are unhappy you can change drivers (trustees) at any time. An A.P.O.T.™ Which you can call "the your name trust" is run by you. You call the shots. Only legal title is in the name of "your name trust." There is a foreign person who is in nominal control (your pilot), but he does exactly what you want.

Q: Are the assets physically in the country where the trust is established?

A: Normally not. You can have a Panama trustee with a bank account in Switzerland or Singapore. You can have access to that bank account anywhere in the world with an ATM (automatic teller machine) card. Securities or mutual funds may have assets all over the world and be quoted in daily papers.

Q: How can I find out my net worth and check on the performance of my assets?

A: You can do this by fax or telephone. Conventional regular statements can be mailed or faxed, but if you are on the Internet, the firm of Marc Harris is able to provide encrypted, strictly private instant statements, upon demand.

Q: If there are political problems (i.e. Wars, revolutions) in the country of the trust, does this affect me?

A: Not at all. The Swiss moved all their gold holdings and bearer securities to New York City when there was a nazi invasion threat. The firm of Marc Harris and the bulk of their 250 employees are currently in Panama. Most investment securities are now held as book entries in clearing houses. These are at major business centers like London, Zurich, Singapore. At the first sign of problems in Panama, all functions of the firm of Marc M. Harris could be easily transferred to existing facilities in a dozen other countries. The customer would never be affected by such changes as e-mail facilities and telephone lines would be electronically adjusted. However, insofar as investment banking and shop-registry functions, Panama has a hundred-year history of stability as a leading offshore banking center. In spite of the USA invasion a few years ago, normal business functions continued and the Americans reimbursed most local property damage.

Q: Can I invest in any stocks, property, or other assets that I choose?

A: Yes. But it is best for you to start with a small discretionary account owned by your A.P.O.T.™. Once you get the hang of using your A.P.O.T.™, you should have a personal meeting with your account executive to go over your objectives. You can visit us at the office abroad that is most convenient for you, or communications can be handled many other ways.

Q: Is everything you do legal?

A: Yes. We have a large staff of lawyers who keep us in compliance with all laws of all the jurisdictions where we operate. We can also put you in touch with our own in-house lawyers and certified public accountants that are licensed in your home country for tax planning and other advice. We can also prepare and certify your financial statements, income tax, and other returns. Naturally, these services are billed to you at cost, which will usually be considerably less than the cost of similar services, stateside.

Q: Do you offer other services?

A: Yes. We offer discount stock brokerage, no load mutual funds, tax and estate planning, corporate, trust, foundation establishment and management, foreign exchange trading, offshore captive insurance companies, newsletter and internet publishing as well as a full range of financial services at competitive prices. We also offer expatriation and new citizenship services. See our web page or send for details.

Q: Do I have to use your people for any or all of the services you offer?

A: No. You have the right to choose what services, if any, you use in connection with your A.P.O.T.™.

Q: What are my reporting requirements in my home country with regard to an A.P.O.T.™?

A: Certain forms need to be filled out and filed. We provide you with these filled out forms. It is your sole responsibility to file them if you choose to do so. Our firm, unless requested by you to do so in writing, reports nothing about your account to anyone.

For further information, visit our web site at http: //www.marc-harris.com.

Reader's Questions And Answers — By Dr. Hill

Reader's question from S. B. in California: I heard Dr. Hill speak in 1988. At that time he seemed quite opposed to Asset Protection Trust deals then being offered by a Colorado law firm. He was almost as negative (as you still are) towards Swiss Annuities. Why the change?

Dr. Hill replies: The asset protection trusts that were touted and marketed by several USA based law firms during the 1980's, and still today, have a lot wrong with them. I am still against them. But just because you don't like the way they make scrambled eggs at one restaurant, doesn't mean you should never try scrambled eggs. These were my main objections:

Too Expensive

The first thing was getting your money's worth. These guys were selling a few pages of boilerplate (pre-prepared text) for $40,000 to $50,000. Besides this, there was an additional $5,000 per year in running costs. Nice works if you can get it — for lawyers and accountants! For years, the much more effective Liechtenstein Foundation had been available from offshore banks, brokers and lawyers for under $3,000 in set-up costs and $2,000 per year to keep it going. For myself, I even found the Liechtenstein foundations over-priced. But until Harris came out with the nominally priced A.P.O.T.™ there were no cheap alternatives for middle class people who shouldn't spend a big percentage of their income on asset protection. So, first and foremost, it was the sucker price I objected to.

Not Secret

Second, any asset protection trust set up and administered by USA-based lawyers or certified public accountants in the country where the settlor (person who sets up the trust) actually lives is nearly worthless. Look at it from a confidentiality point of view: Under the rules of the game (litigation procedures) USA-based accountants have to tell everything they know and disclose all paperwork and correspondence. If they don't tell all your secrets even in a frivolous lawsuit, they can go to jail for contempt of court. The reason is simple. Any person or financial services firm within the USA is subject to the jurisdiction of USA courts or administrative agencies like the IRS. They are obliged to cooperate to make full disclosure in virtually every case that is filed. If they don't they can be jailed or they'll lose their precious license to practice. Lawyers used to have an "attorney client privilege" but in recent years, this secrecy has been seriously eroded. The fact is that several attorneys have been disbarred and/or have gone to jail because they refused to roll over and make full disclosure of client affairs. Judicial exceptions to the attorney client privilege are made wherever there is an allegation of fraud. Accountants have never had any privilege or duty to keep their clients' affairs a secret. Naturally, every creditor or plaintiff will yell fraud where the defendant seems to be living well, but has no visible assets to pay a judgment. The net result is that any facts known to USA-based lawyers, accountants or other service providers plus any written or electronically stored records within the jurisdiction might as well be published on the front page of our local newspaper. Without secrecy, the main benefit — hiding assets to prevent being a target of government agents or plaintiff's lawyers — is seriously diminished.

Tax Neutral

Most (but not all) foreign trusts won't save anything on income taxes. Reporting requirements for tax purposes, if observed, can still hide and protect assets from seizure in a lawsuit, but theoretically should not affect tax liability. There are still a few exceptions or loopholes, but we certainly are not going to reveal them in print. Our past experience has been that bureaucrat and legislators read tax-avoidance materials [like this report] very carefully. Within a year or two, new legislation is passed to close any forgotten tax loopholes we point out. Suffice it to say that neither the $50,000 trust nor the Harris $99 trust will in most cases legally saves anyone a dime in taxes. But remember, I said "in most cases." A good offshore advisor still knows a few tricks that can help you save on taxes legally!

The $50,000 Model Doesn't Do As Good A Job As A $99 Offshore Trust

The asset protection trust set up by USA personnel may protect some assets from a lazy plaintiff's lawyer. It is not completely worthless, but for most people, it will be money down the toilet. A foreign trust set up by people outside the USA will do a better job of it. Why? Simply because records of its existence, being one step removed, are generally unobtainable. Courts cannot jail or disbar a foreigner in the financial services business unless that person visits the jurisdiction where he is sought for questioning.

Diversification — The Final Word

If your purpose is to protect your nest egg from creditors or plaintiffs that are not yet existing, the asset protection trust is one legal way of doing it. It is not the only method. Simply using an alias (alternate identification documents, etc.) to do the job used to be a cheaper and better way. Unfortunately, with the new money laundering laws forced on most of the world by Big Brother, using an alias or pen name to open a bank or brokerage account is not so easy to do any more. It isn't impossible, but these days, it may cost a lot more than $99 to arrange. An A.P.O.T.™ is easy, cheap and still legal. It is not a perfect solution that protects you against all eventualities. Anyone who tells you they have something that is 100% sure is either a liar or a dreamer. The bottom line is that I personally would never have more than ten to twenty per cent of my assets with any one-fund manager, in any one country or in any one legal structure. You never know what could go wrong. But if you keep your big mouth shut, and quietly diversify abroad to lower your financial profile, it can't hurt. You may not avoid all lawsuits and government confiscation, but you'll insure that potential enemies can't take everything you own at one stroke of a pen.

Note: The author welcomes any questions, comments, or corrections! Tell us something we don't know, and even if you offer a service that competes with the Harris A.P.O.T.™ we will print your comments and give you a plug in our next edition. Our purpose is to inform our readers, not push any one product or service.

How the A.P.O.T.™ Works For A Typical Client

ALBERT is a plumber. He makes good money, if you call $250,000 a year good money. He has about a million in securities, two million invested in his home and other real estate, $500,000 in foreign bank accounts, and a million in an A.P.O.T.™. His dad was also a plumber. Albert remembers the time when his dad was sued because twin babies drowned in a bathtub. It was unfortunate for the parents, but logically Albert's dad shouldn't have been held responsible. But the parent's lawyers went hunting for someone with "deep pockets." Dad was the targeted defendant. The parents sued him for $100 Million "wrongful death" and pain and suffering. Dad had installed this bathroom many years earlier. There was no legal requirement to put in handrails. There still is no such requirement. But that didn't stop a jury from deciding that dad's bathtub (lacking handrails) had been negligently installed. Dad got stuck with a judgment for twenty million dollars. His insurance went up to $1 million — and with personal assets of only another few million, this event put him into bankruptcy at the age of 62.

Not wanting all his life savings to be subject to some similar claim, before he found out about the A.P.O.T.™, Albert placed some assets in secret, numbered foreign accounts. He found that he could invest in stocks, bonds, funds or anything else by simply calling his foreign English speaking "offshore" investment bankers from a phone booth or public fax and telling them his wishes. The accounts were in his name though. Albert was always worried that if put on the stand in a trial and asked about property in his name, he would be faced with a difficult choice: He'd have to lie, or to avoid testifying, have to leave the country till the heat was off. If he simply told the truth he'd be ordered to bring the foreign assets back to pay off the creditors.

The Asset Protection Offshore Trust, or A.P.O.T.™, gave Albert an additional layer of protection. He filled out a few forms, and then made arrangements to transfer assets (stock certificates, gold coins, cash, etc.) to the "Dependable Trust Company" as trustee under A.P.O.T.™ #143. As a practical matter, this account was like any account with a stockbroker or investment banker. Only Albert's name was not attached in any way to the assets. He was just the "designated trust advisor." Albert could call, fax or e-mail his personal customer representative at Dependable Trust and give orders of what to buy and sell. If he gave discretionary investment powers to his investment bankers, Albert could find out what had gone up, and what had gone down, and thus monitor his account's performance. The fees and charges or managing his money and for keeping the trust alive were about the same as any "discount broker" would charge for handling a similar sized account. If Albert wanted to buy a house or a car or a tract of land, at home or abroad, he could ask Dependable to do it, and they would. The new assets could be held in the name of the trust, given as a gift to anyone, or even put back in Albert's name. In short, Albert controlled the trust, and would benefit from the assets and income. But a judgment creditor or hostile party would find it incredibly difficult to (A) Find out about the trust or if they knew, to (B) Put a lien on it or grab the assets.

This is not to say that in an extreme case, a local judge might tell Albert to pay the judgement or go to jail for contempt. There are many penniless debtors serving indefinite sentences — especially in domestic relation's cases. Judges do have the power to seize local assets immediately or to coerce people they suspect of having hidden assets: "Cough up or go to jail." But as mentioned in our introduction, plaintiffs and their lawyers always look for visible, easily recovered assets. If they don't see any, they don't normally file suit.

Obviously, the powers of any government agency or tax collector to seize or confiscate assets stops at the international border — unless serious criminal activities (like drug dealing) covered by treaties are involved. Even then, there can be no seizures unless the assets are identified and linked to the "criminal" and court proceedings in the foreign country result in the equivalent of a criminal conviction.

The net result of the exercise was that Albert had X million dollars of assets "offshore" in an A.P.O.T.™. The money is well managed, invested, safe from creditors, and will provide a nice financial cushion for his retirement. Even if hit with an unwarranted claim like the one that bankrupted his father, Albert will be financially secure. Unlike his father, he can have a comfortable retirement.

Can you afford not to protect your assets with an A.P.O.T.™?

For the average middle class professional or tradesman who has accumulated a few dollars, the A.P.O.T.™ is one of several very effective methods of protecting those assets. The fact that this trust and all records pertaining to it are held offshore (in a foreign country with secrecy laws) throws up nearly insurmountable barriers against unjust claims and seizures.

Resource List For The Invisible Investor

By Peter Trevellian

*B*Y adding a resource section like this, we hope to provide useful initial contacts to readers who (before reading this book) may have been totally in the dark. There is a whole brave new world of service providers out there. Some are good some are incompetent.

For the novice, it is impossible to distinguish between the good guys and the sharks. Trial and error can be expensive when you trust people with your secrets and your money. How about recommendations in a book like this? Should you put your trust in what we have to say? **NO!** Don't rely on anything with blind faith! Before you risk any money or tell your family secrets, sniff around. Con men are convincing, but they cannot withstand scrutiny or penetrating questions. We have done some *preliminary screening* for you and we believe our recommended resources are honest, discreet and reliable. But if I personally had a million dollars for every time I was shafted, I'd be a few million richer than I am. An outfit that is solid and reliable today can fold next year. One of the largest banks in the World (Bank of America) barely survived a few years ago. Fortunately, if you read the papers, the relevant Internet postings and a few newsletters, you'll have advance warning in plenty of time to move your ass or your assets out of harm's way. If you smell trouble, forget "loyalty." Just take appropriate action. Move your assets to a safer haven fast! That rule applies at home or abroad.

When looking for the offshore banks or stockbrokers you expect to place your confidence in, should you bring along your home-country lawyer? No! Not unless he is your brother and you trust him with your life. Your home country lawyers and accountants are the last people who should know about your offshore activities. Domestic lawyers, accountants and of course the government have a vested interest in killing any offshore deals you make. Why that? The local service provider want to keep your money and business (and those juicy fees & taxes) in their own office!

Who can you trust as a consultant just to make the initial offshore introductions or contacts? Dr. Hill for sure. Me. I guess. Unfortunately, you have to pay Dr. Hill or myself for your time. Are there others? I am sure there are, but we don't know of them. If you are a consultant or know a good "PT" who has walked the walk, tell us. We will be happy to list them in future editions. Also see our chapter on this subject. But you don't need a consultant to hold your hand. With the lists and information in this book you can do it all yourself. I strongly recommend a trip (or several trips) to the various tax havens to interview your prospective new money managers.

Free Advice

They say that free advice is worth what you pay for it. But I don't agree entirely. If you ask enough questions of enough people, you will get something approaching the truth.

Probably anyone who has lived as a PT for the past few years and has no particular product to push or service to sell is a good source of guidance. You can get information maybe for the price of a good lunch or dinner! This is why going to some **offshore conferences** could be important to you. You can meet the people who live the life and have done it. The pitchmen on stage at a conference (who are all trying to sell you something) are less likely to give you reliable information than your fellow attendees.

Ask questions! It's the only way to learn. Force yourself to be an extrovert. Meet as many new people as possible. Develop some product or service you yourself can offer — or better yet, something you can trade! It is more fun if you are a player, not just a watcher.

These days, people are paying up to US$5,000 for just an introduction to an offshore banker. I think they are stupid because basically, you can walk in the door of most banks with a banker's letter of introduction, "to whom it may concern", and with a passport. You can open an account without any "introduction." Only in Switzerland, where I am not so keen to go anyway, will they generally turn down business from American passport holders. There has been too much heat over money laundering from the American government. Some elite bankers don't want any new business from Americans.

Free Stuff

Free "state of the art" laptop computer & special proprietary software with encrypting and international communication capabilities, **total value US$10,000** is given to new private asset management customers at Harris Investment Advisory, Fax: 011-507-263-6964. globalinvesting@marc-harris.com. The idea is to establish secure communications links with their clients. We discovered their really good computer/modem could be used for net surfing, game playing, and everything else. Shhhh! Don't tell anyone, as this deal is the only one like it in the industry. When an account is opened in person, you walk out the door with the computer in your hand. You even get a lesson or two while at their headquarters on how to use the equipment. They will also ship it to you at your home, if desired. I don't think they want this offer publicized, but as it was the most expensive "free gift" I ever got just for opening a stock brokerage account, I thought I'd better mention it. When you contact them just say "Will you give me the same deal you gave Trevellian, about the free computer I heard about from Invisible Investor?" For more info on this outfit see: Offshore **Service Provider** a few pages ahead.

Free Stuff Via Computer

Now you know how to get a free high quality computer (above). If you don't have a computer and a connection to the Internet, you are not able to participate in the most exciting and useful source of information and communication in the world today. It is a million times better than phones, faxes, or yelling out of windows. There are so many offers on the Internet that you can't count them. For instance: Choose from 10,000 different free catalogs by connecting to http:// catalog.savvy.com/catalog.html. Over 1,000 free newsletters at http:/ /pub.savvy.com/CGI-bin/newsletter. You can get a free email address so that no one can find out where you really live from "hotmail." Send inquiry to meat trevellian@hotmail.com or visit web page www.hotmail.com.

Cheap Phone Calls

Everyone knows about Kallback and similar services. Anywhere in the world you dial a free local number. Then you dial in the number you are calling. Presto you are called back — connected on long distance calls at up to 90% off regular telephone company rates. You can reach Kallback by fax in the USA at 1-206-599-1980, or 417 Second Avenue West, Seattle WA 98119 USA. See their website at http://www.kallback.com. E-mail: info@kallback.com. Dear Reader: For future editions, please send me other recommendations for my "cheap or free" section. If you have a computer, you can make phone calls (with a picture!) anywhere in the world for the price of a local call with new attachments. For the moment they are not as high quality as the sound on your phone, but it keeps getting better.

Cheap Faxes (Outgoing)

If you have a computer, you can send faxes in the USA for 10¢ a page, or worldwide, around 30¢ just enter the fax number you want and follow it with <@faxaway.com>. For full details on this program, see http://www.faxaway.com or e-mail info@faxaway.com.

Cheap Faxes Or Voicemail (Incoming)

JFAX has local fax numbers in most major cities. For US$12.50 per month (if you have a computer) you can get faxes from your friends (or enemies). They won't know (and can't find out) where you really are. You give them a number in London or Paris and the message is transmitted automatically (and instantly) by email to your computer. Call "1-888-GET-JFAX" [From outside USA CALL 1-

212-431-3833], OR EMAIL TO <INFO@JFAX.NET>, or write: JFAX, 60 Spring St., New York City, NY, USA 10012.

Can You Rely On Writers Like Trevellian And Books Like This?

Some books are written to sell the author's product or services. Although this book may (sometimes) sound like I am pushing my own consulting services that's not really true. We can pay the rent and still eat very well if we never earn another dime. Nevertheless, we also like helping the interesting people who have decided to break free of Big Brother by going "PT". We can help you "find freedom in an unfree world" and we like making new friends. Over the years our clients (and their wives or companions) have become our social friends. We trade houses, cars, and information, travel together and have a good time. This group of my clients and ex-clients is the "Inner Circle" of original PT's. I have found that people who like my writing style are apt to like me personally, and I them. Thus, publishing a book like this helps me find kindred souls. The money is secondary. By charging a hefty fee (US$10,000 for two years unlimited consulting), I eliminate most time wasters. Also, poverty has no place in my orbit. What other books do you know of where the author will appear and call (or email) you directly on command, like a genie? I also am open to offers of trades instead of money and I do (among other things) ghost-writing of auto-biographies promotional campaigns and other writing assignments unrelated to "PT."

Not All "Hill" Books Are By The Original Hill

It has also been the experience of my predecessor and myself, Dr. Hill that when a book publisher buys up the rights to re-publish one of our old titles, editorial control is lost. There goes the integrity of a book (sometimes). Different people than the named author do the revisions. They recommend products and services — perhaps for a kickback or commission. The publishers hire new, inexperienced writers to put forth silly, non-workable ideas and suggestions. Sometimes they recommend less than savory service providers do. Sometimes the publishers themselves can't distinguish between crooks and good guys. In this section, as I write this, the year is 1998 and I Peter Trevellian, "pure at heart" can assure you that I am getting no kick-backs from anyone on this list that I "highly recommend." I am going to try and act like the people who award the "Good House-keeping Seal of Approval." Remember that from when we were kids? I will give a recommendation to outfits that I trust. From my comments if I don't commend them at all, you'll possibly be able to avoid some of the sharks. I won't call anybody a crook in this book. Why? Because the worst crooks are the first to sue and cause a guy like me to waste a lot of time and money in court.

As you know, my goal is (and yours should be) to avoid confrontations and litigation, not to say or write things to invite it. But in a private conference, I can tell you the real story about most people you'll encounter in the "Offshore" biz. Run a name or "offering brochure" by me, and I can tell you in about 30 seconds if it is a con or what. Another good source of info on scams is Tony Heatherington who writes columns for *International the Investor Magazine*, the *London Financial Times, and the Offshore Advisor.* All these are listed in this resource section with addresses. Hetherington is really good and knows who to stay away from. Encourage him as I have, to put his many exposes into a book and write him to ask about any "suspect" propositions. I never met him, but have spoken with him on the phone. He has helped some of my clients get their money back from such outfits as one-man banks who promised huge inter-est, but then did a Ponzi (paid off old depositors with new depositor's' money).

You Can Get Help From Me For Free!

This could be very important to you some day: *If you ever have any complaints about any outfit that I have mentioned, write or email me. Tell me the whole story in detail. I may be able to get the outfit that "done you wrong" to give you satisfaction. If I can't get your money back, and it seems to me that they are in the wrong, I will pull my recommendation. This "ultimate weapon" may give you some protection. It is extremely important to me that we never get conned into favorably recommending any service that doesn't deliver as prom-*

ised! There is no charge by me for investigating a complaint. Here is one outfit you should never have to complain about:

Offshore Service Provider
(Banking, Securities Brokerage, 2nd Passports & Financial Guidance)

As mentioned several times in this book, we **highly recommend** the well established offshore money manager and discount stock broker: The Harris Organisation, PO Box 6-1097, El Dorado, Panama City, Panama. Their main office is located at the Balboa Plaza Building, on Balboa Drive — the main drag. Marc's personal office is Room 501. Their telephone number is (507) 263-6900, Fax: (507) 263-6964. globalinvesting@marc-harris.com. In addition to Panama, they have operations in over 10 countries. You can learn a lot about this well established outfit and their services by dialing up their home page on a computer connected to the Internet: www.marc-harris.com. They can fix you up with offshore corporations, foundations, trusts, annuities (if you insist), bank accounts, legal second passports, and above all good advice. They even prepare tax returns and can insure you against the costs of any audit. The first half-hour conference (phone or in person) and a tour of their offices is free. They will even pick you up at the Panama City airport, for free. They are located a block down Balboa Drive from the new Miramar Intercontinental Hotel, the best in town. The best suburban hotel is the Caesar Park. Remember this though. When you go for the free tour and consultation package, although you are under no obligation. To get the most out of your visit, WRITE DOWN WHAT IT IS YOU HOPE TO ACCOMPLISH BY GOING OFFSHORE. Let them know your goals and approximate resources before you arrive. That way if any research is needed it will be done before you get to Panama.

The reason I like this firm so much is that (as explained in our earlier chapter "Kiss of Life) they will take an interest in you as a human being, long term client and partner — not just "gimmee your money and go." They have a staff of lawyers who can help you to be a Boy Scout and do everything legally and by the book — if that is your desire. If you want to do things not recommended by your government, like investing in forbidden places [Cuba? Vietnam?], they may be willing to point you in the right directions and set up trusts or corporations so you don't break the law and invest directly.

Harris shares my philosophy of giving a client a lot of options and letting the client choose. They don't push you into things. But remember this, The Harris Organisation has a lot of personnel (over 200). **It is possible that you might be assigned someone who grates on you or isn't your style of person. If that should happen to you, ask to see that person's supervisor or the C.E.O. Then ask for someone else to work with you.**

The Big Boss, Marc Harris is busy making good investment deals. He doesn't have time to see many new clients. But if you are thinking of letting Harris manage US$1,00750,000 or more for you, you just ask for his personal assistant (Olga or Valerie). Tell them that Peter Trevellian, in his book said that Mr. Harris would be happy to meet high net worth customers personally, even if they only want to place a small amount first, to test the waters.

If you have a legal question, make an appointment with the head of their legal department. He is a former prosecutor and tax law professor from Washington D.C. Also, if you get in touch with Harris and become one of his private clients as a result of reading this book, be sure to ask for your special "state of the art" computer and communications system (that you keep at your residence) worth approximately US$10,000. It will allow you to monitor your offshore investments and communicate confidentially.

What is my connection with Harris? **This is full disclosure.** He is a former consulting client who has become a social friend. He shares my ideas and beliefs. When I am in Panama, I stay at his home — for free. When he, and his wife, and his three children are in my neck of the woods (Thailand or wherever), he gets the same treatment from me. I wrote this book in Panama and felt that if I were personally going to start a business to turn freedom seeking people from ordinary mortals into "PT's" it would be exactly like what he has done with The Firm of Marc M. Harris. I have some of my own money invested with Marc Harris and I get the same good service as all of his clients get — nothing more or less. PS: I did get the free US$10,000 computer from him but all his clients at a certain financial level get it too. See "Free Stuff" above regarding this offer.

Advisors To The Super Rich

We have noticed that most banks and money managers to the super rich are so low profile they don't even call themselves "banks." Marc Harris has told me that within twenty years he hopes that his clients (due to his astute money management skills) will all be super rich, and his firm too, will be accepting only eight figure (over US$10 Million Dollar) net worth clients. For now, Harris will manage as little as US$100,000.

Favored by **British** Aristocrats, Jersey (Channel Islands, Great Britain) Offshore Service Provider **Mourant du Feu & Jeune** is Jersey's leading law firm. It is proud of its pre-eminent position in the Island and of the influential role that it played in developing Jersey as a leading offshore jurisdiction. The firm can trace its history back more than 100 years and was established under its present name in 1947. Today Mourant du Feu & Jeune, together with its wholly owned **Trust Company Mourant & Co.**, employs over 200 staff acting for clients around the world. Today Mourant du Feu & Jeune acts for very high net worth private clients who require money management and an effective legal adviser in Jersey. In the local community, the firm can help would be immigrants who would like to move to Jersey and take advantage of the maximum 20% flat rate income tax. Jersey's close proximity to the United Kingdom and Europe make it an ideal offshore center with excellent communications in a very convenient time zone for British millionaires who want to put their assets (and perhaps themselves) offshore. Minimum accounts US$2 million.

Another money manager favored by the British, and used by the Queen herself is Coutts & Company having offices in London and in the entire major offshore banking centers. Minimum US$1 million.

The **Bessemer Trust Company** or the **Northern Trust Company, both in the USA** (with representatives in all of the wealthier USA communities) may be just the ticket for Americans who want to stay at home and have their money managed by the folks who provide services to many individuals with vast inherited wealth. Trouble is even if they do very well, after taxes and inflation, your mother lode keeps shrinking. Thus "offshore" is obviously better. Minimum US$5 million.

Wealthy **French** people favor **Ferrier & Lullen** of (French Speaking, right across the border, 3 hours from Paris) Geneva, Switzerland, who have been managing the inherited money of French aristocrats for around 500 years. Slightly less exclusive and also in Geneva are **Bank Von Ernst, Hentsch, Bank Julius Bar, Vontobel, and Bank Indo-Suez. They all have many officers who speak perfect English. Remember that Switzerland is no longer advised as an asset depository for Americans. But the above banks all have "safe" branches or subsidiaries in other tax haven locations.** Minimum US$5 million. But all of the above accept smaller amounts on a trial basis.

In Switzerland's postal and telephone system, but not legally in Switzerland, **The Private Bank of Liechtenstein (PO Box 885, Vaduz, Liechtenstein FL9490) and the Bank in Liechtenstein (owned by the Prince) at PO Box 85, Vaduz FL9490)** are both old favorites. They will accept accounts of value over US$1,000,000 and do a decent, conservative job of managing your money.

Of the money managers listed above, in terms of asset management performance, Bessemer (with an office in the Cayman Islands), Julius Bar (Zurich), and Ferrier & Lullen all have averaged between 15% and 25% annual returns for their clients over the past ten years. Marc M. Harris' "aggressive portfolios" do somewhat better. Liechtenstein makes its investors around 12% per year in dollars, over the long term. However, in any of these places you can specify the sort of portfolio you want to invest in: Bonds, equities, high volatility, Asian, small cap, junk bonds, diversified, etc.

Consultants

Chevalier Harry D. Schultz is a venerable newsletter author (International Harry Schultz Letter) and consultant for all PT and investment matters. US$100 per minute. Send advance payment (minimum US$3,000) in US dollars to **FERC, PO Box 622, CH1001, Lausanne, Switzerland or fax (32-16) 535-777** with questions and your phone or fax number. Minimum charge of US$3,000 is for a 30-minute fax or phone consultation. Retainer US$112,000 per year. Harry Schultz is the world's most expensive investment adviser, listed for decades as such in the Guinness World Book of Records. Since his newsletter takes about 200 hours to produce each month and has Sir Harry's genius and input on almost everything, the Investment Newsletter is a much better bargain, at US$285 per year. Or, send US$25 in cash or equivalent to cover postage and handling for a free sample back issue and a current issue. Write Sir Harry that you read about this offer in a book by Peter Trevellian. Chevalier Harry Schultz lives in the South of France, usually.

W.G. Hill (The Legendary Original!) is semi-retired, but tells us he will take on one or two selected consulting clients per year. His annual retainer is US$10,000 (unlimited calls or contact). Add costs of his getting to and staying at places of mutual convenience. If personal meetings are desired. You may contact him (mark fax or e-mail on top "PERSONAL AND CONFIDENTIAL for the Eyes of the Original W. G. Hill Only") c/o the publisher of this book or Fax him in Paris, France at (331) 5301-3119 or London (44-171) 681 1490 or E-mail: drwghill@hotmail.com. Hill normally lives in Japan, France, and Chile. Enclose your message marked "Hill" in sealed envelope. Allow several weeks for initial contact. For guaranteed contact, use duplicate messages to ALL suggested addresses. Top of message must say "To: W.G. Hill."

Peter Trevellian (Author of this book). Cheaper by far than Hill & Schultz, [but the advice, if I say so myself, just as good]. Of course, "Consider the Source!" Since I wrote this book I could say anything I want. But seriously, if you liked my style and think I can help you, my fee is US$10,000 up front. For that you get **two years** of unlimited but reasonable consultation by phone or email on any PT related subject. Personal meetings or one-off conferences or phone consultations at US$1,000 also possible. I am based in Thailand and Switzerland usually, but travel quite a bit. Contact me at trevellian@hotmail.com. If no Internet connection is made, try writing me c/o my mail drop "PT Wales, St. George's House, 31A St. George's Road, Leyton, London E10 5RH, Great Britain" or "PT Cores, C.P. 82, CH 8887, Mels, Switzerland." Put your message to me, Peter Trevellian inside a separate sealed envelope inside the envelope and say "Redirect to Peter Trevellian". Give me a telephone and time where you can be called collect, or an e-mail address, or a mail address. Fax to: (331) 5301 3119 or (31 20) 524 12 26. Fax must say on top "To Peter Trevellian."

How To Get On Mailing Lists For Offshore Conferences

Do this and you will get so many invitations, you might soon want to get off the lists! Here are a few places to write. Just say: "Put my name down for any future international investment conferences you sponsor."

Offshore Investment Conference Organizers

Peter T. Trevellian, PTT Communications, PO Box 6-1097, El Dorado, Panama City, Panama. Or write to the publisher: Address: On the front page of this book. Fax: (507) 263-6964, visit web page http://www.ptshamrock.com.invisible.htmllst. If there is enough interest, Peter Trevellian hopes to organize an annual Invisible Investor, "PT Conference" in attractive vacation spots. Just ask to get on our mailing list.

Other Offshore Conference Organizers who will send you a brochure, upon request.

Oxford Club, at 800-992-0205, 410-223-2643, or Fax: 410-223-2650.

Scope International, Forestside House, Rowland's Castle, Hants, PO9 6EE. See http://www.britnet.co.uk.

Shorex, 4 Heathgate Place, London NW3 2NU, Fax 44 171-482-1100 or infor@shorex.com.

Tax Planning Association UK +44 1732-762-910

International Herald Tribune UK +44 171-836-4802

International Professional Conferences UK +44 161-445-8623

European Study Conferences UK +44 171-386-9322I BC

Legal Studies & Services UK +44 171-637-4383

Key Haven Publications UK +44 181-780-2522

Offshore Investment Magazine, 62 Brompton Rd., London SW3 1BW, UK +44 171-225-0550

International Tax Academy The Netherlands +31-20-626-7726

Professional Education Systems USA +1-715-836-9700

Management Centre Europe Belgium +32-2-543-2100

Institute for International Research USA +1-212-661-8740

Professional Education Systems USA +1-715-836-9700

Offshore Investment Magazine UK +44 171-225-0550, UK +44 171-610-4509

Sample Seminar Announcement

Seminars in conjunction with The Oxford Club "Asset Protection Strategies"

Domestic and Offshore Techniques for Asset Protection, International Estate and Financial Planning. The Oxford Club is a private financial club with more than 70,000 members worldwide. Club members share one common goal: To enjoy financial independence and create a legacy of secure, private wealth for their families and themselves. The Oxford Club sponsors seminars.

A US$50.00 attendance fee includes light refreshments and a free copy of our just released "Fortress of Wealth" report. Topics to be covered will include:

1. Introduction to asset protection
2. Domestic asset protection
   - Nevada Corps., Wyoming and Delaware Corps.
   - Family Limited Partnerships, LLC's and domestic trusts.

- Will include income and estate tax savings from domestic entities. Actual case histories will be discussed.
3. Offshore asset protection
   - Asset protection trusts, offshore corporations, offshore banking, and annuities.
   - Selecting a tax haven and an offshore service provider
   - Privacy, use of the Internet for communications.

There will be ample time for questions during the seminar.

Due to the exclusivity of this meeting, seating is limited. Early reservations recommended. Call The Oxford Club, at 800-992-0205 or 410-223-2643, or fax 410-223-2650.

Trevellian's Note: The reader should note that any free or inexpensive seminar is going to be primarily an "infomercial" aimed at selling them some products or services. Perhaps these services will be of value, but it is best to shop around and fully understand what is needed and the costs of competing services before you buy.

Recommended "Straight Arrow" Tax Lawyer

Marshall J. Langer, tax lawyer with Schutts and Bowen, 48 Mount Street, London, England, WIY 5RE, Tel.: +44 171493 4840, Fax: +44 171493 4299. Very ethical, responsible and professional. Charges are about US$600 per hour. Good for international tax planning, especially for individuals who are considering changing countries, acquiring another citizenship, or expatriation. Langer is author of *The Tax Exile Report* and *The Swiss Report* both published by Scope International. He is also author of *Practical International Tax Planning*, published by Practicing Law Institute, available from Scope International, price £150 / US$250 airmail post free. Langer can also be contacted through Schutts & Bowen's Miami office, Tel.: 305-379-9130, Fax: 305-381-9982.

Tax Havens

The Tax Exile Report by Marshall Langer covers expatriation and the tax consequences of changing residence and citizenship in great detail and has become the authoritative source of information on these subjects for non professionals. The standard reference work on tax havens, expatriation, and so on is *International Tax Planning*, also by Marshall Langer. See the listing under "Recommended Tax Lawyer" for more information.

For a most comprehensive treatment consider reading Diamond on Tax Havens, the original "old standard" for offshore operations. Expensive. It is published by **Matthew Bender, 11 Penn Plaza, New York, NY 10001, USA.**

One expensive but very good book on the subject is Tax Havens And Their Uses, Special Report No 186, by Carol Doggart, published by The Economist, a respected British business magazine at **25 St James's Street, London SWIA IHG, UK.** Price £75.

Butterworth's Tax Haven Encyclopedia is a loose-leaf binder on the subject. It is available from Hasbury House, 35 Chancery Lane, London, WC2A TEL, UK at £155 (plus updates) but can be found in most major business libraries. They also produce another large loose-leaf book ion immigration law in the UK.

Almost every major accounting firm publishes useful free booklets for distribution to clients and potential clients, meaning you! These cover tax laws and business conditions in selected jurisdictions. You can get these for free. Just call the "librarian" of the firm in any major city for a list of their publications. Try any major Certified Public Accountant, known as "Chartered Accountant" in the Commonwealth. For instance: Touche Ross, Price Waterhouse, Peat Marwick, Pannell Kerr Forster, Arthur Anderson, Arthur Young, etc. Find them in the yellow pages or commercial phone book listings.

Scam Alert: Prime Bank Guarantees — Loan Broker Services With Upfront Fees

Be warned. There is no such thing. This is a classic swindle. For details you may get a special report on Prime Bank Guarantees from the publisher at US$100. But we recommend you simply stay away from any scheme where you will supposedly get a vastly higher interest rate than usual. All are scams. That's really all you have to know. The same is true of deals where you pay a point or two up front to get a loan. All you will get is a stall, and you will never see your 1% or 2% fee ever again. On a legitimate loan, the fees are paid out of loan proceeds.

Recommended Newsletters

One of the most offbeat publications we have come across is the *Expat Newsletter*. The price of a one-year special half-price dis-, count trial subscription is US$70. Their monthly rag has wonderful classified ads on places to rent, dating & mating agencies and many other weird and wonderful things. Recommended. Send subscription fee to the publisher or US$5 for a sample issue (you must mention Invisible Investor). PO Box 1341, Raffles City, Singapore 9117. The editor calls himself "Willie Wonka" but I doubt that's his real name.

Harry Schultz International Newsletter is issued every four to six weeks. This newsletter is an interesting mixture of investment advice, political updates, and philosophy. It is the only newsletter in the world that has a regular PT section by the guy who originated the concept! I strongly suggest a trial subscription (print, fax, or E-mail) to this stimulating newsletter of original ideas. It's also a mind-boggling guide to profitable international investments (stocks, bonds, metals, and futures. One-year subscription for US$285 or a free sample copy sends US$25 to cover postage and handling. Please send your inquiry and payment to the publisher or **FERC, PO Box 622, CH1001, Lausanne, Switzerland or fax (32-16) 535-777.** Indispensable for the PT. The world's original international newsletter and the oldest in continuous operation — for over 35 years.

International Living Newsletter is a wonderful monthly bulletin with interesting ads. A subscription is not expensive, but write for the current rate as it is due to change shortly before we go to press. This newsletter offers many ads on vacation home rentals and exchanges etc. as well as great travel articles, plus a section on travel bargains. News of interest to PT's and nomads not found elsewhere. Highly recommended! Send US$5 for sample back issue (if you mention Peter Trevellian) to **Agora Inc. 824 East Baltimore St, Baltimore, MD 21202, USA.**

Adrian Day's Investment Analyst is from one of the few intelligent financial journalists in the world whose perceptive stories and sound financial advice has often produced good results for me. Introductory subscription, US$78/year. Free sample available if you mention Peter T. Write to **PO Box 6644, Annapolis, MD 21401, USA.**

Larry Abraham's Newsletter Insider Report comes highly recommended by Harry Schultz and by us. Send US$5 for a sample issue to **Insider Report, PO Box 84903, Phoenix, AZ 85071, USA.** The writer, an American expat lives in Santiago, Chile.

Marc Harris Investment News & Marc Harris Financial Analysis. These two newsletters are free to his money management and brokerage firm customers. They are in the US$120 per year range for outsiders. Send US$10 to publisher for **a free trial subscription** of at least 3 issues. [Special Note: If you actually bought and paid for this book, or received it as a gift, you are entitled to a free trial subscription. Just mention you bought the Invisible Investor book (say where & how much you paid) and send E-mail request to newsletter@marc-harris.com or by fax or mail with US$10 handling costs to our publisher.

Ken Gerbino's Newsletter also comes recommended by Harry Schultz. Send US$5 for sample issue to **Suite 200, 9595 Wilshire Boulevard, Beverly Hills, California 90212, USA.**

The Reaper. An eccentric investment and PT Philosophy newsletter written by R.E. McMaster that has our very high recommendation. Send US$10 (to cover postage cost) for free trial subscription. Write to R.E. McMaster Box 6-1097, El Dorado, Panama, or Internet www.thereaper.com where you can read back issues for free.

My Personal Favorite Newsletters

International Living (about travel destinations and with great ads) and *Bottom Line* Costs only US$30 (in USA) US$45 (abroad) a year. Has over a million circulation's, and has intelligent and useful hints on investing, travel, sex, relationships, etc.

If I wrote a Newsletter (which I don't because its too much work!) it would look exactly like ***Bottom Line/Personal.*** This eight pager is published twice a month by Boardroom Inc., Box 2614, 55 Railroad Ave., Greenwich, CT 06836-2614. Boardroom also publishes Bottom Line/Business, Bottom Line/Tomorrow, Health Confidential, Moneysworth and Tax Hotline. You can subscribe at the special introductory rate for I.I. readers of **US$29.95 for a year** — total of 24 issues. This is the biggest bargain in the newsletter industry. Absolute Highest Recommendation.

Special Reports For PT's

PTO-Portable trades & occupations... By: Peter Trevellian & W. G. Hill

Don't have enough money to live abroad PT style, without working?

Here's over 101 Ways You Can Make Serious Money Anywhere In The World Without Special Education, Visas, Permits or Licenses. Each job or service in PTO has an estimated minimum earnings' potential of US Dollars US$100,000 per year. You can realistically achieve this result after one year of persistent effort. For those who don't aim high financially, you can earn as little or as much as you need. Not everyone is comfortable with the idea of being a multimillionaire. But as Mae West once said, 'I have been poor and happy and I have been rich and unhappy. Rich and unhappy is happier.' Special-first time offered! £60 / US$100 for this beautifully leather bound report. Approximately 300 pages packed full of information. Order from the publisher. US$100-. ****High recommendation for those who want to work abroad. Trevellian just wrote this one.

PT

The one, the only, the original! Learn the PT way to avoid all taxes, government interference with your life, ex-wives, lawsuits, and hassles. Better than 10 visits to your lawyer or a shrink. Worth its weight in gold, this is the Hill classic! Of course we give it our highest five-star recommendation. Order from publisher, US$100-.

PT Vol. 2

Freedom and Privacy, Tactics. Read PT, and you'll crave Vol. 2.

Addictive reading. The practical application behind the philosophy. Not entirely written by the original Hill, but still very good. *** Order from publisher. US$100-.

The Passport Report

Legally obtain 'second," foreign passports in more than 100 countries. The book they tried to BAN, still available for the moment. High recommendation **** Order from publisher US$100.

Think Like A Tycoon

Tried and tested methods of making very big money in property deal with no personal investment. An absolute brilliant and workable opportunity. High recommendation **** for the young entrepreneur in real estate. Order from publisher US$100-.

The above Hill special reports are all £60@ or US$100@. Package deal: "Order all five books for the price of three." For postage add US$15 per book extra. Order by email: shamrock@netcomuk.co.uk, Fax: +44 171-681-1490 or regular mail to: **Cores Services**, P. O. Box 118, CH-8887 Mels, Switzerland.

The World's Best by Marian V Cooper. This is a "how to" source book for the international traveler. It offers a wide range of recommendations like the best beaches, banks, bars and bird watching in the world, and that was just the BS! Three hundred pages of goodies for £10 or US$20. Also by the same author and publisher.

Travel and Retirement Edens Abroad by Peter A. Dickinson. This one explores the best and most economical places for the mature person to settle. Mr. Dickinson's favorite "Garden of Eden" is San Remo, Italy, famous for its mild climate, low costs, no taxes, and unlimited range of activity. We are in total agreement with his assessment. He also has an interesting newsletter that deals with the same subject. Send US$10 to cover postage and handling for a free sample issue of this and International Living to **Agora Books, 824 E Baltimore Street, Baltimore, MD 21202 USA.**

The Hong Kong Bank (contact branch nearest you) has an excellent free series of books on investing and doing business in most countries. In many countries, the Hong Kong and Shanghai Bank is known as The Midland Bank (a subsidiary) or British Bank of the Middle East. It's the Crocker Bank in the US.

Information Libraries Run By Consulates and information services of the US, Great Britain, Australia, Canada, etc. are all good places for free information on a variety of topics of interest to tycoons. Of course, there will be a governmental bias in their material, but if you read between the lines and ignore the propaganda, you can get some valuable data.

Book Catalogs

Scope International is the publisher of most works of the original W.G. Hill (as well as some attributed to Hill and actually done by others) plus a variety of books and reports on personal freedom and tax havens. Some are exceptionally good; others are exceptionally boring or full of misinformation. If you order Scope books through me, Peter Trevellian, they will be at the same price Scope offers them, but we will recommend the good ones and save you from the stinkers. The Hill books listed above are the good ones.

For catalogs of other unusual and hard to find books about personal freedom, individual liberty, alternate identification, survival, etc., I recommend that you send (list below) US$5 or equivalent in any currency (refundable with first order) to cover postage and handling to any one or all of the following:

Loompanics Unlimited, PO Box 1197, Port Townsend, Washington 98368, USA. Web page: www.loompanics.com and e-mail at: loompanx@olympus.net. Many interesting books you won't find elsewhere. Strongly recommended.

Paladin Press, PO Box 1307, Boulder, Colorado 80306, USA, pala@rmii.com, or www.paladin-press.com/ Phone for orders 800-392-2400. Note: As of 1997 a 75-page catalog is free to USA addresses. This is the outfit that published *The Hit Man* and was sued by victims of someone who used methods in the book to murder a relative. They won the case because the Supreme Court still recognizes *freedom of the press* but were nearly put out of business by the legal defense fees. They have been carrying our books off and on for 30 years. Strongly recommended.

Eden Press, PO Box 8410, Fountain Valley, California 92728, USA. reids07@ix.netcom.com. Write for their highly recommended catalog of "underground books". This is an outfit of Barry Reid, author of *the Paper Trip -How To Get A New Identity.* Many wonderful and informative books in this collection. Highest recommendation.

Laissez Faire Books, 942 Howard Street, San Francisco, CA 94103, USA. An excellent free catalog. I especially *recommend The Amazing Bread Machine* which is about a man who invents a terrific product, markets it, becomes a millionaire and then goes to jail for violating various technical laws. It is fiction but rings true, reminding me of the stories that Victor Posner, Leona Helmsley and Michael Milken have to tell.

Newspapers And Magazines For Expatriates

Free Ones

The International Investor comes free to anyone interested in offshore investments. Many good articles and ads. Write to **The Financial Times Business Information Ltd. 102-108 Clerkenwell Road, London ECIM 5SA, UK.** Highly recommended, considering the price.

The Offshore Adviser, by the **same publisher**, is another free newspaper for investment advisers, stockbrokers, lawyers, or accountants based outside of the UK. **Free.**

For an interesting **free** monthly magazine concerning refugees and stateless persons, and how the United Nations High Commissioner for Refugees spends its budget of one half billion dollars per year, ask for a subscription to Refugees. This magazine is glossy, full of photographs and will make you glad that you have several passports and are not refugees! Ask for it in any of the following languages: English, Italian, Greek, Spanish, Japanese or German. An interesting feature is regular stories of famous refugees such as the scientist Albert Einstein or Victor Hugo, the French novelist. There are also articles of direct interest to the passport seeker from time to time. Write to **UNHCR, PO Box 2500, CH-1211 Geneva 2 Depot, Switzerland. Recommended. The price is right!** [Free]

The following are not free, but worth looking at:

Resident Abroad, "The Magazine For Expatriates", contains terrific classified ads and good articles. This thick, slick, monthly magazine costs about £50 per year or £36 in the UK. Most subscribers are British, but American Expats will find it useful. Write to **Resident Abroad, 27 Park Street, Croydon CR0 IYD, UK. Ask for a sample back issue. Include US$5. Or look for it in the larger news agents or magazine stores in Europe. Recommended.**

Investment International is another good magazine. Write to Consort House, 26 Queensway, London W2 3RX, UK.

TRAVEL INFORMATION MANUAL FOR AN UP. For an up-to-date, thick monthly bulletin of about 400 pages on passports, visas, vaccinations, exit permits, currency controls, and pets. In addition, how many cigars you can import duty free and information on about a zillion stupid rules and regulations you never knew existed, go to any major travel agent and ask to look at their TIM or *Travel Information Manual.* **Highly Recommended!** It is the joint publication of the 14 member airlines of the IATA. Almost all airline ticket offices and travel agents subscribe. It offers a complete explanation of the visa requirements for every country on earth. However, unlike *The Passport Report*, it says nothing about how to obtain passports, etc. The purpose of the TIM book is mainly to enable airline employees and travel agents to check the documents of passengers and refuse passage to those whose documents are not in order or who are carrying things that are illegal in the destination country. In many cases, airlines must pay huge fines for people they transport who arrive in a country without proper papers. You probably won't need your own copy of TIM if all you want to do is look up the facts for a few countries. However, if you really want one, maybe you can arrange for an out of date copy from your local travel agent although there are approximately 100 revisions to the information in each successive edition. Alternatively, you can subscribe for a year at 258

Dutch Guilders or buy a single copy at 57Dutch Guilders (approximately US$37). Write to **TIM, PO Box 902, NL-2130EA Hoofddorp, Netherlands.**

***** Highest recommendation if you travel a lot.

Other Recommended Mainstream International Newspapers

The International Herald Tribune [Full of wonderful "sucker" ads], Paris. Available in most five star hotels for free.

The Financial Times [Less lively than the Wall Street Journal except for the excellent weekend editions, which are especially good and have feature articles], London. Available in most five star hotels for free.

The Wall Street Journal, New York [Very interesting Page One feature stories]. Available in 5 star hotels frequented by Americans for free.

The European [New Newspaper — We hope it survives], London.

All of these are available at all international hotels and magazine stores.

Also, almost every international Anglophile community has local English language newspapers that are very good for finding apartments, handymen, concerts, art exhibits, and making local contacts. Try the concierge desk of the big hotels where they are usually available for free.

Recommended Travel Books

When you visit a new country, the best way to know what to do and see is by purchasing a good travel book. Many such books are a waste of time and money. I once bought a guidebook where much of the ink was wasted on fancy phrases like, "the dining room is papered in a nonchalant mauve . . ." Who cares? I want a practical guide for good values, good times, and an intelligent discussion of such things as prices, quality of food and service. What are the special local attractions? Where is a coin-op laundry? Cook's Tours representative or an American Express office for cashing checks and receiving mail?

For down-to-earth travel books and guides to good value I highly recommend:

South American Handbook published annually. **In my view this is the world's best travel book** and the best value for money published today if you are going to visit or live anywhere from Argentina to Mexico, or the Caribbean. Highest recommendation *****. This portable, pocket-sized 1500(!) page book has everything, all beautifully organized and indexed. It costs about US$40. You can find it at most bookstores. If not, to order by mail in the UK write to **T&T Publications, 6 Riverside Court, Bath BA2 3DZ, UK. In USA: PASSPORT BOOKS, 4255 West Touhy Ave., Lincolnwood (Chicago) Illinois 60646-1975, e-mail:** NTCPUB2@AOL.com**.**

Arthur Frommer US$25-US$35 A Day travel guides are inexpensive paperbacks, priced at around US$20 each. They cover most countries and major cities in an efficient, budget conscious style. Frommer does another series called the *Frommer Dollarwise Guides.* These are less oriented towards starvation, budget-minded travelers, but still discuss the best places to see, things to do and place to stay with an emphasis on getting good value for money. Highly recommended. I have been using them personally for 30 years! Both series are available in all English language bookstores. If you can't find the one you want order by mail from 1230 **Avenue of the Americas, New York City, NY 10020, USA.**

Let's Go budget travel guides are an easy to follow alternative. *** They are updated regularly and usually tell you exactly what to expect. These guides are written by traveling students forced to live on a small stipend by the publishing company in return for their troubles. You can count on their honesty. They offer guides, 22 in all, covering Europe, Canada, the US, Mexico, Central America, South East Asia, and the Middle East and have vast amounts of good information for PT's, such as train schedules, hours of admission at tourist sites, maps, museum guides, etc. They are available in most bookstores or by mail from *Let's Go,* **1 Story Street, Cambridge, MA 02138, USA. In England: Macmillan, Houndmills, Basingstoke, Hampshire, RG21 2XS.**

Lonely Planet Shoestring travel guides tend to focus on the other half of the world i.e. not Europe and North America. They are published out of Australia and offer the best budget travel advice for all of Asia and Africa as well as Australia and New Zealand. They can be found in most bookstores or order from **Embarcadero West, 112 Linden Street, Oakland, CA 94607 USA** for North America or **PO Box 617, Hawthorn, Victoria 3122**, Australia for the rest of the world.

Michelin, Baedeker, Fieldings and Birnbaum's travel guides are "so so."

Vacation Home Exchange Organization And Directories (Highly Recommended)

While many individuals may be afraid to let strangers use their homes, home exchangers are not the same as rental tenants. Normally the people who trade homes for a month or three are experienced exchangers who will take the same care of your home and property as you do. They will exchange references with you. Since you are using their place, and perhaps their car, while they use yours, there is naturally a high degree of responsibility. This author has had many wonderful experiences exchanging properties in Paris, London, Hong Kong, South Africa, Bangkok, San Francisco, and Monaco. The beauty of an exchange is that instead of an expensive hotel room, you get a fully furnished apartment, books to read, etc. If you are lucky, the owner of the home you trade for will leave you a list of the best restaurants and reveal many non-touristy secrets of his city. Plus, depending upon the terms of the exchange you may get fringe benefits, like the use of a summer cottage, a regular cleaning person, a car, boat, horse, etc. You can always advertise for an exchange in a newspaper of the town where you want to go, but the home exchanging clubs are probably better deals. The people in them tend to be upper middle class retired folks or teachers with attractive places to offer. If you have an open mind and will consider offbeat locations you might otherwise not have on your list of first choices for visiting, you will definitely enjoy some enriching experiences. I have done home exchanges personally more than a dozen times (Peter

Trevellian). We used Yahoo and a word-search for vacation+home+exchange and turned up 899 listings of people who wanted to exchange all over the world. The Internet is the greatest way to find anything.

The Arthur Frommer publishing organization has a paperback called *Swap and Go*. It's full of info on the subject of home exchanges. They have a superb bargain offer including this book, *Europe on US$40 a Day* a one-year subscription to their newsletter, *The Wonderful World of Budget Travel and the Frommer Guide to New York City*. The price of the entire package is US$25. Send to **US$25 A Day Travel Club, Frommer/Pasmentier Publications, 1230 Avenue of the Americas, New York, NY 10020, USA.**

Generally, home exchange organizations will either sell you a directory, meaning you write to the people listed in it, or you can list yourself and expect to receive many tempting offers for the periods you designate, and from the places you want to go. The cost of such services are quite inexpensive, about US$20 for the directory and another US$10 to be listed in it. The largest organization is **International Home Exchange Service, PO Box 3975, San Francisco, California 94119, USA,** Tel: 415-0300. It has about 4000 subscribers.

Travel Bargains

Experienced travelers know that seats on the same plane starting and stopping at the same points can vary tremendously in cost. This author once had an argument with a client who said, " I always go first class because I can afford to. "A few weeks later, we were sitting side by side on a first class flight, getting exactly the same service, heading for the same destination. He had paid US$2600 for his ticket while I had paid US$500 for mine. For what was saved by not just buying a point to point ticket, yours truly could buy a new car. Of course one doesn't get much of a car for US$2100. Not doing a bit of comparison shopping for airline tickets, cars or any major item is to my mind, extremely foolish, no matter how much money you have. I hate to be taken for a ride. Here are a few secrets known to all experienced travelers:

4. Always ask your travel agent to look for the cheapest way to travel. Go first Class if you must, but try to get it at a discount. Usually a travel agent can do better than the first price quoted. Always ask your travel agent to look for a cheaper way.

5. Look at ads particularly in Sunday newspapers (travel sections) and in travel/entertainment/leisure magazines. In the USA, the New York Times and the Los Angeles Times have dozens of pages of discount travel ads every Sunday. Best ads in Europe are in Time Out published in London and available in magazine stores worldwide. Time Out ads are always offering bargain flights, package tours, cruises, home exchanges, and so on. The best deals on discounted plane tickets can usually be purchased in London, Singapore or Hong Kong. Particularly recommended are: **Trailfinders, 42-50 Earls Court Road, London, W8 OFT, UK**, Tel.: 44 71-938-3366, Fax: 44 71-937-6059. They specialize in round-the-world tickets, usually good for one year, with a huge number of stopovers. The price of such a ticket can be as low as £717, or slightly over US$1,000. Send for a free Trailfinder magazine.

6. Overflight routings should be checked. For example, sometimes one can get a super bargain flight from say London to San Francisco. Assuming where you really want to go is London-Salt Lake City, a good travel agent may be able to sell you a San Francisco ticket at the bargain rate, and you simply get off the plane in Salt Lake and throw away your coupon to San Francisco. If you have a lot of chutzpah, you might sidle over to a line of people waiting to buy SFO tickets in Salt Lake and try to sell your (discounted) coupon for San Francisco. As I wrote this, I made a tentative reservation to fly from Central America to Amsterdam. The price was US$1250. The price to go from the same starting place to Zurich was however US$850 with a stop in Amsterdam. I will save US$400 by buying the ticket to Zurich and getting off in Amsterdam. Then I will still have a free ticket to Zurich, which would otherwise cost about US$150. I will surely try to sell it in Amsterdam for US$100. You have to check

in, get a boarding pass, and then hand the boarding pass to your buyer. Why? Because they check your passport-name and your ticket name at the time you check in and get boarding pass. After that, you can make the substitution in passengers.

7. Due to IATA monopolistic price controls, a flight including a hotel package may be considerably cheaper than a flight without accommodation. You can always throw away or give away any hotel room vouchers you won't be using. I once bought a New York to Paris round trip with seven nights in a decent hotel for the same price as a point-to-point one way flight only. As I didn't want to come back in a week, I used the New York to Paris coupon and threw away the return trip portion. I still came out ahead — by the cost of seven nights in the hotel or about US$600.

8. Casino Gambler Flights are usually subsidized. Thus, if you are going to the US, East Coast or West Coast, you could probably get a super-bargain "High Roller" flight to Atlantic City, New Jersey or Reno, Nevada. If South Africa is your destination, tie it in with Sun City. There is a big Harrah's club in Auckland; New Zealand and they have gambler special vacation packages. You can probably get a big discount deal on a round trip ticket to anywhere with a casino.

9. Business conventions, academic conventions, all may have group package flights and hotel deals. These are less costly than a do-it-yourself point to point ticket.

10. Travel passes, such as the Eurorail Pass in Europe or the Unlimited Flight Passes available to foreign passport holders in most countries, always work out cheaper than buying point to point individual tickets, if you are going to be moving around quite a bit.

11. Look into becoming a travel agent or owning a share in a travel agency. Travel agents always get discounts on everything. There is no reason why you couldn't be a part-time travel agent. You can't just print up a calling card and get away with passing yourself off as a travel agent. Why? Because you need an IATA ID number. But if you know a travel agent that will let you use their number, well — why not?

12. Currency conversion deals. Where a currency has appreciated suddenly, as the US dollar did in 1997, the pricing of tickets in the home currency remains the same, but a ticket purchased somewhere else could be had at half price. For instance, due to the recent high value of the Yen, a sensible Japanese person who wanted to go to Europe or the US would take a short flight to anywhere outside of Japan and then be able to get his air tickets for half the price of those bought within Japan in 1991. In countries with a two tier market in currency, like South Africa, it is possible to change money with a friend there and buy an air ticket with "cheap money" to give yourself a 75 per cent saving.

13. Other sources of discounts? They exist for anyone in the hotel or travel business and are obtained by showing a calling card identifying you as such. Then too, there are special prices for those with "student ID". Your author has been carrying around student ID for forty years, as a result of enrolling in some adult education course or other. For the over 55 there are "Senior Citizens Discounts" for which your author will also soon be eligible. In summary, with a little effort, your travel and hotel accommodation bills can be cut by half without compromising your comfort in the slightest.

14. Last minute bargain specials can offer tremendous savings. My personal best deal came when passing a travel agency in Genoa, Italy. I saw advertised in the window a three-week Mediterranean cruise "Leaving Genoa in Three Days". The announcement was in magic marker on a handwritten poster. It said, "US$12 per day per person in a four-person cabin, with window on the sea." I went in to inquire. It turned out to be on a new Russian ship. They were having trouble filling it up because a similar ship had just sunk off the coast of Australia. The usual rate for a cruise with full meals and free nightlife activities was at least five times that price. I quickly called up a friendly ex-wife and told her to pack up the kids for a surprise fun trip to Cairo, Tel Aviv, Odessa, Istanbul, Dubrovnik, Athens, Cyprus, Palma de Majorca, Morocco, Libya, Sicily, Monaco, etc. The price was certainly right! I couldn't stay at home for US$12 a day.

Moral, if you keep your eye open for bargains and are flexible, you can usually find them. Sometimes calling a cruise line direct and asking about last minute bookings works wonders. I have bought last minute tickets at 20 per cent to 50 per cent off the regular price several times. As Woody Allen once said, "The only sin in my family was paying full retail price for anything!" Travel books and newsletters often have sections on how to get different travel bargains. A book may cost a few dollars but it could save you thousands. Knowledge is cheap ignorance is expensive.

Inspirational And Informational Books

Bridge Across Forever and *Jonathan Livingston Seagull*, by Richard Bach, published by William Morrow, New York. International best seller available in most bookstores. Highest recommendation.

The Good Earth, by Pearl S Buck. Great story about the capitalist tradition in ancient China, yes China. Considered a classic. Out of print but you shouldn't have much of a problem finding it in the public library. Same ****

How to Retire at Age 35, by Roger Terhorst, Bantam Books. You also can find this one in almost any bookstore, if not order it from Bantam.

How I Found Freedom in an Unfree World, by Harry Brown, published by Avon Books, 959 Eighth Avenue, New York, NY, USA. **Highest recommendation!** *****

Data Save

The Safe Deposit Company for PT's
("One Year Free" offer **Exclusively to Invisible Investor Readers**)

Our company offers a more personalized, deluxe quality service than any other company in the world plus these special features:

- Valuables, or sensitive documents stored in your own private, double locked, electronically guarded strong box, within a fortified, constantly attended and monitored, purpose built structure in the central business (banking) district.

- Armed Guards present at all times. 24-hour per day access
- Free Courier Service To & From Anywhere in the World (at cost) with 24-hour delivery by our personal, trained staff or by commercial services including registered mail.
- Insured vs. loss to US$10,000,000 (Extra Cost)
- Easy personal access by regular scheduled daily flights worldwide, by train or by boat.
- No earthquakes, floods, tornadoes or other natural disasters common to area.
- Stable Political System
- We will keep safe and secure your computer disks, bearer shares, valuable papers, collections, or coins. Anything (except contraband) can be received, held, and delivered for you.
- Escrow Services Available: We can deliver cash (or bank checks) vs. securities, or accept cash in exchange for goods delivered within the limits of local legal restrictions.
- Your identity Unknown to Safe Deposit Company if desired — access by code word, phrase, or Key.
- You never need appear personally to deposit or collect box contents.
- No signature or identity documents required to open or close box account.
- Registered Mail to Country is safe
- Absolutely Judgment Proof Asset Protection
- Immune to court orders or claims from any nation outside of jurisdiction.
- Unlimited Deposits or withdrawals from your box
- Mail and bank statements can be received here and automatically deposited to your box or disposed of as per your instructions.
- Cost for deposit space of up to 1 Cubic Meter (size of small closet) US$500 per year. With our special "one year free" offer, US$500 pays for two years.
- Banking introductions and securities trading arrangements made as part of service.
- Death Instructions accepted (to avoid probate).

- Security guards and escort to and from airport can be provided at cost, with round trip first visit and once a year thereafter for "free." As round-trip ordinary taxicab to airport is US$50, you can see how anxious we are to serve and please you!

Send check for first year payment (US$500), money order, cash, or your credit card number. Wire transfers by arrangement. You may prepay up to ten years and get up to ten years additional, free! Send funds or any further questions to: data save, Apartado 6-1097, El Dorado, Panama City, Panama. Facilities at Calle Manuel Maria Icaza 7. Phone: 011-507-269-4828, Fax: 011-507-223-7919. Recommended by PT****

Banks With A Home Page On The Internet Web

Recommended banks marked with an (*)

(Get detailed information from each listed bank by writing them at city given or via www.)

ANDORRA (La Massana)
•*Banc Agricol I Comercial d'Andorra
AUSTRIA (Vienna)
•Allgemeine Sparkasse Oberosterreich •Bank fur Arbeit und Wirtschaft •BKS - Bank fuer Kaernten und Steiermark •Bank Austria •Creditanstalt •Die s Bausparkasse •Erstes Wiener Tele-Zentrum •GiroCredit Bank AG der Sparkassen •Hypo Landesbank Vorarlberg •OeKB - Österreichische Kontrollbank •P.S.K. Telebanking •Österreichische Nationalbank •Raiffeisen-Bankengruppe Österreich •Raiffeisen Bankengruppe Vorarlberg •Raiffeisen Banking Group •Raiffeisen Bank Kitzbuhel •Raiffeisenbank Kleinwalsertal AG •Raiffeisenbank Kötschach-Mauthen •Raiffeisenbank Mauthausen Schaerding •Raiffeisenbank Oberdrauburg •Raiffeisenbank Oberdrautal-Weissensee •Raiffeisen Bankengruppe Sterreich •Raiffeisenbank Wolfurt-Schwarzach •Raiffeisenlandesbank Niederösterreich-Wien •Raiffeisen Zentralbank Austria AG •Steiermärkische Bank und Sparkassen AG
BELGIUM (Brussels)
•AxionWeb •BACOB Bank •BBL Web'Bank •Banking Center of

LUXEMBOURG •CERA Bank •Cooperation Bancaire pour l'Europe •Cortal Belgique •Crédit Communal •Crédit Général société anonyme de banque •Gemeentekrediet •Fortis World Wide site •Generale Bank •Kredietbank

CYPRUS
•Bank of Cyprus Group •The Cyprus Popular Bank Ltd •Hellenic Bank Group

CZECH REPUBLIC (Prague)
•Czech National Bank

DENMARK (Copenhagen)
•Amagerbanken •Den Danske Bank •Den Fri Bank •*Jyske Bank •Lån & Spar Bank •SparNordjylland •Unibank

FINLAND (Helsinki)
•Aktia Bank •Bank of Finland/Suomen Pankki •Merita Bank •Osuuspankki •Postipankki

FRANCE (Paris)
•Banco di Olig •Banque Cortal •Banque Directe •Banque Paribas •Banque Populaire •Banque Populaire de Bourgogne •Banque Populaire du Centre •Banque Populaire de Franche-Compte •Banque Populaire de Lorraine •Banque Populaire de la Region Nord du Paris •Banque Populaire Savoisienne •Banque Saradar France •Banque Sofinco •La BAREP (Banque Réescompte et de Placement) •BNP •BRED •Crédit agricole d'Ile de France •Crédit Agricole de Toulouse et du Midi Toulousain •Crédit Commercial de France •Crédit Local de France •Crédit Lyonnais de France •Crédit Mutuel •Crédit du Nord •Groupe Banques Popularies •Société Générale •Société Marsellaise de Crédit

GERMANY (Frankfurt)
•Advance Bank •Bank24 •Bankgesellschaft •Bausparkasse Mainz •Bayerische Landesbank •Bayerische Vereinsbank •Bundesverband Deutscher Banken •Comdirect Bank •Commerzbank AG •ConSors Discount-Broker •Consors Schmidt Bank KGaA •Deutsche Bank •Die bayerischen Volksbanken Raiffeisenbanken •Dresdner Bank Investment Group •Die Deutsche Bank •Direkt Anlange Bank •Franken WKV Bank •Frankfurter Sparkasse 1822 •Freyberg & Hambros •Gries und Heissel •Hamburgische Landesbank •Hypo-Bank •IfBG

•Kreissparkasse Calw •Kreissparkasse Bayreuth-Pegnitz •Kreissparkasse Gelnhausen •Kreissparkasse Köln •Landesgirokasse Stuttgart •LBS - Landesbausparkasse Württemberg •Quelle Bank •Rabobank Deutschland AG •Raiffeisenbank Grafenau-Regen eG. •Santander Direkt Bank AG •Snet - Sparkassen •Sparda-Bank Hamburg eG •Sparda-Bank München •Sparkasse Erfurt •Sparkasse Neu-Ulm-Illertissen •Sparkassa Schwerin •Stadtsparkasse Augsburg •Stadtsparkasse Bamberg •Stadtsparkasse Bocholt •Stadtsparkasse Hannover •Stadtsparkasse München •Stadtsparkasse Nürnberg •Vereinsbank •Volksbank Hannover •Volkbank Ketsch eG •Westdeutsche Landesbank
•CHANNEL ISLANDS (Jersey)
•Bank of Scotland (Isle of Man) Ltd. •Barclays Offshore Banking •HSBC Private Banking (C.I.) Limited •Royal Bank of Canada (Channel Islands) Ltd. •Standard Bank Isle of Man •TSB Bank Channel Islands Limited
•ENGLAND (London)
•Abbey National •Alliance & Leicester •Banco di Olig •BankNet Electronic Bank •Bank of England •Barclays Bank •Birmingham Midshires •Bradford & Bingley Building Society •Bristol & West Building Society •Cheltenham & Gloucester •Co-operative •HSBC Holdings •Halifax Building Society •Lloyds Bank •Midland Bank •Nationwide Buidling Society •National Westminister Bank •Northern Bank Limtied •Northern Rock •TSB Bank •Woolwich
•NORTHERN IRELAND (Belfast)
•Ulster Bank*
•SCOTLAND (Edinburgh)
•Bank of Scotland •Royal Bank of Scotland
GREECE (Athens)
•Alpha Credit Bank •Astir •Ergobank •ETBA S.A. Hellenic Industrial Development Bank •Piraeus Bank •XIOSBANK
HUNGARY (Budapest)
•Magyar Külkereskedelmi Bank
IRELAND (Dublin)
•Allied Irish Bank Group •AIB/First Trust •Bank of Ireland •Bank of Ireland Trinity Branch •EBS Bank •First National Building Society

•Irish Nationwide, Ltd. •Northern Bank •Ulster Bank
ITALY (Milan)
•Banca Antoniana •Banca Commerciale Italiana •Banca del Salento
•Banca di Credito Cooperativo dell'Alta •Banca di Credito
Cooperativo Cascia di Regello •Banca di Credito Cooperativo di
Carate Brianza •Banca di Credito Cooperativo di Civitanova Marche
e Montecosaro (MC) •Banca di Credito Cooperativo del Piave e del
Livenza •Banca di Credito Cooperativo dell'Alta Brianza •Banca di
Credito Cooperativo Faenza •Banca di Credito Cooperativo di Piove
di Sacco (PD) •Banca di Piacenza •Banca Popolare di Sondrio •Banca
di Credito di Trieste •Banca di Roma •Banca di Sassari •Banca
Nazionale del Lavoro (Fil. di Pescara) •Banca Passadore & C. •Banca
Popolare dell'Emilia Romagna •Banca Popolare dell'Etruria e del
Lazio •Banca Popolare di Bari •Banca Popolare di Lodi •Banca
Popolare di Polistena •Banca Popolare di Ravenna •Banca Popolare
di Sondrio •Banca Popolare Veneta •Banca Sella •Banco Ambrosiano
Veneto •Banco di Napoli •Banco di Sicilia •CARIPLO S.p.A
•CariPrato spa •Cassa di Risparmio della provincia di Teramo •Cassa
di Risparmio di Carpi •Cassa di Risparmio di Cesena •Cassa di
Risparmio di Firenze •Cassa di Risparmio di Forli •Cassa di Risparmio
di Imola •Cassa di Risparmio di Mirandola •Cassa di Risparmio di
Parma e Piacenza •Cassa di Risparmio di Pisa •Cassa di Risparmio
di Prato •Cassa di Risparmio di Tortona •Cassa di Risparmio di Udine
e Pordenone •Cassa Rurale di Molina di Ledro •CREDITO
BERGAMASCO •Credito Cooperativo •Credito Popolare Salentino
•Istituto Bancario San Paolo di Torino
LIECHTENSTEIN (Vaduz)
•*Bank in Liechtenstein •*Liechtensteinische Landesbank
•*Verwaltungs - und Privat-Bank AG
LUXEMBOURG (Luxembourg)
•*Banque Générale du Luxembourg •*Banque et Caisse d'Epargne
de l'Etat •Fortis Bank Luxembourg (formerly Banque UCL)
•Kookmin Bank Luxembourg S.A. •*Robeco Bank S.A.
MALTA (Valetta)
•Mid-Med Bank, Ltd. •Bank of Valleta Group
NETHERLANDS (Amsterdam)

•ABN AMRO Bank N.V. •Friesland Bank •ING Bank International •Interfinance Ltd. •Kredietbank (Nederland) N.V. •Postbank •Rabobank

NORWAY (Oslo)

•Bankplassen •BNbank •Fokus Bank •Gjensidige Bank •Kreditkassen Christiania Bank og Kreditkasse

POLAND (Warsaw)

•Pomorski Bank Kredytowy S.A. •PPABank S.A.

PORTUGAL (Lisbon)

•Banco 7 •Banco Espirito Santo •Banif - Banco Internacional do Funchal •Caixa Ceral de Depositos •Credito Predial Portugues •Grupo BFE

RUSSIA (Moscow)

•Ami Bank •Arsenal Bank •Bank of Moscow •ICFI •Inkombank •IntehBank •MontazhSpetsBank •Most-Bank •Neftechim Bank •Novosibirsk Municipal Bank •Promstroybank of Russia •Rossiyskiy Kredit Bank •UNEXIM BANK

SPAIN (Madrid)

•Argentaria •Banco Central Hispano •Banco Bilbao Vizcaya •Banco de Espana/Bank of Spain •Banco Espanol de Credito S.A. •Banco de Finanzas e Inversiones, S.A. •Banco de Tiempo Espanol •Banco Inversion •Banco Sabadell •Banco Santander •Bankinter •Bilbao Bizkaia Kutxa •Caixa de Catalunya •Caja de Arquitectos •CajaCanarias •Ibercaja •la Caixa •Kutxa •OpenBank

SWEDEN (Stockholm)

•JP Bank •Nordbanken •Ostgota Enskilda Bank - Linkoping •S-E-Banken •Sparbanken Sverige (Swedbank) •Stadshypotek •Svenska Handelsbanken •Swedbank NetTrade •Trygg Hansa

SWITZERLAND (Zurich)

•Banca della Svizzera Italiana •Banque Cantonale Vaudoise •Bank von Ernst •CREDIT SUISSE **(Emphatically Not Recommended)** •Kreditanstalt Grabs •Maerki, Baumann & Co. AG, Privatbank •Schweizerischer Bankgesellschaft •Schweizerischer Bankverein •Sparkassa Berneck •SBC Warburg•St. Gallische Kantonalbank •Swiss Private Bank •Thurgauer Kantonalbank •Union Bank of Switzerland •Zürcher Kantonalbank

AUSTRALIAN & NZ BANKS WITH WEB HOME PAGES

AUSTRALIA (Sydney)

•Advance Bank Australia Limited •Adelaide Bank •ANZ Bank*•ASB Bank •Australia and New Zealand Banking Group •Bank of Melbourne •BankSA •Bankers Trust Autralia, Ltd. •BankWest •Commonwealth Bank of Australia •Macquarie Bank •Metway Bank - Australia •National Australian Bank •Reserve Bank of New Zealand •State Bank Of New South Wales Ltd. •St George Bank •Westpac.

NEW ZEALAND (Auckland)

•ASB Bank Limited •Countrywide Bank •National Bank of New Zealand, Ltd. •Reserve Bank of New Zealand •Trust Bank of New-Zealand

ASIAN BANKS ON INTERNET

HONG KONG

•Bank of America (Asia) Ltd. •Dah Sing Bank •Dao Heng Bank •DBS Bank •Hang Seng Bank •International Bank of Asia •Jardine Fleming Bank •Rabobank Hong Kong •Standard Chartered •United Bank of Hong Kong Ltd. •Wing Lung Bank

INDIA [Not recommended for Offshore Banking- Inefficient and bound up by red tape]

•Bank of India •Industrial Credit and Investment Corp. of India (ICICI) •IndusInd Bank •Reserve Bank of India •Standard Chartered Bank •State Bank of India

INDONESIA (Jakarta)

•Bank Andromeda •Bank Bali •Bank BDNI •Bank Bira •Bank Dagang Nasional Indonesia •Bank Duta •Bank International Indonesia •Bank Niaga •Bank Umum Servitia •Bank Universal •BankJaya •Direct Banking •Lippo Group •Standard Chartered •Tamara Bank

JAPAN (Tokyo)

•Asashi Bank •Bank of Nagoya •Bank of Saga •Bank of Tokyo •Dai-Ichi Kangyo Bank •DC Card in Japan •Export-Import Bank of Japan •The Fuji Bank •Japan Development Bank •Joyo Bank •Long Term Credit Bank of Japan •Mitsubishi Bank •OITA •Sakura Bank •Shonai Bank •Shonai Bank - English Site •Sumitomo Bank Limited •Tokai

Bank •UC Card in Japan

MALAYSIA (Kuala Lumpur)

•Allied Bank •Arab-Malaysia Bank •Bank Numiputra Malasia Berhad •BHL Bank •Hong Leong Bank Berhad •Southern Bank Berhad •Standard Chartered

PAKISTAN [Same comment as for India]

•Standard Chartered

PEOPLE'S REPUBLIC OF CHINA (P.R.C.) [Forget it unless you are doing business there]

•Bank of China

PHILIPPINES (Manila)[Friendly but local bankers can't walk in a straight line & chew gum at the same time!] •Asian Development Bank •Far East Bank & Trust Co. •PCI Bank •Standard Chartered* [best bet].

SINGAPORE [A Hidden Gem. Singapore Banks are IMO the best places in the world today for secrecy and efficiency. If you live in USA Panama is more convenient, but Singapore is 1st World, and a nicer place to visit: Great food, great shopping — but expensive!]

•AFC Merchant Bank •Citibank of Singapore •Development Bank of Singapore •OCBC Bank •Overseas Union Bank •*Standard Chartered •The United Overseas Bank Group of Singapore

SOUTH KOREA (Seoul)

•The Banking System in Korea •Cho Hung Bank •Cho Hung Bank - English Site •The Commercial Bank of Korea •Daedong Bank, Ltd. •Hana Bank •Hanil Bank •Industrial Bank of Korea •Jeonbuk Bank •Kookmin Bank •KorAm Bank •The Korea Development Bank •Korea Exchange Bank •Korea First Bank •Korea Long Term Credit Bank •Kwangju Bank •Peace Bank •Pusan Bank •Seoul Bank •Shinhan Bank

SRI LANKA

•Hatton National Bank •People's Bank of Sri Lanka •Standard Chartered •VANIK Incorporation, Ltd.

TAIWAN R.O.C (Republic Of China)

•China Trust Commercial Bank •Hua Nan Commercial Bank •International Commercial Bank of China •Standard Chartered

THAILAND (Bangkok)

•Bank of Ayudhya •Central Bank of Thailand •Government Savings Bank •Laem Thong Bank PCL •Siam Commercial Bank •Standard Chartered •Thai Farmers' Bank PLC

BANKS — SOUTH AMERICA, CENTRAL AMERICA, & THE CARIBBEAN

ANTIGUA
•American International Banking Group •European Union Bank •Horizon Bank International
ARGENTINA (Buenos Aires)
•Banco de Galicia y Buenos Aires •Banco Frances del Rio de la Plata, S.A. •Banco Los Tilos •Banco Mayo •Banco Privado de Inversiones, S.A. •Deutsche Bank Argentina, S.A.
BARBADOS
•Altamira International Bank, Inc. •Central Bank of Barbados •Excelsior International Bank Corp.
BERMUDA (Hamilton)
•Bank of Butterfield *Bank of Bermuda*
BOLIVIA
•Banco Central de Bolivia •Banco Nacional de Bolivia S.A.
BRAZIL (Rio) [No anti Laundering Laws — yet!]
•Banco Bamerindus Sociedade Anônima •Banco Boavista •Banco Bozano, Simonsen, S.A. •Banco Bradesco S.A. •Banco CCF Brasil •Banco Central do Brasil •Banco Credibanco, S.A. •Banco da Bahia •Banco de Boston •Banco do Brasil •Banco do Estado de Bahia •Banco do Estado do Ceará •Banco do Estado do Rio Grande do Sul •Banco do Nordeste do Brasil, S.A. •Banco Excel Economico •Banco Graphus •Banco Icatu •Banco Itaú •Banespa •Banco Pontual •Brazilian Development Bank •Caixa Econômica Federal •Finasa Banco Mercantil de Sao Paulo •Unibanco •Unicred-Rio
BRITISH VIRGIN ISLANDS
•VP Bank (BVl), Ltd.
CHILE (Santiago)
•Banco Bhif •Banco Central de Chile •Banco Concepcion •Banco de Chile, S.A. •Banco de Crédito e Inversiones •Banco Sud Americano

COLUMBIA
•Banco Colpatria •Banco de la Republica de Colombia •Banco Industrial Colombian
COSTA RICA (San Jose)
•Banco Banex, S.A. •Banco Central de Costa Rica •Banco de San Jose •Banco Nacional de Costa Rica •BanCrecen •Consorcio Bantec
CUBA (Havana)
•National Bank of Cuba
DOMINICAN REPUBLIC (Santo Domingo)
•Banco Mercantil •Banco Popular
ECUADOR
•Banco del Pacifico •Banco del Progreso •Banco Central del Ecuador •Filanbanco
FALKLAND ISLANDS
•Standard Chartered Bank * [They'd never look for your money here!]
HONDURAS (Tegucigalpa)
•Banco Central de Honduras •Banco Ficohsa •Banffaa
JAMAICA (Kingston)
•Bank of Jamaica •NCB Group
GRENADA
•National Commercial Bank of Grenada Ltd.
NICARAGUA (Managua)
•Bancentro •Banco de Finanzas •Banco del Cafe •Casa Nacional de Inversiones
PERU (Lima)
•Banco Central de Reserva
PUERTO RICO (San Juan)
•Banco Popular •Roig Commercial Bank •Westernbank Puerto Rico
TRINIDAD AND TOBAGO
•Republic Bank Limited
URUGUAY (Montevideo) Banking Center of South America
•Banco Comercial Montevideo •Banco de Credito •Banco Santander
VENEZUELA (Caracas)
•Banco Consolidado

Titles Of Nobility

Have you always wanted to be a Count, Knight, Prince, Duke, or Earl? There are many crooks in the business that will sell you worthless paper. Through purchase, Marriage Blanche, or adoption, you can legally get a title from the lowest (Lord of the Manor) at about £5000 to the highest (Prince Pretender to the Throne of Albania) if not already taken. Recently, a dukedom in Sicily was for sale, carrying with it a castle, moat, fortifications, small private army, art collection, antique furniture, the right to appoint Abbots of certain churches and about a thousand acres of vineyards. The price was a mere US$2 million. A bargain for the land alone. Quite a few opportunities to obtain ceremonial titles exist in France, Germany, Italy, and other republics. Of course you can't buy a title that has any legal status in a Republic. Why? Because the feudal system of titles and special privies for the nobility has been abolished. In any modern monarchy or principality, noble titles are not for sale.

There are opportunities carrying with them real status and an actual (usually ceremonial) role in government. These situations exist in Spain, Belgium, Netherlands, Luxembourg, Liechtenstein, Monaco, Thailand, and The Vatican. There, hereditary monarchs and an aristocratic class still exist and have certain privileges recognized by law.

Titles are arranged by purchase, marriages, appointment, donation, or adoption. They can be passed on to your heirs, and you in turn can adopt other people. Fashion magnates Gucci, Pucci, The Prince of Liechtenstein, The King of Sweden, Lord Rothschild, the Seigneur of Sark and in fact virtually all present day aristocrats, or their ancestors, acquired their titles by adoption, direct purchase or by doing financial favors for those with the power of appointment, just as you would be asked to do. Don't waste your money on professional advice unless you are prepared to spend at least £3000 on the project to gain a title. IMO any title you have to pay for isn't worth having!

The use of a legal aristocratic title is sometimes an economic benefit. Obviously, in promoting some snob-appeal item the Prince of

Liechtenstein's personal cuvee, estate bottled wine will command a higher price than "Padrone Corleone's Chianti" or any other vin ordinaire.

All providers of noble titles have proved unreliable or are scammers. After dealing with hundreds of bogus nobility deals we cannot recommend any legitimate source of titles except one. It is incredibly simple, totally legal and an absolutely free way of getting the noble title of your choice. Your "title", which becomes your legal name, can then be included on your driver's license, passport, letterhead, etc. Send the publisher US$50 cash; ask for Noble Title papers. I will send you all the instructions and forms so you can be addressed as "Prince," "Baron," "Earl," or whatever you want. The whole concept doesn't fit in with my concept of low profile living, but if you want to pretend you are a "noble" I can show you how to do it legally and for US$50. Write to Peter Trevellian. This whole sort of thing isn't recommended for people who want to be unmemorable, low profile PT's.

Offshore Services

Some are good, some are incompetent, and many are thieves. The lack of regulation offshore and in Cyberspace gives people the freedom to say anything, to offer anything.

Passport Providers for instance are 99.99% crooks who will take your money and disappear. We have personally lost a great deal of money by dealing with these people until we discovered legitimate suppliers. Some of the crooks advertised in respectable publications like the International Herald Tribune and the Economist. If they don't just disappear with your money, they give you forged or stolen documents instead of a valid passport. Generally, protect yourself by **picking up your documents** (i.e. new passport) **at an official government office** like a consulate. Or go through a consultant who really knows his way around. Generally you shouldn't pay out any serious money until the passport is in your hand. Escrow arrangements are OK to protect both sides in a deal. A legitimate passport provider can't be expected to do all the work, present you with your new passport, and have you change your mind or attempt to negotiate a lower price at the last moment. An escrow is where a third party holds the funds, documents, and doesn't make delivery until authenticity is verified and the money is counted. The safe deposit Box Company in Panama whose ad appeared a few pages back provides escrow service. You don't have to go there to use their services. We can also recommend reliable 2nd Passport providers and escrow services in Europe. Suggestion: Get a referral by someone who has dealt successfully in this field. While the author doesn't "do passports," he may be able to point you in the right direction — towards legal programs, reasonably priced. The typical deals offered in ads are either scams or grossly overpriced.

Money Managers, the number of crooks and Ponzi Scheme operators in this field is down to around a third. But you wouldn't want to risk any serious money by sending it to a post office box if one in three operators are fly-by-nights. Use a solid established bank or stockbroker in a country with bank secrecy. The Harris Organisation, Marc Harris in Panama and elsewhere is OK. Private Bank in Liechtenstein is OK. For other recommendations, consult with Dr. Trevellian. Visit them personally. Don't be shy about asking for audited statements and / or evidence that an employee fidelity bond protects you. Check references.

Comments, questions, additions, and constructive criticism should be sent to:

Dr. Peter T. Trevellian, PTT Communications
PO Box 6-1097, El Dorado
Panama City, Panama
Fax: (507) 263-6964

trevellian@hotmail.com

As Benjamin Franklin once said, "If we don't hang together, we will hang separately!" As a reader of this book you are already a PT. You are now a member of a unique group of libertarian individualists who believe in limited government power, free enterprise, tolerance, personal privacy, and above all, the freedom of the individual to do what he wants so long as he does not harm others. If you have any good ideas or practical tips to share with fellow PT's, please send them to the author. If you know of commercial products or free things of interest to us all, please send them in so I may list them in future "Resource Sections." Hopefully we will have an Internet Web Page of our own by next year.

LIFETIME RECHARGEABLE ATM CARD
PLUS ANONYMOUS BANK ACCOUNT!
WE CALL IT THE "PLASTIC CASH LIFELINE"™
NEW PRODUCT NOT AVAILABLE FROM ANYONE ELSE!
ONLY 150 OFFERED
FIRST COME FIRST SERVED...

"THE GREATEST PRIVACY AND ASSET PROTECTION TOOL I'VE COME ACROSS, BAR NONE! INFINITELY MORE CONVENIENT AND USEFUL THAN THE SPARBUCH!" W. G. HILL

HOW MUCH WOULD YOU PAY FOR AN ANONYMOUS, JUDGMENT PROOF ACCOUNT FROM WHICH YOU CAN DRAW UNLIMITED AMOUNTS OF CASH ANYWHERE IN THE WORLD, 24-HOURS A DAY?

Imagine this situation: Your kid is going to college in Paris (or anywhere in the world). You want her to have ready access to cash for emergencies. You give her a plastic card **"PLASTIC CASH LIFELINE"™** that enables her to withdraw up to the local equivalent of US$20,000 (you set the amount anywhere from US$2,000 to infinity). The card can be used anywhere in the world to access the cash, in any Automatic Teller Machine. No identity cards need be shown. No one aside from you can find out where the money is, or how much is in the account backing this card. If the card is lost or stolen, no one else can use it because it can be activated only by a secret PIN code. The bank does not know the identity of the owner of the funds. If the funds are not used, they can be transferred anywhere in the world by wire transfer. You can raise or lower the amount in the account at any time. The **"PLASTIC CASH LIFELINE"**™ makes it easy to supply a dependent, friend, relative anywhere in the world with a weekly, monthly or annual allowance. You can give a **"PLAS-TIC CASH LIFELINE"**™ card to an employee you send abroad to cover his expenses. It is a plastic "smart" card where the person setting it up decides how much money to "back" the card with and whether or not to replenish to funds.

Another example: You owe your business partner a settlement of US$200,000. You wish to settle up confidentially with him using your offshore funds. You transfer the US$200,000 to and present him with a plastic card **"PLASTIC CASH LIFELINE"**™ (no name on it) that is backed by US$200,000. This money can be accessed (in cash) from any ATM machine. In some countries goods and services can be charged as if it was a credit card. The card is no good without the PIN code. The PIN code is useless without the card. If your creditor wants the money in the form of a check, gold bullion, shares of stock or bonds delivered at any bank anywhere in the world, he can arrange for the transfer without your knowing about the destination of the funds once you authorize the transfer of the bearer share corporation to his control.

Final Example: You are moving to (or already living in) a country full of grasping, corrupt public officials who can be relied upon to tax, confiscate seize and freeze everything in sight. There are also kidnappers and others around who might cause you trouble if they knew you had access to large sums of cash. You want to be able to access a few hundred dollars in cash spending money every few days in a low profile way. You get a **"PLASTIC CASH LIFELINE"**™ and for the rest of your life you have access to cash anywhere in your home country or abroad — quite anonymously. You go up to an automatic teller machine, insert the card, press buttons asking for the screen to print out in your language and spew out the cash you want. You identify yourself only by PIN number. No signature or identity documents are ever required for cash withdrawals.

You don't need to "trust" anyone. After paying the US$5,500 total lifetime fees for setting your **"PLASTIC CASH LIFELINE"**™ up; you can make the transfer of funds to a major international bank in a first class offshore banking center. If anything goes wrong or the account is refused, your set up fee will be refunded in full, immediately. If you are a consulting client of either Dr. Hill or Dr. Trevellian, by special arrangement they are authorized to hold all your introductory and opening balance funds in escrow and guaranty that your funds won't be touched until you have your **"PLASTIC CASH LIFELINE"**™ in your hand and have tried it out to successfully access your funds.

Details: How "Plastic Cash Lifeline"™ Works:

We supply you with a ready-made or shelf "bearer share" Corporation. You can use this corporation for other purposes, but if you want to keep your connection with the **"PLASTIC CASH LIFELINE"**™ a secret' it is recommended that you do not use the corporation for any other purpose (like owning your secondary residence). We will be glad to set up other bearer-share corporations in any name you want for other purposes. Your new bearer share company starts out with a bank account containing a balance of the equivalent of US$5,000. Only the name of your corporation appears on the ATM card. Your signature is never required. The bank does not know your name or identity. You can use a ready made off the Shelf Corporation for instant access. Alternatively you may choose any name (not already in use in that country) for your corporation. It will take a few weeks extra for a new corporation to be formed, The cost of the entire **"PLASTIC CASH LIFELINE"**™ package at US$5,500 may be less than others charge just for setting up a corporation or inferior asset protection plan. All this and more are yours for the asking.

Privacy Yes, Crime No! Important Note: This bank account may not be used for laundering money or to further any activity defined as criminal at the site of the bank account. If in doubt, ask us! Under new international "know your client" regulations, your lawyer (not us) who forms the corporation and provides nominee directors will need for his files a copy of your passport and a brief biography of yourself. This information will stay in his confidential, privileged files. You may use a "pen name" in dealing with us. The bank holding the funds to back the **"PLASTIC CASH LIFELINE"**™ does *NOT* see nor will they ever have a copy of your passport, photo, or signature. It would be a bad idea, but you can if you wish, make deposits to your account direct and in person at any of the branches of any international bank. You could even arrange to make check or wire transfer withdrawals in person but this would compromise your anonymity. Thus deposits or transfers should be made only through your lawyer. A reasonable amount of activity is included with the set up costs at no extra charge. Details will be supplied upon establishing an account. Having a reputable lawyer (specially recommended for you) as your go-between to handle all transactions via a trust account insures anonymity.

Withdrawal Limits: In most countries, there is a limit of approximately US$500 per card use. But there is no daily limit, and no limit on how many times you can use the card to withdraw cash. Some countries and some ATM machines may have different rules. Generally speaking, you can empty out your account at any time. This is not a good idea because if the balance drops to zero, the account is closed and you may lose your set up costs. A minimum balance of US$2,000 is required to avoid charges, and we recommend that except for emergencies, the balance be kept at more than the absolute minimum.

Do You Want Your Own "Plastic Cash Lifeline"™?

You pay Cores & Co. at the address below, an 'Introduction Fee' of US$4,000 for providing you with further details. In a sealed envelope you will receive an introduction to the legal firm who will handle all details for you at an additional cost of $1,500. Cores & Co. need never see your personal details, like address, photo, ID, nor do we learn the name of your new corporation. We are not a party to your transactions, monetary or otherwise. After the introduction is made, you then send $1,500 to cover your attorney's fees, and a minimum of $5,000 as your initial deposit. Alternatively, you can make your arrangements via a financial consultant known to us: These include Dr. Hill or Dr. Trevellian.

The entire US$5,000 is already or will be deposited into your Bank. This could be a bank of your choice, but we recommend you start with the bank suggested by your lawyer as it has an excellent history of reliability and client service. In about 3 weeks, you will receive your ATM card, not a visa card. Visa or other credit / debit cards can be arranged, but these have to be in an individual's name. If the anonymous feature of the **"PLASTIC CASH LIFELINE"**™ is of no use to you, we suggest you let us know. We can make cheaper setup arrangements for a simple offshore account to a named and identified individual who merely wants an Amex Gold Card or other credit card. To make later deposits, funds are transferred to either your lawyer, or directly to the account of your corporation.

Annual Charges: Just as with most credit cards, there are annual renewal charges. These are fully explained in the "Introduction" letter.

You will be able to withdraw cash anonymously, up to certain limits, out of a wall anywhere in the world where the ATM system is operative. Presently there are tens of thousands of locations accessible all over the world, with new ones opening every day. You can immediately withdraw up to US$3,000. Only US$2,000 is required, (after opening,) to maintain your ATM Card Account in good standing. You just put the card in any Automatic Teller Machine at any bank & enter your pin number to take out cash. Each time you use the ATM you will incur bank charges around US$5 per transaction. But we have found you come out far ahead because charges and exchange rate spreads are much greater on cashing traveler's checks or changing cash into local currency. In a few countries you will be able to use your **"PLASTIC CASH LIFELINE"**™ card as a charge card.

Only a person who has the ATM Card and who knows the PIN code can make withdrawals. The **"PLASTIC CASH LIFELINE"**™ is far better than the bearer savings account or Austrian Sparbuch! With a Sparbuch, for any transaction you must go to the bank (Austria,) in person or risk loss by sending it via mail. Your Sparbuch balance is in a minor currency (Schillings) linked to the Deutschmark. With the Anonymous ATM Card, you can get CASH 24-Hours a day, 7 days a week anonymously, anywhere in the world! The **"PLASTIC CASH LIFELINE"**™ is linked to the USA Dollar. "The greatest privacy tool, bar none " says, W.G. Hill.

While there can be direct access to the Bank account by fax, mail instructions, phone or otherwise, we strongly recommend that (for anonymity) all such activity go through your lawyer. He may also be useful to you in other areas, but your relationship will be strictly attorney-client. Only in the rare instance [never has happened yet] that you do not like the lawyer we introduce we can offer a second choice. You are protected by attorney client privilege! The lawyer is a citizen of and resident in a tax haven country (not Switzerland!) with bank secrecy. He will never visit your home country. We feel it is best for many of our clients if they have no signature power over the account. Nor do they "own" legal title to it. The client will hold the bearer shares in a vault under certain arrangements not amounting to ownership. Your home country lawyer can explain the asset protection advantages of such an arrangement. You can of course take delivery of the bearer shares at any time, but in some countries, physical possession of such shares (if discovered) might have negative consequences. Under the standard arrangements, any funds are JUDGMENT PROOF. Tinker with the deal and this important protection may be lost.

TAX STATUS: You must get a local opinion in your home country as we are not tax lawyers. However, in most countries, the arrangement described here is a tax neutral, non-reportable event much like keeping cash savings in your mattress. As the **"PLASTIC CASH LIFELINE"**™ is not "owned" by you, it is not reportable in countries that require an annual balance sheet to be filed. As it pays no interest, it is not reportable in those countries requiring an annual disclosure of offshore income. You are responsible for complying with your own local rules and regulations.

If you live in a country where confiscation is common and where keeping your serious offshore money separate from your spending money is an important consideration, the **"PLASTIC CASH LIFE-LINE"**™ has been designed with you in mind.

To Re-capitulate:

- No ID required to access funds in cash...
- No Signature required to access your funds in cash anywhere in the world!...
- Only US$2,000 to maintain accounts in good standing without bank charges...
- 24-Hour Instant access worldwide to your CASH funds...
- Your name unknown to everyone except your own "offshore" lawyer
- Deposit & Withdrawals in Anonymity...
- Limited Supply available. The program since limited to 150 will not attract the negative attentions of mass marketed programs that some insecure governments feel are a threat...
- Double Protection of Bank Secrecy plus Lawyer Confidentiality...
- Chose your corporate name or use 'off the shelf'...
- Set your own cash balance after opening deposit of US$5000...
- Totally Anonymous & Transferable...
- Your identity unknown to bank, further protected by bank secrecy and lawyer client privilege...
- No reporting requirements that we know of...
- Better than the Austrian Sparbuch...
- Wire transfers or checks into and out of account...Flexible arrangements for known customers
- Extremely Low Profile...
- Carry in your Wallet Like an ordinary card...
- Originally developed for several select clients at cost to them of US$200,000...
- FREE Info packet (send $10 to cover postage and handling)...
- Personally used and recommended by W.G. Hill and Peter Trevellian...
- Total Set-up Cost: US$5,500 plus US$5,000 minimum opening deposit...

- Once 150 are gone, the program closes down and that's it...
- Comes with complete instructions and all particulars...

To open, send your check for $4,000 introduction fee [or ask us about your preferred method of transferring funds] to:

P. T. Wales
St. George's House
31A St. George's Road
Leyton, London E105RH

Great Britain
Fax +33 1 53 01 31 19
E-mail: Ptshamrock@ptshamrock.com

Our introduction fee is not co-mingled with your **"PLASTIC CASH LIFELINE"**™ new account and will be deposited in an unrelated bank in a different country. FULL REFUND GUARANTEED IF ACCOUNT NOT SET UP AND CREATED AS ABOVE.

Confidential Mailing Address And Business Center

Telephone +33 1 53 01 31 18 — Fax +33 1 53 01 31 19

Cores AG is a confidential high-tech communications service. We show you how to use unbreakable encryption techniques, facilitate communications, and protect your privacy. We are a corporate PT, (Permanent Tourist- Prior Taxpayer, etc.) serving PT's around the world. We are a broad-minded and have proved ourselves trustworthy to many clients (including Dr. Trevellian) over the past 15 years. Naturally, our services may not be used to promote financial or other frauds or to further activities defined as criminal in Switzerland. We cannot be involved with shipments of weapons, contraband, or certain other matters. It is best to be candid when opening your account as we can then tell you if your proposed activities will be acceptable to us. You may use a fictional or penname while using our service. Mail can be picked up electronically. We would like a contact address, telephone, or fax number for emergency. But this is not always necessary. Some incoming mail, for example, bankbooks and credit cards, may need ID provided at our end to ensure that it goes to the correct party. We retain mail for one month after your.fee falls due for renewal. If we do not hear from you by then, your mail is discreetly disposed of if it is of a personal nature, or returned to source for official items. Any company or individual using our service must insist that anyone sending cash to this address must send it registered, (recorded is not sufficient). Also any valuables that can not be replaced should be treated in a similar fashion.

Our Basic Mail Only Service is for a 1 year minimum at £100 / US$160 per annum. This is a special introductory offer. If you wish to prepay, you may due so for a maximum of three years payable in advance upon initial application.

Alternatively you may wish to utilize our 'Full Service Option' that includes all normal business services. For instance, our business center address, the receiving of telephone messages, faxes, plain text e-mail and encrypted e-mail message forwarding. All-inclusive at £500 / US$800 per annum.

Cores AG

At a very reasonable cost Cores AG provides a Prestigious Swiss (or other European) Receiving and Transmitting Address including Fax, Phone, Voice mail, Anonymous Re-mail, and regular mail. We offer the latest in communications technology, with guaranteed secure Privacy and Efficiency. For sensitive business and personal communication we provide you with "State of The Art Encryption" facilities. Only you and you're chosen recipients can encode and decode your messages. Each of you has your own unique, secret electronic key. No clipper chips here! No intruder can decode what you send and neither hackers, investigators, nor your recipient can discover where the message is coming from unless you tell them. We can't read your messages and not even you can decode them once they are encrypted and sent! Only the intended recipient can instantly and automatically decrypt on his computer. Our PGP™ {Pretty Good Privacy} System (free with our full service) will amaze you.

The range of confidential and sophisticated services we offer the "PT" or offshore operator are found nowhere else, yet we charge only onetenth of the cost of our European competitors! We supply at no extra cost, your own Internet Lifetime e-mail address. It's yours to keep forever with no annual charges.

No ID is required to open an account. Our service is strictly personal and highly confidential. For an added degree of security, your 'secret' codes and forwarding instructions are kept in a different 'legal' jurisdiction — not Switzerland. This provides even greater privacy. In other words, we do not keep our 'files' in the same location where your communications are processed.

Opening Your Account Is Fast & Easy!

To open your account and prepay for one year (minimum), at our bargain introductory rate simply fill in the attached application. Our Basic Service is just £100, (SFr. 235) per annum and includes our box number. Mail collected for the week is posted on Monday of the following week. For our Full Service Option, enclose Swiss Fr 1175, Sterling £499, or US$799 by Bankers Draft, Postal Money Order, Traveler's Checks, Money Orders, or Cash. We will also accept bank to bank wire transfers of funds and Credit Cards. However for confidentiality, this is not advised. Alternatively, you may elect to establish an address at our branch offices either in Liechtenstein, or Sark, in the Channel Islands.

Special Services

Your wish, is our command. Do you have any special requests? For instance, to be picked up at Zurich International Airport in a Rolls Royce? Charter a jet for a day trip from London to Liechtenstein and return? Do you require to be met at Nice International Airport, take a helicopter to Monaco, board a 100-meter Yacht, and cruise to Malta? How about the counting and exchange of cash for goods and services in a Swiss Bank Vault, with armed security guards? Just about any service you desire, and a few new wrinkles you haven't even thought of, can be arranged through Cores AG's vast source of contacts.

Most of our clients have been with us for years. Until recently, all new clients were from referrals only. Now we are expanding and can offer even more. **Please note** This service is available to established 'Full Service' clients only. Upon opening your account, please fax your requirements to the attention of Mr. Peters. Include an alternative request in the event Plan A is unavailable. If your requirements are of a highly confidential nature, please forward via post, to the attention of Mr. Peters. Clearly mark on the outside bottom left hand corner of the envelope, 'Strictly Personal & Confidential.' Include a fax number or a contact address where we can get back to you with a quote for your requirements. Satisfaction guaranteed.

Confidential Bank Introduction

Through our many years conducting business 'off-shore,' we have developed a unique stable of banks and bankers located in various 'Tax-Haven' and Bank Secrecy locales. For a modest fee, we provide an introduction to the right banker and bank for you. Services include, but are not limited to; 'Managed Accounts,' or an account with a Diners Club or other Credit Card, (secured by a small deposit). Alternatively, a basic account, or what we call, the 'TIN CAN' or 'secret off-shore' account is available. (The account is the one that's hidden from your spouse or creditors.) Ask for our Bank Introduction Information sheet. The £25 cost is applied towards our fee should you elect to proceed. Please specify the 'Tin Can' introduction or the 'Managed' account introduction when requesting our information sheet. Request both reports for £35.

Anonymous Mobile Telephones

We can supply you with a mobile phone with an anonymous name for total privacy, including G.S.M. (Digital) international roaming and automatic bank payment facilities. For more information please request our information sheet "Anonymous Mobile Phone Systems". Please remit £10. Most countries available!

UK Anonymous Transposable Numbers

For a fee of £300 we can arrange for a special UK number that is untraceable from source. This can be attached to a conventional or mobile phone, and can be moved around at will from one phone to another. More information available upon request. Send £10.

Cores AG Services E-Mail Address

Ptshamrock@ptshamrock.com

(Please note this is the quickest way to communicate with us. Alternatively, if time is of the essence, please fax us at +33 1 53 01 31 19).

PTO-Portable Trades, Occupations & Opportunities

**Special Report- Brand New & Hot Off The Press! **

© 1997 - By: Peter Trevellian & W. G. Hill

Suppose you don't have enough money to live on after leaving your home country to become a PT. Don't look for a freedom-devouring job!

You can use your brain in place of financial assets! This new book explains how to survive and prosper in a strange country even if you are poor, and don't have the proper papers.

Subtitled, 101 Ways You Can Make Serious Money Anywhere In The World Without Special Education, Visas, Work Permits or Licenses, this is the answer. Do you want to be a PT but do not have a lot of capital? Each job opportunity or service described in PTO has estimated minimum earnings' potential of US$100,000 per year. You should achieve this after one year of persistent effort. For those who don't aim high financially, you can earn more or as little as you think you need. Not everyone is comfortable with the idea of being a multi-millionaire. But as Mae West once said, 'I have been poor and unhappy and rich and unhappy. Rich is better.' This book will give you bountiful "PT" plans and help you set goals that are realistic for you. Special-first time offered! £60/or US$100 for this beautiful leather bound report. Approximately 300 pages jam-packed full of information. We would be very surprised if you did not earn at least 1,000 times the price of the book by using it as your inspiration and entrepreneurial guidebook. Send for PTO now. Enclose US$100 plus US$15 for airmail postage. Full money back guaranty of satisfaction.

Or, For Further Information Contact:

London Fax: +44-171 681 1490

Paris Fax: +33-1-5301-3119

E-mail: Ptshamrock@ptshamrock.com
or
Shamrock@netcomuk.co.uk

VISIT OUR WEBSITE: WorldWide Web-http://www.ptshamrock.com/invisible.html

**PT Wales
31A St. George's Road
Leyton, London E105RH
Great Britain**

INDEX

Printed in the United Kingdom
by Lightning Source UK Ltd.
109148UKS00001B/309